THE

Good
Life

THE
Good
Life

Sally Gordon

J. M. DENT & SONS LTD,
LONDON · TORONTO · MELBOURNE

A QUARTO BOOK

Published by
J. M. Dent & Sons Limited
Aldine House
33 Welbeck Street
London W1

First published in the UK in 1981
Copyright © 1981 Quarto Limited
ISBN 0 460 04516 4

This book was designed and produced by
Quarto Publishing Limited
32 Kingly Court, London W1
Art Director: Robert Morley
Editorial Director: Jeremy Harwood
Art Editor: Moira Clinch
Editor: Jane Struthers
Designer: Roger Daniels
Illustrators: Edwina Keene; Chris Forsey; Ian Jackson;
Marilyn Bruce; Colin Newman, Linden Artists; Rodney
Shackell; John Woodcock

All photographs by Trevor Wood with the exception of:
Ian Howes 87; Harry Smith Collection 51t, 109, 112t & b,
115, 119; Sutton Seeds 65b, 67t, 95; Colin Molyneux
207c & b.

Art Assistants: Martin Chambers; Nick Clark;
Neville Graham; Dennis Thompson

Filmset in Britain by Servis Filmsetting Limited and
Flowery Typesetters Limited
Colour origination in Hong Kong by Rainbow Graphic
Arts Company Limited
Black and white origination in Hong Kong
by Hong Kong Graphic Arts Service Centre
Printed in Spain by Graficromo S.A.

Contents

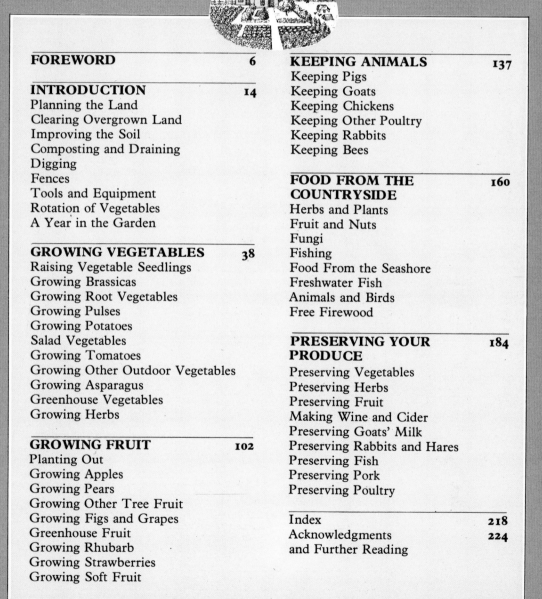

Foreword

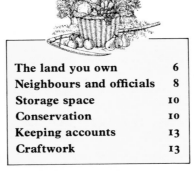

THIS BOOK is for those who wish to approach a 'good life' gently and gradually, rather than in headlong flight. It is for those who would like to try their hand at growing some fruit and vegetables, producing their own honey or eating their own eggs, drinking milk from their goats and making their own dairy produce, or rearing their own pigs or rabbits so they can enjoy their own home-produced meat. It is for those, too, who would like to make more use of the free produce that may be found in the countryside – in the hedgerows, woodlands and rivers or by the seashore.

It may be that once you have embarked on such home production, and begin to look at both your land and the countryside differently, you will want to turn the hobby into a way of life, shifting the emphasis so that it becomes your full-time job, and you do some other part-time work to supplement your income. At least if you approach it this way round, you will know what you are in for and what to expect – the dangers and pitfalls as well as the compensations and satisfactions. And you will know, too, whether you have sufficient dedication and instinctive feeling for such a life. For it is those people who really love this way of life; who actively enjoy cleaning out a smelly goat shed, or going out to

feed the pigs and shut in the chickens in all weathers; who find satisfaction in digging over a rough patch of land or spending hours up a ladder pruning a neglected apple tree, that are the most likely to make a success of it.

The all-important message, however, must be to go at it slowly. Do not try to grow all your own fruit and vegetables, and keep all the animals discussed in this book in your first year of operation. Without previous experience, it simply cannot be done (at least, not effectively) and you are even more likely to end up with ulcers than your erstwhile colleagues who stayed in the city! Instead, tackle it little by little, finding what you enjoy doing, and giving yourself time to learn by your mistakes. This, after all, is the most valuable experience of all, and the best way to gain knowledge.

The land you own

You need very little land indeed to produce at least some of your own food. A tiny backyard – even a terrace or a patio – can yield some produce; the important point is that if you decide you want the land you own to be productive, you must use it as efficiently as possible. Everyone, of course, will have different ideas and

6

different views on the best way to use it, so if you get offered advice, be grateful for it, assimilate it and sort through it – then do exactly what you want to do! Your land, after all, should yield what you and your family like to eat, not something recommended by a neighbour that appeals to none of you.

Another important factor is to try to put back into your land what you take out of it. No ground will go on producing crops or supporting livestock of any type unless it receives proper treatment and usage. Your aim is to get the best possible return from the land, but not to exploit it so that it eventually becomes stale and useless. This is not as daunting or terrifying as it may sound; it merely means acquainting yourself with the needs of the soil, the effect of growing various crops and keeping livestock in terms of what they take from, or give back to, the ground, and the ways in which they can benefit or react upon one another.

If you do find that the home production of food along these lines becomes your main way of life, it may be that you will find yourself faced with a decision whether to stay in your present location and use the land you have there to the full, or whether to move somewhere with greater scope. Many people find that adopting this sort of life allows them to live in the area they have always wanted to be in, and this could be said to be another of its advantages.

Neighbours and officials

The relationships you manage to establish with those who live close by can make a surprising difference to the success of your operation – however big or small it may be. Those people who have lived in the area for some time often have valuable hints and advice on what does and does not grow well in this particular location, and knowing this can save you a great deal of time, money and exasperation! There is no point in battling to grow some particular type of vegetable, however much you like it, if the soil and conditions are simply not right. Far better to divert your energy into growing something else that does favour the prevailing conditions.

Show due consideration for your neighbours at all times, particularly if they are very close and also if they are not interested themselves in growing their own crops or keeping animals. There is nothing more annoying for somebody than suddenly to find their early morning peace shattered by the crowing of a cockerel or their afternoon quietude ruined as they sit directly in the flight path of your bees returning to the hive. Site your animals so that such eventualities do not occur, and take the trouble to inform your neighbours, courteously, of what you are doing, or better still, plan to do.

It is very often possible to establish a kind of exchange-and-barter system with neighbours or like-minded home-growers, although this is a relationship it is best to allow to evolve, rather than to plan or push. It is, after all, very difficult to strike just the right balance yourself in terms of growing the right amount of everything, whilst trying at the same time to produce as much variety as possible. It is often far easier to produce a glut of one particular crop, and providing that your neighbour is producing a glut of something else, you could well work a mutually beneficial exchange. This can be put into effect whether you and your neighbour have no more than a pocket-handkerchief-sized vegetable plot, or whether you are both going in for home food production on a major scale. It can extend to

livestock too, with you perhaps keeping goats and providing your neighbours with milk, while they have chickens and supply your daily egg ration. Just see gradually what suits you all best and then try to come to some arrangements along these lines.

If you intend to make the operation as large as possible and to keep livestock as well, you will often find the farmers in the area will be willing to offer advice and help, particularly if you approach them humbly and not as if you actually know the answers already. All farmers love the land they work, and they would infinitely prefer to see someone else make a success of farming their bit of ground, rather than ruining it, and themselves, in the process. The old-timers of the district, too, are always worth listening to – they can often tell you where the best field mushrooms are to be found, what kind of edible plant life grows on nearby wasteland, or what fish can be found in the local streams and rivers, as well as giving you time-honoured tips about how to grow the biggest and best vegetables of all.

There is another area in which you may find neighbours or neighbouring farmers can be a help, and that is over the question of machinery. Again, if you are going into small-holding on a larger scale than merely making the best use of a small back garden, you will inevitably find that, sooner or later, you need the help of some specialized tool or item of machinery – a rotavator maybe, or a cement mixer. The first thing to do, of course, is to see if there is any firm in the vicinity that hires out such equipment. You may be lucky; more often you will not be, for the hiring of equipment (or at least the equipment you want, it seems) does not appear to be a widely practised business. To buy the item will undoubtedly be expensive, but if two of you have a use for it, you have already halved the cost. Thereafter, you may well find others who want to use it too, and before you know where you are, you will be in the midst of a highly profitable tool-and-machinery-hire business!

Many of us have an almost in-built horror, or mistrust, of official bodies, and this is likely to be highly developed among those who have adopted a way of life that almost by definition excludes officialdom and bureaucracy to a large degree. Nevertheless, the government organizations that exist to offer advice to small-holders (however small!) should not be ignored, for they are able to give thoroughly practical and truly invaluable advice on every aspect of growing produce, keeping livestock and generally making the best use of the land available. In the United Kingdom, the Ministry of Agriculture and Fisheries will come and advise, or send leaflets on numbers of subjects, to all who ask them, and their advisory service (ADAS) has made the difference between running an economic and a non-economic operation to many people. Contrary to what you might think, they are actually in favour of this type of small operation and will do all they can to help. They are not, as is so often thought, trying to catch you out, or wanting to snoop around your property in order to make official complaints. Instead, they are genuinely interested in helping you to make a success of what you are doing.

An important point, incidentally, is that you should always check with your local authorities (or Ministry of Agriculture representative) when planning to keep livestock. There are rules and regulations adhering to the keeping of all farm-type livestock, and in some areas you are not allowed to keep such animals at all. Some animals must not be transported on public roads or highways

*If you have any surplus stock you can sell it by
advertising it on a board by the roadside, or
anywhere else which is prominent. However, you
must check first that you are not infringing any
by-laws by doing so.*

unless the transporter has a proper licence. It is much better to discover such things before you go to the expense of obtaining the animals and their accommodation.

Do not let the seeking of advice from others – official bodies, farmers, old-timers or like-minded neighbours – completely dull your own wits or quell your ingenuity. You will be at your most successful, and satisfied, when you find new, quicker and more economical ways of doing things, and there are any number of short cuts to be taken in an operation of this sort. Discuss such ideas with others by all means; it often takes the stimulation of discussion to develop ingenious new methods of gathering your apple crop, inventing a new poultry feeding system or streamlining a milking operation.

Storage space and outbuildings
The amount of storage space and outbuildings you will need will depend very much on the scale and scope of your home production operation, but it is a factor worthy of consideration. Many of the activities outlined in this book do take up a fair amount of space, and if you do not want them to invade and soon take over the interior of your house, you must think of some alternatives.

You will not, for example, be able to eat all the vegetables and fruit you grow as you harvest them, and indeed you would not want to, for the whole point of such production is to be able to enjoy your home-grown produce the full year round. Root vegetables can be stored in their natural state (see page 186), but for this you either need to allocate them a patch of ground (for clamping), or you must store them in some sort of weather- and rat-proof shed. This should not be a garage, or at least, not one where you also keep the car, for they may easily become tainted with petrol fumes. Other vegetables and fruit will need different storage facilities; if you mean to store them by bottling, or by turning them into chutney, pickles, sauces, jams and so on, you will need considerable shelf space in a cool, well-ventilated, but shady place. Alternatively, or ideally, in addition you will need a deep freezer, and there are two major considerations attached to this item of equipment. The first is the siting of it, and the second is to decide if you have sufficient kitchen space and facilities to process the amount of produce you mean to put into it (bearing in mind this could include the preparation of such livestock as poultry and rabbits, too). A deep freezer will ideally be sited as close to the kitchen as is practical – perhaps in an adjacent scullery, utility room or garage.

Kitchen space and facilities usually amount to no more than a common-sense reorganization of the space available to give sufficient work-top area to deal with the preparation, processing and packaging of the produce ready for the freezer, as soon as it comes into the kitchen.

The housing of the livestock discussed in this book is dealt with as the care and keep of each animal is considered, but again there are further space considerations. If you intend to keep goats, you should give some thought to the milking conditions, for ideally you should have some sort of dairy, however makeshift or Heath Robinson-like it may be. As will be discussed in greater detail later, goats should not be milked in the shed in which they are kept, because conditions are simply not hygienic enough; therefore you really need another shed for milking. If this can incorporate facilities for dealing with the milk, cooling it, etc (see page 145), so much the

better, for again this will take up a great deal of space in your kitchen. Certainly, the cooling of large quantities of milk does not fit conveniently into a very small, but doubtless very busy, kitchen.

Consider, too, if you have sufficient room to keep the eggs as they come in, storing them in such a way that they can be used in strict rotation. Egg trays or boxes can take up quite a lot of room on a shelf or in a larder, yet they must be kept somewhere cool, where there is no danger of the eggs being smashed. If you intend curing pork, you must have somewhere large enough to hold the brine tank so it is not constantly in your way, and then somewhere else cool and away from flies, to hang the meat. Similar facilities are needed for hanging game. A smoker large enough to take reasonable quantities of meat or fish is not a tiny item and must be housed somewhere.

Food to be fed to the animals is most economically bought in bulk or large quantities, but then it takes up a lot of storage room. Hay and straw, if needed, are bulky items to store, and yet they must be kept undercover (again, in a weather-proof shed) if they are to keep in good condition. If they are allowed to turn mouldy, they will be useless, and at their current cost, this would be the greatest possible waste of money. Other more concentrated foodstuffs must be kept in rodent-proof containers, and these too should be housed in a shed or outbuilding of some sort. Anything rodent-proof must be made of galvanized metal, ideally, with a lid that fits right over the container. Failing this, a heavy, thick wooden barrel will keep the rats out for some time; plastic will keep them out for no time at all.

In conclusion, you are likely to need some sort of outdoor, undercover, storage space, and this becomes almost imperative if you are keeping livestock of any kind. The closer the buildings are to the house or to the animals' quarters, the more convenient you will find them, but always make use of any old shed or outbuilding that is already there on your property. Repairing existing buildings – making them waterproof by nailing some asbestos sheeting on the roof or boarding-up a no-longer needed, broken window – is generally much cheaper than erecting a new building. And if you are lucky enough to live in a house with an attic or a cellar, make full use of this added storage space, erecting a system of shelves (or wine racks, perhaps?) if there is enough room.

Conservation
Conservation of energy and the environment are much-talked about subjects, and ones perhaps to be a little wary of, for they are highly loaded and highly emotive. The alarmists tell us that the earth's resources are running out (and doubtless they are right), but still the subject must be kept in perspective. That is not to say that it is not worthy of consideration; it is, and indeed, if alternative systems of creating energy or ways of preserving the environment can be found, so as at least to prolong the existence of natural resources for as long as possible, so much the better. In the pursuit of such alternatives, however, it is quite easy to get carried away with the excitement about the possibilities, for example, of windmills and watermills to generate power and heat. Unless you really know what you are doing, you can spend a great deal of money on such schemes, but end up achieving very little.

Using oil is undoubtedly the most efficient and

*T*he Good Life: these are examples of
just some of the different types of
produce you can grow, collect or
preserve, on even a small piece of land,
from raspberries to goats cheese to wood.
With careful planning it is possible to
eat your own fresh or preserved food all
the year round, especially if you follow
the directions for preserving which are
given later in the book.

Amongst the many types of livestock, geese in particular are very endearing, and also make excellent watchdogs. However, if you intend to eat your animals eventually, don't get too fond of them or killing them might be a traumatic experience.

economic way of heating our homes and water, in terms of giving the most heat from the smallest amount of raw material. But, as we all know, oil is currently prohibitively expensive, and it is also so vital to life itself, being the basis of so many essential products, that the fact it may soon run out is a frightening thought. In an attempt to allay this fear, many people are installing wood-burning systems to heat their homes and their water, but the long-term effects of this are just as frightening. If wood-burning stoves were to be used on a massive, national scale, our wood resources would soon run out. Trees are an integral and essential part of the environment as we know it and not just from an aesthetic point of view; without them, it – and probably us, too – would not survive. This is why all responsible people who use wood at all owe it to future generations to replant trees – and which one of us does not use wood in some way?

The trouble with considering conservation on a small scale – that is, in a way that we can influence individually – is that we are likely to come up against a personal conflict of interests or economics. The cheapest form of using energy to heat our homes, run our machinery and so on, may well turn out to be the one that most threatens the earth's resources. We must all come to terms with this for ourselves and in our own particular ways.

One possible and very practical way, however, of helping to conserve energy (and, incidentally, in the long term, saving money too) is to consider the possibility of using solar energy. The only real application of this is to heat the water in our homes; it tends not to work for space heating as the heat created can not be stored, but it is extremely efficient for raising the temperature of water. In climates which enjoy continuous sunshine, it is quite possible that no other system will be needed to keep the water at a desired temperature; most places in the United Kingdom will need some additional system, but still the solar panels can be used to raise the temperature of the water coming into the house a good 10° F (5° C) the entire year round, and this can represent a great saving in cost.

The moderately-talented handyman can install a solar water heating system himself, although he would probably be wise to get some professional advice if planning to do so. The cost of installation is not cheap; current figures say it takes about five years' operation to recover the cost of the installation, but once this has been done, it really is free fuel.

The important point of installation is obviously the positioning of the panels to ensure they get the maximum benefit from any sun there may be or, in the absence of sun, full reflection from the sky. Thus they must not be overshadowed at all and ideally should face south. It is important, too, that the system has some sort of cut-out or, failing that, a warning alarm system, for those times when the temperature outside drops below the level of the temperature of the water going through the panels. In the same way that the solar panels collect the heat, they will also collect the cold, thereby freezing the water inside.

If you do not feel you could install a solar heating system yourself, be a little circumspect about which firm you choose to handle it for you. Because it is still a relatively new area, there are neither the same standards, nor the same elements of competition amongst firms, that will be found among those who install more conventional water heating systems. Try, therefore, to ensure that all the claims being made about any particular system or installation are correct, for you may have little recourse if they are not.

Keeping accounts

If you are growing a certain amount of your own fruit and vegetables and keeping the odd chicken and a hive of bees more as a hobby than a money-saver, there is no real need to keep any sort of accounts – unless you want to, of course. If, however, you are running the operation on a larger scale, it is a good idea to follow some accounting routine, or else it is quite possible to indulge in massive self-deception about how much money you are saving. The cost of animal food, fertilizer, fuel, equipment, machinery and the like must all be noted and balanced against the cost of the food you produce, should you have had to buy it. By keeping such accounts, you will be able to discover those areas which are really not economic, and either abandon them or alter them in some way.

A slight warning however: it may well be that you find your operation, particularly as far as keeping livestock is concerned, saves you very little money. You will not be producing free food by any means, although your eggs, milk and meat should cost you less than if you were buying them. What you have to remember here is that you are producing food of infinitely better quality than it is possible to buy. The eggs are richer, the milk fresher and the meat more tasty. Add to this the satisfaction you are getting from looking after the animals and watching them flourish in your care and it must be worth something!

Later on, I have recommended also that you keep records relating to the livestock – how many eggs you get each day, numbers of young in a litter or brood, the date they were born, etc. It might help, too, if you keep similar records of the fruit and vegetable production so that you can see what does particularly well, when it is time to replace fruit trees, bushes and so on. It is this sort of observation and practice that could ultimately make the difference between an operation that is relatively cost-effective and one that is little more than a money-waster.

Craftwork

As has been explained, this book concentrates on enriching the quality of life through the satisfaction of growing your own crops, keeping your own animals, and searching the countryside and seashore to provide good, wholesome food for your table. The bigger the scale of your operation, the more of a craftsman or -woman you are likely to become. Fence-erecting, concreting, brick-laying, carpentry and forestry are just some of the skills you are likely to acquire. Having found that you can turn your hand to such trades with relative impunity, you might like to take the 'good life' a step or two further (and perhaps head that much further towards self-sufficiency, too) by practising even more crafts. The possibilities are endless – from weaving baskets to building boats, making your own soap (with lime and wood ash), your own cosmetics (from herbs) and your own candles (from beeswax) to producing your own textiles from spinning and weaving and making them into clothes to wear. Many such crafts could be used to help supplement your income as well as providing you with satisfaction and good things. Be as ambitious as you like; ultimately the only commodity you need be short of in your 'good life' is time.

Introduction

WHATEVER SIZE AREA of land you have available for your home production of food (the growing of fruit and vegetables and/or the keeping of livestock), careful planning and judicious use of the space can make a great deal of difference to its productivity. A comparatively small garden, well-planned and worked, could prove infinitely more productive than a larger amount of land where things are just allowed to happen at random. Give careful initial thought, therefore, to the siting of everything you want to include, even if you are not planning to do so straight away. Many features of the plan – the vegetable garden, fruit patch, pig sty and goat shed, for example – are likely to be in one permanent site, so you want to be sure you have chosen the best possible place, both in terms of convenience to you and best conditions for them.

Below are a few guidelines for the siting of each productive element discussed in the following pages, but bear in mind that the leeway you have in each instance is enormous! Your vegetable garden, for example, can be as large or as small as you want or are able to make it; it has been proved possible to provide a family of four with fresh vegetables each week of the year from a plot that measures 3 × 4 metres (10 × 12 ft). How much space you need for your chickens depends on whether their site is to be permanent or whether you are able to move them around, and similarly with goats – are you going to take them out during the day and tether

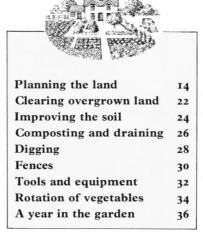

them on nearby wasteland, or are they to stay permanently on one patch of ground, in which case they will need more space and supplementary feeding? Providing you use your common-sense in the early stages, and erect firm and solid fencing for any livestock you want to confine to one area, you will find all rules are bendable.

The vegetable garden

The plot you choose for growing vegetables should not be overhung or heavily shaded by large trees. Vegetables grow best if they get the maximum amount of sun possible; few will really flourish in shady conditions, although that is not to say they will not grow at all. Shelter from strong prevailing winds – particularly those from the north or north-east – is desirable, and is probably best provided by a solid fence or a low hedge. A hedge, though, should have a path sited between it and the edge of the vegetable plot, and all protruding roots from the hedge must be cut through each year when you dig over the plot, or else they will rob the vegetables of essential nutrients from the soil.

The size and shape of the plot will of course depend on the space you have available, as well as to how much time you are willing to devote to working it, but a rectangular shape is generally the most convenient. Working will be cleaner and easier if the patch is surrounded by solid paths (ideally some material such as brick, concrete or paving slabs, rather than compounded earth which is bound to get muddy during the winter). These should

Above: this beautifully laid-out vegetable garden is probably larger than most smallholders need. Nevertheless, it is a good example of how to arrange such a garden. **Right:** herb gardens used to be a feature of old-fashioned gardens, but if space is at a premium, you can grow herbs in a flower border. **Far right:** this espalier tree has been very well trained against a south-facing wall.

be wide enough to take a wheelbarrow. If the patch is very large, similar paths sited at intervals across it would be a good idea too.

The siting of the vegetable garden in relation to the house is not a major consideration; some people like to have it close by, others favour a spot away from the house to which they can retire. However, bear in mind that it is probably preferable to have the vegetable garden, rather than the pig sty or the chicken run, close to the house! It will be convenient if the tool shed is close by and also the greenhouse and cold frames (remember the sloping side of the cold frames should face south, if at all possible). It will help, too, if you allocate some space, perhaps next door to the cold frames, for seed beds, and the compost heap should also be sited within easy access, although this is perhaps the element of the vegetable garden that is best placed at the furthest corner from the house. It does not have to be within the vegetable garden at all of course, but you will find it convenient if it is not too far away.

If the vegetable garden must be sited on an irregular shaped plot of land (and this will often be the case), try to divide it so there is a rectangular patch within it. This, you will find, to be the most convenient shape to divide in order to work the crop rotation plan (see page 35). The remaining patches of land could be used for the perennial crops, such as asparagus and globe artichokes, which remain in the same spot year after year.

As with the siting of the greenhouse (see page 88), there are advantages and disadvantages to planting rows east/west or north/south. Rows that run north/south get the maximum amount of sun, catching it on one side in the morning and on the other in the afternoon. Rows that run east/west tend to be shaded by those on either side for part of the day, but they are better for crops that are going to be grown through the winter under cloches. The decision could be made for you if the plot is on a slope; it is better to plant rows across the slope, than up and down it.

The fruit garden
Different considerations apply to the fruit garden and to the two types of fruit – soft fruit and tree fruits. Although it is perfectly possible to dot soft fruit bushes around the garden wherever there is space for them, you will find it considerably more convenient to keep them all together in one spot. Apart from general cultivation, harvesting, etc, it is far quicker and easier to provide netting protection from the birds over a large number of

bushes, than over just one or two (and they must be protected in this way if you want a decent crop of anything). If you are growing a lot of soft fruit of this type, consider growing it in a fruit cage, which allows you easy access, whilst keeping the birds off the fruit.

If the spot chosen for the soft fruit is close to the vegetable garden, try to site it so that it affords the minimum amount of shade to the growing vegetables. Some soft fruits, such as blackberries, loganberries and raspberries, are shade-tolerant, so they can occupy shadier parts of the patch.

Remember that once planted, soft fruit remains in this position for several years, so try not to site any in a place that you might want to incorporate into the vegetable garden, or use for something else in a year or two's time.

Tree fruits should not be sited with the soft fruits as they will soon overshadow them and rob them of important soil nutrients. Tree fruits, instead, can be incorporated into an overall garden plan (unless you have room for, and want to plant, an orchard) and they can be placed either where there is room for them, or in a spot where you want to introduce some shade. They can be planted too, to give a pleasant aspect from the house, perhaps by hiding or screening some less aesthetic feature. Remember to choose tree fruits carefully, making sure they have been grown on the rooting stock that will give you the size of tree you want (see page 102); otherwise you could end up with a giant that over-shadows everything!

The more delicate tree fruits – apricots, peaches and nectarines – together with vines, should be sited against a south-facing wall for the best results. Walls can also be used for growing cordon or espalier trees of apples and pears, or for some of the soft fruits that need training and supporting as they grow.

The herb garden

This is probably the element that needs the least consideration and takes up the smallest amount of space. Herbs can be grown anywhere that is convenient and where there is room for them. If you have a choice, however, they are best sited close to the kitchen, so that they are readily to hand when you want them as you are cooking. Grow them in a small plot, so you can reach them all easily, and one with lots of sun.

Chickens

As briefly mentioned earlier, just where you site your chickens in the overall plan will depend as much as anything on which method you choose to keep them. Free-range chickens need only a permanent house and this can be sited anywhere. If there is a building suitable for a hen house already installed on the property when you take it over, then this is undoubtedly the best place for the chickens!

If you intend to keep your chickens in a permanent run (as opposed to free-range), it might be advisable to site this a little way from the house as it is not likely to be the most aesthetic of all your garden features. The size of it is really academic; allocate as much space as you feel you can spare. Common-sense will tell you whether the chickens have enough room. In fact, they do not need a great deal of space in the run, although they will peck over as much land as you give them; it is far more important to ensure that you provide 10–15 cm (4–6 in) per bird around the feeding trough or hopper, and about

Planning your land: before you begin to plant anything on your land, you must draw up a plan to decide how it can be used to its best advantage. **Below:** this is a suggested plan for a small plot of land, which is devoted almost entirely to growing vegetables and fruit. Only chickens are kept as livestock, to supply fresh eggs and meat. The compost heap is close to the hen house and the fruit and vegetable beds. **Right:** a larger plot of land. This allows for more suggested features, such as a permanent pig sty and a movable hen house within an orchard, so the chickens can scratch around. The extra land means that more vegetables and fruit can be grown, giving a bigger variety and a larger harvest. **Bottom:** this idealized plot not only has space for pigs and chickens, but goats, bees and even a horse. The extra vegetable plots allow a larger system of crop rotation to be employed. There will also always be one plot lying fallow, which can be used for grazing livestock.

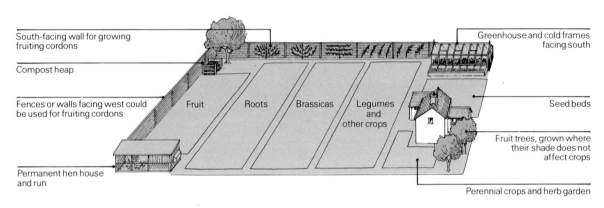

South-facing wall for growing fruiting cordons

Compost heap

Fences or walls facing west could be used for fruiting cordons

Fruit

Roots

Brassicas

Legumes and other crops

Permanent hen house and run

Greenhouse and cold frames facing south

Seed beds

Fruit trees, grown where their shade does not affect crops

Perennial crops and herb garden

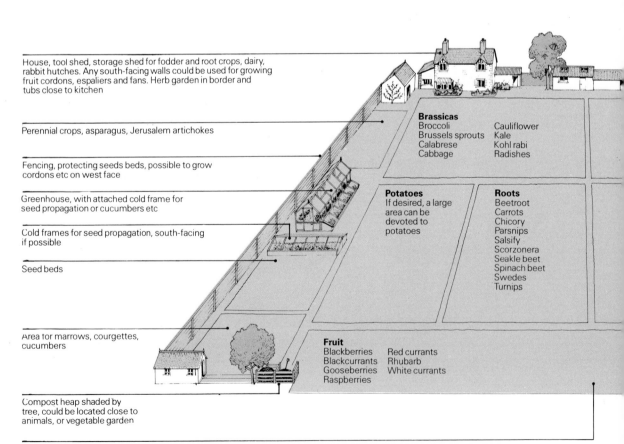

House, tool shed, storage shed for fodder and root crops, dairy, rabbit hutches. Any south-facing walls could be used for growing fruit cordons, espaliers and fans. Herb garden in border and tubs close to kitchen

Perennial crops, asparagus, Jerusalem artichokes

Fencing, protecting seeds beds, possible to grow cordons etc on west face

Greenhouse, with attached cold frame for seed propagation or cucumbers etc

Cold frames for seed propagation, south-facing if possible

Seed beds

Area for marrows, courgettes, cucumbers

Compost heap shaded by tree, could be located close to animals, or vegetable garden

Brassicas
Broccoli
Brussels sprouts
Calabrese
Cabbage
Cauliflower
Kale
Kohl rabi
Radishes

Potatoes
If desired, a large area can be devoted to potatoes

Roots
Beetroot
Carrots
Chicory
Parsnips
Salsify
Scorzonera
Seakle beet
Spinach beet
Swedes
Turnips

Fruit
Blackberries
Blackcurrants
Gooseberries
Raspberries
Red currants
Rhubarb
White currants

Fruit-growing area, could include a caged area for protection from birds

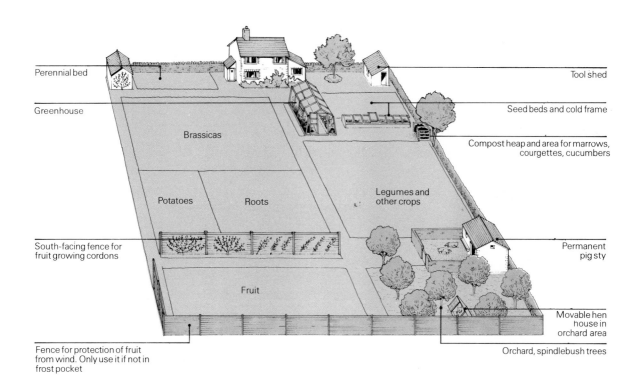

Perennial bed

Greenhouse

Brassicas

Potatoes

Roots

South-facing fence for
fruit growing cordons

Fruit

Fence for protection of fruit
from wind. Only use it if not in
frost pocket

Legumes and
other crops

Tool shed

Seed beds and cold frame

Compost heap and area for marrows,
courgettes, cucumbers

Permanent
pig sty

Movable hen
house in
orchard area

Orchard, spindlebush trees

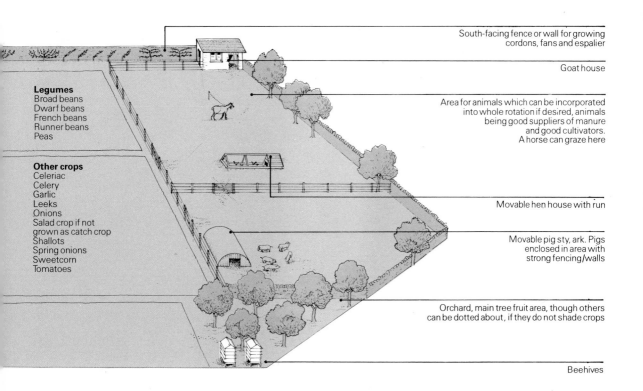

Legumes
Broad beans
Dwarf beans
French beans
Runner beans
Peas

Other crops
Celeriac
Celery
Garlic
Leeks
Onions
Salad crop if not
grown as catch crop
Shallots
Spring onions
Sweetcorn
Tomatoes

South-facing fence or wall for growing
cordons, fans and espalier

Goat house

Area for animals which can be incorporated
into whole rotation if desired, animals
being good suppliers of manure
and good cultivators.
A horse can graze here

Movable hen house with run

Movable pig sty, ark. Pigs
enclosed in area with
strong fencing/walls

Orchard, main tree fruit area, though others
can be dotted about, if they do not shade crops

Beehives

Care of animals: keeping animals can be a great joy and can provide you with entertainment as well as food. Before you acquire any livestock though, do not forget that they must be cared for every day, and are a very big tie and responsibility. However they can be very educational for children.

20 cm (8 in) per bird roosting space in the hen house (see page 147).

As I have discussed more fully later, if you can allocate two patches of ground to the chickens, there is more chance of keeping both of them in better condition than if you have only one, as they can be rested in turn. Think of siting these two plots side by side; if there are two entrances to the hen house, this can be used for both runs and the fence dividing them would provide a boundary for both patches.

Other poultry
Requirements for other types of poultry – ducks, geese, turkeys – follow the same common-sense factors. As all poultry must be shut up by night and let out by day, it might be slightly more convenient for you if you site them relatively closer to one another. It could make feeding a quicker operation, too. If you want your geese to act as watchdogs, and make the loudest of all possible noises whenever anyone enters your property, put them near the gate; if you want a more peaceful life, put them further away – down at the bottom of the garden, for example! Ducks, of course, need a pond. They need a house, too, but very little additional ground space.

Goats
If you intend to run the goat shed on a deep litter system – that is, to keep adding more and more bedding to the floor and then mucking it out when it becomes almost impossible for you to get into the shed – it is probably best to site it some way away from the house, just in case the smell is a little more pervasive than you may like! There is no real reason for the goats' living quarters to be near the dairy, if this is a separate unit, although if the two were to be close, it could mean that the twice-daily visits for milking would be less unpleasant for you in very cold or wet weather.

There are no special size requirements for a goat run, even if this is to be their permanent home (although it

must be very strongly fenced if they are to be turned loose in it). Goats are infinitely adaptable and will live happily in most circumstances and conditions.

Having given them sufficient room to wander about and graze without bumping into one another all the time, the only consideration regarding the size of the area is how much you want to supplement their feeding. The smaller the grazing area, obviously the more additional feed you will need to supply. Also, if this area is to remain as grass and not become a bare patch of land, it will need resting from time to time, which means you must either allocate another patch of land, similarly fenced, to the goats, or you must have access to wasteland or hedgerows where you can take them out and tether them during the day. If you tether goats, incidentally, they should be moved twice a day as they will not eat greenstuff that they have fouled, and you should not place them too close to bushes or long patches of tough grass, in which the rope could get entangled. If this happens there is a risk that the goats could strangle themselves.

In wintertime, it is best to keep goats on a piece of land that has been concreted (again it does not have to be very

big) if the ground is liable to become very muddy, as this could lead to various feet disorders.

Rabbits

Space requirements for rabbits are minimal; each rabbit needs a hutch that has only to be about 90 cm wide × 60 cm deep × 60 cm high (3 ft × 2 ft × 2 ft). This should be increased somewhat when breeding from a doe, and if young rabbits are to be kept together in a cage, then they will also need more room. You can allocate some garden space to a rabbit, but there is no need for this, and it certainly does not need to be a permanent feature.

The siting of the hutches in terms of height off the ground, shelter from winds and so on is discussed on page 153. If they are properly looked after, there should be no smell at all from the hutches, which means there is no reason for not putting them close to the house. The most sensible place to put them is obviously wherever you find it most convenient to have them: close to the house for quick access or for observation; close to the compost heap for quick disposal of hutch cleanings (although this would not be so good if there were a lot of flies round the compost heap) or close to the hay and straw store for quick collection of bedding and feed; the choice is yours.

Pigs

If you are keeping pigs to help you cultivate a very rough area of land, you will move them and their movable sty around as necessary. If, however, as is probably more likely, you keep them in a sty with a permanent yard, this again will be sited wherever you find it most convenient. It is probably best placed a little way from the house, to protect you from the smell and the noise.

Pigs do not need a great deal of space if they are not relying on the land for their food. All they need is adequate space to rootle around a bit and to make themselves a nice, deep dust or mud hole. Further considerations do come into play, though, if you are planning to let your sow have a litter of piglets. As discussed later, she is likely to have about ten babies, and these have to be weaned when they are between five and eight weeks old. At this point, they will need separate accommodation from her, and depending on how long you mean to keep the young pigs, it may be necessary to split them up still further. Ten healthy, squealing piglets is a large number to keep in one fairly small yard, and overcrowding can lead to all sorts of unpleasant problems.

Bees

These are the livestock that take up the least amount of ground of all, their only housing or space requirement from you being the provision of a hive. There are some points to bear in mind about the siting of bee-hives, however, and these are discussed on page 157. In addition to those mentioned, most people will probably wish to put the hives a distance from the house, so that regularly-used paths from the house to various parts of the garden do not clash with the bees' most usual flight path to and from the hives.

Clearing Overgrown Land

IF THE LAND on which you want to grow fruit and vegetables and keep an assortment of livestock is a tangle of bushy undergrowth, it has first to be cleared. This is an arduous task in which mechanical aids can certainly help, but in which results will mainly be achieved by sweat and toil.

The basic and most useful tools and items of equipment are discussed below. If you are intending to keep goats, it may be worth your while to get them now because they will do most of the work for you. They will eat their way through quite a lot of undergrowth, even stripping the bark off trees and killing them, if you let them. Pigs will also clear the land.

Attack tangly clusters of undergrowth with a scythe (power ones are available). Brambles, thin-stemmed bushy clumps and young saplings should all fall under the scythe; use the shorter-handled sickle or a slasher in awkward or confined places and on tougher stalks and stems. Remove all the fallen branches and other pieces of wood, chop them into manageable sizes and store them for use as firewood in the winter.

Having cleared the ground of the undergrowth, decide if you want to remove any trees. This is probably a job for an expert, although instructions for felling a tree are given on page 182. If you do it yourself, remember the operation is only slightly better than useless if the stump is left in the ground. Removing this is a major job in itself; stumps can be dynamited out of the ground or pulled out with a special winch (again, both jobs for an expert). If you do it yourself, it probably means digging them out with a mattock and a spade. Expect to be at it for some little time!

As neglected land is best broken up for initial cultivation by a rotavator, all large stones, boulders,

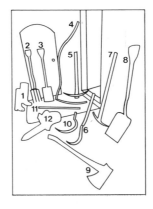

Clearing land: these are the basic tools which are needed to clear ground by hand. You should always buy the best tools available, not only because they are the easiest to use, but because they will last the longest. Always wear tough boots to protect your feet. **Above: 1** wellington boots; **2** fork; **3** spade; **4** scythe; **5** pickaxe; **6** slasher; **7** mattock; **8** shovel; **9** axe; **10** sickle; **11** crowbar; **12** chainsaw. **Below:** mowers are used to cut grass on land which has been cleared of debris. The smallest piece of stone can break the blades.

builders' rubble, bits of brick, wire, or binder twine must first be removed, or these will spell instant destruction to the blades of the machine. Go over the entire area, picking up these items and putting them in a barrow or trailer. Large boulders may have to be levered up out of the ground (you will need help for this). Remember to lift all heavy items carefully, bending your knees and lifting with your back straight, rather than stooping over the object, thereby running the risk of straining your back muscles. Very heavy boulders could be hauled out of their resting place or moved away by towing them with a trailer – even a car, if it is fitted with a proper tow bar attachment.

Do not necessarily dispose of all the apparent debris you have picked off the ground. Bricks and large stones or slates can be very useful in building paths, raising all sorts of structures slightly off the ground, and so on. Stack anything that might be useful later in an out-of-the-way place.

Once the ground is cleared, those areas you want to cultivate in any way can be rotavated (the alternative being to dig them over; see page 28). Again, goats allowed to graze the area for a week or so will do much to remove harmful weeds – at least disposing of seeds, if not the deep-seated roots. Before cultivating, if the weed growth is very heavy, you can go over the ground a few times with a flamegun – but only if you know how to use one properly, and it is really necessary. Certainly it will destroy weed seeds, but it will also destroy the natural organic matter that can do much to improve the ground.

Various types of rotavator are available, but their basic purpose is the same – to turn over the ground. Do not try to rush the machine over the surface area, as it will not reach deeply enough into the ground.

MOVING A BOULDER

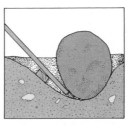

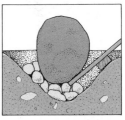

1 Using a strong pole, work it under the boulder. Put a brick under the pole, and use it for leverage

2 Still holding the pole, begin to place large stones under the boulder to raise it from the bottom of the hole.

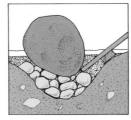

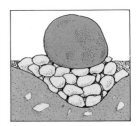

3 Having raised the boulder, lever it in the same way from the other side. Continue adding stones to raise it.

4 Finally the stone will bring the boulder up to the level of the ground, at which point it can be rolled away.

Improving the Soil

THE SOIL on any plot of land is made up of a series of layers. The top layer, or top soil, is of the most immediate importance and it is its nature that most affects the successful growth of fruit and vegetables.

Top soil may be categorized into five main groups, although these could be endlessly further sub-divided, as few soils fall so neatly into one category. The groups are sandy, loam, clay, chalky and peat. One method of assessing soil type is to mix it with water and leave it in a jam jar overnight; another is to identify the various plants that are growing on the land and then check in a gardening encyclopedia to see what kind of soil they require to flourish.

Sandy soil
This is light and easy to dig over – the soil offering little resistance to a spade or fork and not being heavy or sticky to lift. It may be identified by picking up a handful; it will feel gritty and slip easily through your fingers. In windy weather, the surface is easily blown away. Water drains through sandy soil so quickly that it can soon become very dry. In addition, vital nutrients are washed away. The nutrients should be replaced and the ground made more water-retentive by digging in large quantities of well-rotted compost or farmyard manure.

Loam
This is the ideal soil for all types of cultivation. It is darker than sandy soil (owing to its humus content) and crumbly rather than gritty. A handful rubbed between the fingers will feel smooth; moisten it slightly and it should not feel gritty, nor should it stick together in lumps.

Clay
Clay soils are heavy to work, sticking to the spade and your boots. A handful pressed between your fingers will stick together in a lump and after a heavy rainfall, puddles will remain on the surface of the ground for a considerable time. In a long, dry spell, clay soils can become very hard. They can be improved by being dug thoroughly in the autumn, leaving large lumps in the surface which will break up in the frost. Dig in large quantities of any available organic material – such as well-rotted compost, farmyard manure or leaf mould. When the soil has dried out in the spring, it can be broken down to a fairly fine tilth.

Chalky
Chalky soil is best identified by its grey-white surface – particularly noticeable during a dry spell and by the fact that such soil largely prevails in the surrounding area. Water generally drains quickly through it; water-retentive qualities can be improved by digging in lots of organic material.

Peat
Such soil is found in relatively few areas, and is the result of centuries of growth and decomposition of certain types of plants. Thus it is generally highly organic, and provided it drains well, it will be easy to work and extremely fertile. In areas where peat has formed over non-porous sub-soil, the soil will become easily water-logged and is usually acid.

Improving the soil
In addition to their type, soils are either alkaline, neutral or acid and this, too, will affect the growing of crops. This aspect of soil can be assessed by using a soil-testing kit, available from any garden shop. The soil tested will register a number on the pH scale. A neutral soil has a pH of 7; above this the soil is alkaline and below it, acid.

Most vegetables favour a slightly acid soil with a pH reading of 6.5. Brassicas prefer a pH of 7 to 7.5, whilst marrows, potatoes and tomatoes like a pH of 5 to 5.5. Most fruit likes a neutral or slightly acid soil.

As a broad generalization, most soils tend to be acid rather than highly alkaline, the exceptions being chalky soils and some clay ones (but by no means all). Over-acid soils can be corrected by applications of lime. It should be sprinkled over the soil as long as possible before growing the crop, but after the ground has been dug in the autumn or winter. It can then be left to be washed through the ground by the winter rains. Most soils should be limed every three years.

Testing top soil in a jam jar: before planning out your piece of land, you must discover what sort of top soil you have, because some vegetables and fruit will only grow well on particular types of soil. There is no point in wasting time and money in growing produce on soil to which it is not suited. Shake a small quantity of your garden soil in a jam jar of water, and leave to settle overnight. Gravel and coarse sand will sink to the bottom and will be topped by a layer of gritty material. Above this will be the clay. If the gravel and sand makes the largest layer, the soil is sandy. The middle layer indicates the amount of loam present; if it constitutes about forty per cent in all, the soil is a good loam. If the top layer of clay is equal in depth to the other two layers together, you have a clay soil.

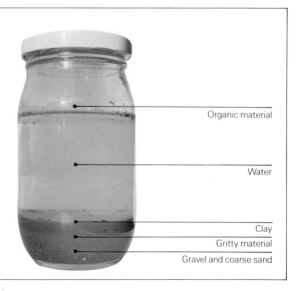

Organic material

Water

Clay

Gritty material

Gravel and coarse sand

TESTING THE PH FACTOR OF SOIL

As well as discovering the type of soil you have, you can ascertain its pH level using a soil-testing kit. Take small amounts of soil from different parts of your land and place them in test tubes. By adding different solutions, you can discover the pH balance of your soil. Then, using the charts provided in the kit, work out whether any lime should be added to correct the pH balance of the soil. You will also be able to decide which fertilizer to use.

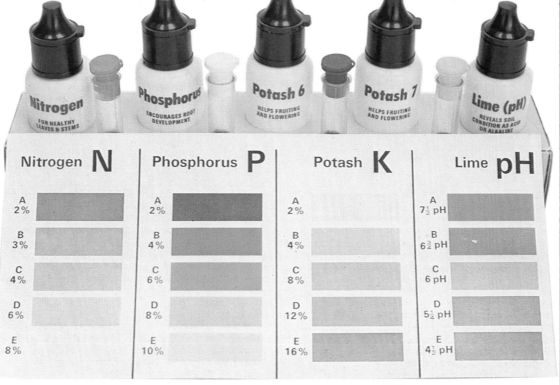

Nitrogen N		Phosphorus P		Potash K		Lime pH	
A 2%		A 2%		A 2%		A $7\frac{1}{2}$ pH	
B 3%		B 4%		B 4%		B $6\frac{3}{4}$ pH	
C 4%		C 6%		C 8%		C 6 pH	
D 6%		D 8%		D 12%		D $5\frac{1}{4}$ pH	
E 8%		E 10%		E 16%		E $4\frac{1}{2}$ pH	

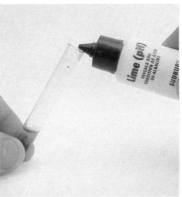

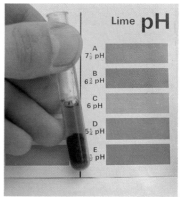

1 Take samples of soil from different parts of your land, allow them to dry, remove any foreign bodies and crumble the soils. Fill a quarter of each test tube with different soils and label.

2 Holding each test tube carefully, add a few drops of solution, according to the chemical for which you are testing. Shake the mixture for 30 seconds and then leave for 10 minutes.

3 When the soil has settled to the bottom of the test tube, match the colour of the solution to the appropriate colour chart. The result gives the pH level of the soil.

Composting and Draining

DURING THE COURSE of their growth, all plants take certain nutrients from the soil. Unless these are returned, subsequent crops will fail. Whenever possible, soil should be revitalized and its stocks of plant food replenished using organic manures and fertilizers. Inorganic or chemical types generally produce more immediate results, but in some cases they can give long-term, lasting damage to the soil.

In many situations, it is possible to keep the soil constantly healthy by adding little more than farmyard manure and garden-made compost, usually dug in during the autumn. Mulches of these materials – that is, a layer spread over the soil – help to prevent the soil drying out.

Garden-made compost
This is produced by compacting together all manner of organic waste – dead plants and flower heads, vegetable peelings and remains, fruit skins, crushed egg shells, hedge and grass cuttings, and so on. These should be layered in a container interspersed occasionally with an activator, which helps the decomposing process by feeding the bacteria. The chemical that brings this about is nitrogen which can be supplied organically by a layer of poultry or other animal manure, fish meal, dried blood or sewage sludge.

Begin the compost with a layer of coarse twigs or stems to allow the air to circulate from the bottom (air is essential for the decomposing process), then add organic waste as it is available in even layers. Press them down and dampen them if they are excessively dry. Do not try to compost perennial weeds or annuals that are full of seeds, any diseased materials (such as the infected roots of a cabbage, for example) or scraps of food that are greasy – the seeds will grow and the infections spread. Anything that is very thick or woody should be chopped

or squashed first and lawn mowings should be mixed with other materials rather than spread in a solid layer, which will form an effective air-excluding barrier, thereby preventing the bacteria from working.

Compost is generally most successful if built quickly, preferably in the spring and summer when the warmer atmosphere speeds up the decomposing process. At this time of year it will be ready in a month or two, at which point it will be brown, moist and crumbly with a uniform appearance and texture throughout. It will take at least twice as long to reach maturity in winter.

Farmyard manure
This is most likely to be horse, cow, pig or poultry manure, mixed with the original bedding of straw, or wood shavings, and may be used to add valuable humus to the soil. It is of great value to the fruit and vegetable gardener, although it seldom has such a high plant food content as well-made compost. This is particularly so if the manure has been stacked out in the open, as the rain will have washed away much of the soluble nutrients. Poultry manure is usually best added to the compost heap, rather than straight to the soil, as it tends to be rather dry.

Other organic manures
Leaf mould: this is produced by composting dead leaves and can be used to add humus to the soil. Very often, there will not be enough leaves to warrant composting them on their own, in which case they can be added to the general compost heap. However, if large sources are available they can be layered in a heap. Press them down well and dampen them if they are very dry. Do not build a pile much more than about 1 metre (3 ft) high and turn it three or four times a year. It will take a good 18 months or so to decompose sufficiently, by

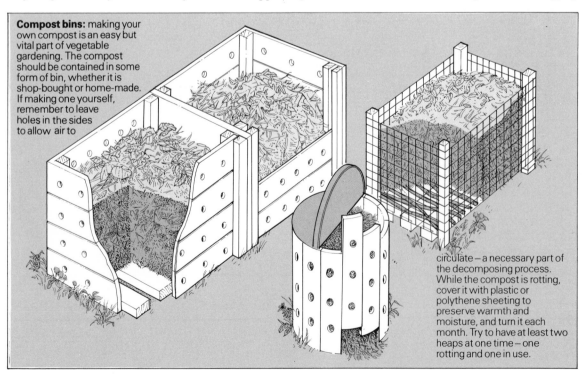

Compost bins: making your own compost is an easy but vital part of vegetable gardening. The compost should be contained in some form of bin, whether it is shop-bought or home-made. If making one yourself, remember to leave holes in the sides to allow air to circulate – a necessary part of the decomposing process. While the compost is rotting, cover it with plastic or polythene sheeting to preserve warmth and moisture, and turn it each month. Try to have at least two heaps at one time – one rotting and one in use.

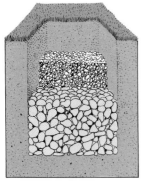

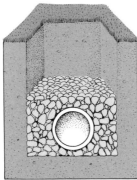

Draining with a sump: a drain-trench can be dug in the sub soil sloping from the highest to the lowest point, and leading to a sump. It must be as deep as it is wide and have a layer of rubble in the bottom, with smaller pieces of clinker. The sub and top soil is then replaced.

Draining with a pipe: to make this system more effective, lay a stone or plastic pipe (into which slits have been cut) in the trench before filling it up with rubble and clinker. The water soaks through the porous stone pipe or through the splits in the plastic and away through the sump.

which time it will have shrunk to about half its size.

Seaweed: people living in coastal areas can collect seaweed, which is a good provider of plant foods. It should be left to endure one or two rainfalls to wash away the salt and then dug into the soil in the autumn or winter.

Sewage sludge: this is sometimes available from the local authorities and can provide a rich source of manure. Check it does not contain any harmful waste matter, though.

Peat: dark brown- or black-coloured peats are useful for enriching the humus content of the soil but contain little in the way of plant food. Light-coloured peat indicates that the decomposition process is not so well advanced.

Bonemeal, dried blood, fish meal and hoof and horn: these animal products are all used as top dressing to soil, or added to enrich the soil at sowing time, and therefore are valuable, although expensive. They add no bulk or humus to the soil, but enrich its content.

Draining poor soil

Soil with poor drainage can often be corrected by regular digging and incorporating lots of organic material to the soil. If the ground still appears to be waterlogged, or if puddles hang about for days on the surface, try raising the level of the plot, by still more digging and adding bulky organic matter.

Better drainage can sometimes be achieved by draining the ground above the plot. Dig a ditch at the end of this, sloping it down into a sump (a deep hole, the bottom of which should be beneath the level of the water table) filled with rubble. Mark the position of the sump in some way as it will probably need periodic cleaning out to remove silt and other rubbish.

Herringbone system: you can make your drainage system more sophisticated by laying proper drains in the trench, arranging them in a herringbone pattern of smaller pipes leading into a main pipe, and from there into a nearby stream or a piece of land where drainage is not a problem.

Digging

DIGGING is an essential part of annual soil cultivation. It improves the soil's condition by aerating it and making drainage qualities more efficient, while also making it easier for moisture to reach and be absorbed by the plant roots. It provides an opportunity to clean the soil of old plant roots and weeds, and to incorporate organic material into the growing area.

Heavy clay soils should be dug in the autumn; not only will they be harder to dig later, but they will not reap the benefit of the winter elements. Leave the soil in large lumps on the surface to expose the maximum area. If you miss this time, wait until the spring winds have dried out the soil. Lighter soils can be dug later.

A plot intended for growing fruit and vegetables may be single or double dug (see below). You will find either method strenuous and tiring, particularly if you tackle it incorrectly. Follow the method shown in the diagrams and always lift less on the spade than you think you can manage. Stand upright, stretching your spine at frequent intervals, and tackle the job slowly.

Single digging is the most usual method of digging, and it is one which is quite adequate for most cultivation purposes.

Double digging is most usually done on long-neglected ground. Heavy clay can benefit from double digging as it will help to improve drainage considerably. A new vegetable plot will yield better crops straightaway if it is double-dug.

As you dig, remove the roots of any perennial weeds. Annuals can be dug into the soil to add to the humus.

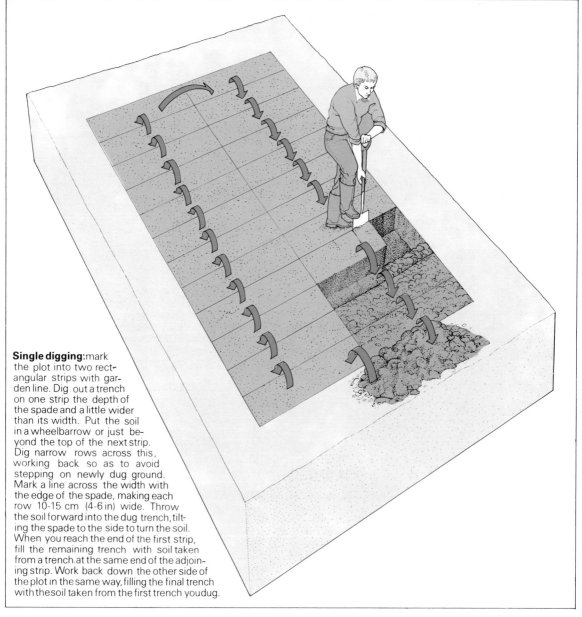

Single digging: mark the plot into two rectangular strips with garden line. Dig out a trench on one strip the depth of the spade and a little wider than its width. Put the soil in a wheelbarrow or just beyond the top of the next strip. Dig narrow rows across this, working back so as to avoid stepping on newly dug ground. Mark a line across the width with the edge of the spade, making each row 10-15 cm (4-6 in) wide. Throw the soil forward into the dug trench, tilting the spade to the side to turn the soil. When you reach the end of the first strip, fill the remaining trench with soil taken from a trench at the same end of the adjoining strip. Work back down the other side of the plot in the same way, filling the final trench with the soil taken from the first trench you dug.

DOUBLE DIGGING

1 Mark out the plot into two strips. Dig the first strip the depth of the spade but twice the width. Take out the soil. **2** Dig over the soil in the bottom of the trench. Do not remove the soil. **3** Add an even layer of organic matter. **4** Dig the next row, making it the depth and width of the spade. Throw soil forward to fill first trench. Dig out two rows of top soil to form **new** trench, two spades' width.

Fences

EVEN THE SMALLEST patch of land or smallholding will need some fences – if only to mark its boundaries. Fences have all sorts of other uses too; they can act as windbreaks to protect delicate fruit bushes or vegetables; they can form a screen which would hide untidy areas of the garden such as the place where you are making compost, or to keep bees, perhaps, away from areas of activity; they are essential for containing livestock such as chickens, goats or pigs in a specific area, and they can act as supports for canes, vines or other climbers.

There are many different types of fencing. Some of the ones most frequently used are illustrated opposite, but there are others you might like to consider. An electric fence, for example, can be useful in keeping pigs and goats in a contained area and it is easy to move from place to place. Fences used to contain livestock must always have some sort of a gate incorporated into them to give you access to feed, clean and inspect the animals. This can be erected quite easily in an electric fence; drive two strong posts into the ground wide enough apart for your access. Then cut the wire between them and slide a plastic handle onto one end. Twist the final piece of this wire into a hook and twist the wire on the other post into

Left: a growing hedge is one of the most pleasing of all fences aesthetically and it can form an effective barrier, too. Quickthorn and holly make good thick fences, quickthorn being one of the fastest to grow. Protect young hedges from animals such as goats, who will demolish them. As a hedge grows it can be laid (as illustrated) by cutting into the base of growing stems and bending them over. In some cases the whole hedge will be growing; in others, separate upright stakes are driven into the ground and the living branches woven between these.

Below left: high walls are undoubtedly the most effective barriers for keeping pets, livestock and children in, and unwanted intruders – animal or human – out. However, they can present a

rather harsh and stark appearance. Attaching a wooden trellis to them and training climbers up this, can do much to soften the appearance. A south-facing wall is particularly useful for growing delicate fruit, such as peaches, apricots and figs.

Below: post and wire structures, such as those illustrated here, make effective supports for climbing fruit canes and trees. Consider growing these against a post and wire fence; it will make an infinitely more pleasing barrier.

a loop. When you hook these together, the circuit will be reconnected. Pigs will need a two-stranded electric fence to contain them securely; goats will need three, but the bottom wire does not have to be live.

There are many permutations on the post-and-rail fencing. Flat wooden boards can be used instead of rails and these can be attached alternately to opposite sides of the vertical posts to give a different effect. Post-and-rails are certainly one of the most attractive forms of fencing to look at and they form an extremely secure barrier, but once erected, they are permanently positioned. They are also among the most expensive types of fencing.

Consider what function you want the fence to serve before selecting the type of fencing to use. This way you can choose the most suitable fencing for the job – although you may find that the financial aspect exerts a strong influence. Remember that boundary fences often have to keep pets and children in, as well as other people's livestock and destructive wild pests, such as rabbits, out. Bear in mind, too, that solid fencing will block out all light from the area it casts into shadow, possibly putting growing fruit and vegetables into deep shade. Above all, any fence you erect is always only as good as its weakest point, and if used to contain livestock, they will find this almost before you have turned away!

TYPES OF FENCE

Dry stone walls: no cement is used in the construction. They are attractive and very stable if properly built. Semi-dry stone walls, in which cement is used in the centre (where it is hidden from view) are stronger, but they retain the dry effect.

Post-and-rail fence: relatively crudely constructed. A neater appearance is achieved by cutting the ends of the horizontal posts at a 45° angle and splicing these together. In some fencing, mortice joints are used to join the horizontals to the verticals.

Hurdles: very useful in making quick, temporary fencing to contain young livestock, for example, When not needed, hurdles can be neatly stacked against the wall of a shed or garage, where they will not take up too much room.

Wattle hurdles: can be purchased or you can make them yourself by weaving split hazel branches between vertical posts. They provide a more solid-looking fence than ordinary hurdles, but would be used in the same circumstances.

Wire netting fences: often used for containing stock. Widely spaced pig wire is very strong; closer mesh wire is easier to handle and perfectly adequate for poultry.

Barbed wire fencing: there is seldom any justification in using this. It looks unattractive and can inflict very unpleasant injuries on livestock. In most circumstances, ordinary wire fencing will provide just as effective a barrier.

Tools and Equipment

THE FOLLOWING SELECTION of tools are those you are likely to find most useful in fruit and vegetable production. When buying gardening tools, it tends to be a case of 'you get what you pay for'. In other words, the more expensive ones will generally be made of better (stronger) material, and will thus not only last longer, but will also do their allotted job more efficiently. Examine them carefully, feeling to make sure the grip or handle is comfortable to hold and that they are the right weight for you.

Having bought good equipment, make sure you keep it in good condition. Scrape off all clinging soil before putting the tools away, and store them neatly, preferably by suspending them from hooks in the tool shed. Keep metal hinges oiled and greased and sharpen all blades at least once a year.

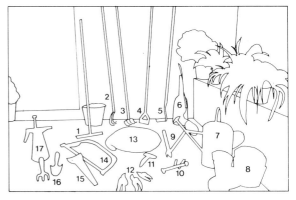

More tools and equipment: as with all garden tools, it is false economy to buy poorly-made tools which will break much sooner than their more expensive, but better-produced, counterparts. However, do not make the mistake of buying very sophisticated equipment when much simpler tools will do the job equally well. **Left: 1** rake; **2 & 3** cultivators: **4** Dutch hoe; **5** draw hoe; **6** sprayer; **7** watering can; **8** flower pots; **9** loppers; **10** garden twine and stakes; **11** dibber; **12** secateurs; **13** hose; **14** log saw; **15** pruning saw; **16** trowel and fork; **17** hand sprayer. **Right:** it is important to spray plants as this gives them the moisture their leaves need and keeps them free of dust. You can also spray them for insect control or to prevent disease. **Below:** instead of using a ladder, you can trim and prune top tree branches using a pruner with a handle extension.

Rotation of Vegetables

THE FIRST PRINCIPLE of growing vegetables is that the crops in each group should be grown in a different part of the vetable garden each year. This crop rotation is important for two main reasons: the first is that different crops like different soil conditions. Peas and beans, for example, like ground that is rich in freshly dug-in, well-rotted manure, whereas if roots such as carrots and parsnips are grown in such soil, the result is a crop of twisted, forked, divided vegetables, as they go in search of the organic matter. The second reason is that the pests and diseases that plague individual groups of vegetables will remain in the ground, ready to attack again. They do not, however, affect vegetables in the other groups.

The most usual crop rotation operates on a three-year plan, although if you can divide the plot up into four patches and operate the four-year plan, so much the better. On the three-year plan, the three principal groups are the root crops (as specified on page 50, but also including potatoes and chicory), the brassicas (as specified on page 44, but including radishes), and a combination of the legumes and other outdoor crops which, besides beans and peas, include celery, celeriac, leeks, the various onions, sweetcorn and tomatoes. The salad crops not mentioned in these groups can be grown as catch crops (between the rows of longer-maturing vegetables, or as successional crops) – that is, as a quick crop to utilize the land after it has been cleared of a major crop and before the next one is sown. Marrows, courgettes (large and small zucchini) and pumpkins can be included in the legume and other outdoor crop section, but if you have a patch of spare land or a space on a compost heap, they are best grown here, for they take up much valuable space in the vegetable garden proper. The perennial crops such as globe artichokes and asparagus have to be alloted a permanent space as they

will crop in the same site for a number of years. Jerusalem artichokes can be included in the roots group, but they are so pervasive that they are really best grown on a small patch of otherwise useless ground, perhaps in front of the garden shed or so as to hide the compost heap and other work areas from view.

If you intend to operate a three-year rotation plan, and have therefore divided the main part of the vegetable garden into three roughly equal-sized plots, allocate the first plot to the root crops, the second plot to the legumes and other outdoor crops and the third plot to the brassicas. The following year move the vegetables down the line, so that the first plot has the brassicas the second has the root crops and the third the legumes and other outdoor crops. In the final year of the plan, the first plot will have the legumes, the second will have the brassicas and the third will have the roots.

Even better crops will appear in your garden if you follow a system of digging lots of well-rotted manure or compost into the ground before planting the legumes, applying general fertilizer to the ground before planting the roots and applying both fertilizer and lime before planting the brassicas. The roots will benefit from the manure dug in for the legumes because by the time they are planted it will have become well rotted and incorporated into the ground, thus making the soil moisture-retentive, rather than very rich. Potatoes, which can react very badly to lime, are not planted until two years after the lime was applied to the ground, but the brassicas, which thrive in alkaline conditions, have had full benefit from it. Bear in mind when planting, incidentally, to site the potatoes and tomatoes as far away from one another as possible.

If you are able to operate a four-year plant you can either separate out the peas and beans from the legumes

WATERING EQUIPMENT

Watering plants is obviously a very important part of your work in the garden. If the plants do not have enough water their growth will become stunted and they may wither and die. As well as the traditional watering can, there are various attachments which can be fitted to hose pipes and will reach into awkward spots. They will also vary the force of water. **Below: 1** A basic hose pipe nozzle, which is hand-held. It can give a spray or a gush. **2** Simple sprinkler which covers a small area at a time, and is stuck in the ground. **3** A rotating sprinkler which covers more ground, and sometimes has adjustable nozzles. **4** The more sophisticated oscillating sprinkler covers an even bigger area. **Right:** when transplanting leeks, dib a hole, put in plant but do not firm it in. Instead, fill the hole with water. When it drains away it will have brought the soil into the hole.

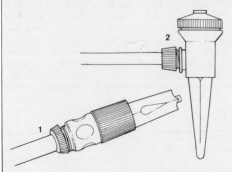

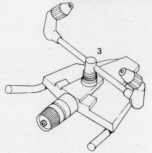

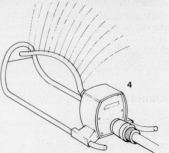

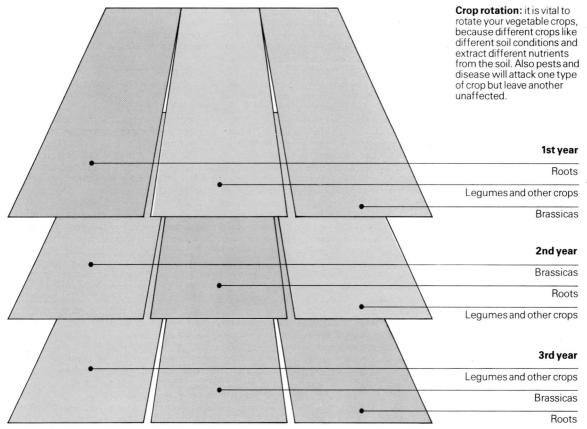

Crop rotation: it is vital to rotate your vegetable crops, because different crops like different soil conditions and extract different nutrients from the soil. Also pests and disease will attack one type of crop but leave another unaffected.

1st year
Roots
Legumes and other crops
Brassicas

2nd year
Brassicas
Roots
Legumes and other crops

3rd year
Legumes and other crops
Brassicas
Roots

and other outdoor crops, or you can treat potatoes as a separate group, perhaps using that plot also for marrows and courgettes and some of the spinach crops. The most important things to remember in any rotation plan are to ensure that brassicas and potatoes never follow themselves in the same sites in successive years (and if at all possible not more than once every three years is infinitely better) and to plant quick-growing, successional crops after harvesting a major crop whenever possible. If brassicas follow brassicas, you could easily get a build-up of the disease club root (see page 49) in the soil and once there, it will remain for several years, making it impossible to grow brassicas at all. Likewise with potatoes, you could encourage the pest eelworm (see page 64) in the soil, and this too will remain for some time.

Remember too that some crops which take a fair time to reach full maturity can be regarded as quick-growing when using them as successional crops. Carrots and beetroots, for example, which would take perhaps four months to reach full size, can nevertheless be harvested much quicker as young, exceptionally delicious baby vegetables. In some instances you will find too that there is time to grow a quick-maturing crop after harvesting the previous one, and before planting the next one outlined in the rotation scheme.

The year in the garden
The calendar of work outlined on the following pages is meant only as a general guide and outline to the principal crop-producing activities of sowing, planting and

harvesting. It is very unlikely that anyone will find themselves doing all the activities as specified at each season – time and room would make it impossible! There are also many crops which can be sown in regular succession throughout the spring and summer months, but if you do this, you will be inundated with that particular vegetable, and also you will not have much room left in the vegetable garden to grow anything else! Sow all vegetables as and when it suits you (within their particular season), therefore, in order to get a reasonable amount and assortment of vegetables, rather than a glut of any one type.

As mentioned above, the activities covered in this calendar of work are really only the principal ones of actually growing and producing crops. Remember that, in addition, you must hoe the fruit and vegetable gardens regularly to keep weeds under control and that all crops must be watered regularly in dry weather. Stake and tie plants as necessary to support them as they are growing, and protect emerging seedlings from birds by tying threads of cotton above them or by covering them with cloches. In addition, protect young crops from frost in the winter and early spring with cloches.

Inspect all crops regularly to make sure they are not suffering from any disease; if they are, deal with it immediately to prevent the condition getting worse or spreading, and burn any infected plants you pull up. Dig up and compost all plants once the harvest is finished, so that the land can be used for another crop. No part of the vegetable garden should lie fallow, particularly during the main growing season.

THE YEAR IN THE GARDEN

	IN THE GREENHOUSE	IN THE FRUIT GARDEN	
SPRING Early spring	**Water all greenhouse crops regularly throughout the spring.** **Sow** pepper, chilli and tomato seeds and raise them in a propagator.	**Plant** apricots; figs; vines and rhubarb. **Sow under glass or indoors** seeds of alpine strawberries. **Prune** apples; apricots; sour cherries; plums, gages and damsons. **Pollinate** apricots.	**Raise new plants** of rhubarb. **Harvest** rhubarb.
Mid-spring	**Transplant** aubergine (eggplant) and cucumber seedlings to their permanent growing sites. **Sow** melon seeds and raise them in a propagator. **Prune** vines and established fruit trees. Train the new growth. **Pinch out** growing tips of vines.	**Harden off** alpine strawberries. **Train** new growth of vines; peaches and nectarines. **Mulch** apples; apricots; sour cherries; peaches and nectarines; pears; gooseberries; vines; raspberries and rhubarb. Put straw under strawberry plants. **Harvest** rhubarb.	
Late spring	**Transplant** pepper, chilli, melon and tomato seedlings to their permanent sites. **Mulch** all greenhouse crops. **Shade** greenhouse roof as necessary. **Pollinate** fruit trees as necessary. **Support** growing aubergine and cucumber plants.	**Transplant to permanent site** alpine strawberries. **Thin fruits** of apricots and gooseberries. **Harvest** rhubarb.	
SUMMER Early summer	**Throughout the summer water and feed** all greenhouse crops regularly and **syringe** crops with water in very hot weather. **Pollinate** grapes and melons. **Thin out** tree fruits. **Support** growing pepper, chilli, melon and tomato plants. **Harvest** cucumbers.	**Prune** figs, peaches and nectarines; gooseberries; red and white currants. **Thin fruits** of apples; plums and gages; peaches and nectarines; gooseberries. **Harvest** strawberries; blackcurrants; gooseberries and rhubarb.	
Mid-summer	**Thin out** fruits of grapes and melons. **Harvest** aubergines, cucumbers, tomatoes, peppers and chillies and tree fruits.	**Plant** strawberries. **Prune** apples; peaches and nectarines; pears. **Thin fruits** of pears (if necessary) and grapes. **Train** blackberries; loganberries and raspberries. **Raise new plants** of strawberries. **Harvest** apricots; sour cherries; peaches and nectarines;	strawberries; alpine strawberries; blackcurrants; blueberries; gooseberries; summer fruiting raspberries; red and white currants and rhubarb.
Late summer	**Harvest** aubergines; cucumbers; tomatoes; peppers and chillies and tree fruits.		
AUTUMN Early autumn	**Water and spray all greenhouse crops regularly.** **Harvest** aubergines; cucumbers; tomatoes; tree fruits; melons and grapes.	**Prepare** the ground for planting tree fruits and canes. **Mulch** damsons, plums and gages and blackcurrants. **Thin fruits** of figs. **Raise new plants** of blackcurrants;	gooseberries; currants. **Harvest** apples; damsons; figs; pears; strawberries; alpine strawberries; blackberries and loganberries; blueberries; grapes and autumn-fruiting raspberries.
Late autumn	**Harvest** aubergines; tomatoes; tree fruits and grapes. **Pull up and compost** all annual plants when harvesting is finished. **Prune** fruit trees and vines. **Plant** fruit trees and vines.	**Plant** apples; apricots; plums, gages and damsons; peaches and nectarines; blackberries; loganberries; blackcurrants; gooseberries; red and white currants. **Prune** blackcurrants and	raspberries. **Protect** strawberries with cloches (to give a late crop). **Harvest** apples; damsons; figs; pears; strawberries; alpine strawberries; autumn-fruiting raspberries.
WINTER Early winter	**Water vines and tree fruits throughout the winter.** Apart from this there is really nothing to do in the early part of the winter.	**Plant** apples; apricots; sour cherries; pears; raspberries. **Protect** strawberries with cloches. **Prune** apples; apricots; peaches	and nectarines; pears; currants; blueberries; gooseberries; grapes. **Raise new plants** of raspberries. **Mulch** red and white currants.
Mid-winter			
Late winter	**Change** the border soil. **Sow** seeds of aubergine and cucumber. **Prune** vines and tree fruits.		

IN THE VEGETABLE GARDEN

Prepare seed beds and permanent growing sites for sowing as soon as weather conditions allow. **Sow under glass or indoors** seeds of globe varieties of beetroot; asparagus peas; leeks; self-blanching celery and ordinary celery.	**Sow in seed beds** seeds of calabrese. **Sow in permanent site** seeds of kohl rabi; maincrop carrots; parsnips; salsify and scorzonera; first-early peas; mange tout (snow peas) and petit pois; American cress; lettuce; radishes;	salad and pickling onions; onions from seed, and summer spinach. **Plant** early potatoes and Jerusalem artichoke tubers. **Harden off** summer cabbage; cauliflower. **Transplant to permanent site** red cabbage.	**Harvest** purple sprouting broccoli; savoy; red cabbage; kale; spinach beet; swedes (rutabagas); turnip greens; chicory; lettuce; celery; leeks; winter spinach. **Protect** early crops and young seedlings from cold weather with cloches as necessary.
Sow under glass or indoors dwarf, French and haricot beans; tomatoes for outdoors; celery; celeriac; marrows; courgettes (zucchini) and pumpkins; okra; New Zealand spinach; sweetcorn. **Sow in seed beds** seeds of purple sprouting broccoli; brussels sprouts; summer cabbage; kale.	**Sow in permanent site** kohl rabi; maincrop carrots; parsnips; salsify and scorzonera; spinach beet; turnips; broad beans; second-early peas; mange tout and petit pois; chicory; lettuce; radish; leeks; salad and pickling onions; onions from seed; onions from sets; garlic; summer spinach.	**Plant** second-early potatoes; globe artichoke suckers. **Harden off** white sprouting broccoli; globe varieties of beetroot; asparagus peas; tomatoes for outdoors; celery; celeriac; leeks; onions from seed. **Transplant to permanent site** globe varieties of beetroot; carrots; turnips.	**Harvest** purple sprouting broccoli; spring cabbage; savoy; red cabbage; kale; spinach beet; swedes; turnip greens; lettuce; salad onions; leeks; winter spinach. **Begin** earthing-up emerging potatoes.
Sow under glass or indoors seeds of cucumber; celery. **Sow in seed beds** autumn and winter cabbage; savoy; cauliflower and white sprouting broccoli. **Sow in permanent site** kohl rabi; maincrop carrots; salsify and scorzonera; seakale beet; swedes; turnips; kale; broad beans; dwarf,	French and haricot beans; runner beans; late peas; mange tout and petit pois; cucumber (but protect with cloches); salad and pickling onions; onions from seed; okra (but protect with cloches); New Zealand spinach; sweetcorn (but protect with cloches). **Plant** maincrop potatoes; asparagus crowns.	**Harden off** dwarf, French and haricot beans; runner beans; marrows, courgettes and pumpkins; okra; New Zealand spinach; celery; sweetcorn. **Transplant** dwarf, French and haricot beans; asparagus peas; celery; celeriac; onions from seed; okra; sweetcorn (but protect with cloches).	**Thin** carrots; parsnips; turnips; dwarf, French and haricot beans; lettuce and all types of spinach. **Harvest** purple sprouting broccoli; spring cabbage; savoy; red cabbage; swedes; turnip greens; broad beans; first-early peas; asparagus; lettuce; radish; salad onions; leeks; winter spinach. **Continue** earthing-up potatoes.
Water all crops regularly during dry spells. Support growing plants. Sow in seed beds seeds of red cabbage. **Sow in permanent site** seeds of Chinese cabbage; kohl rabi; globe varieties of beetroot; long-rooted varieties of beetroot; dwarf, French and haricot beans;	first-early peas; asparagus peas; lettuce; radish; salad and pickling onions. **Harden off** cucumbers. **Transplant to permanent site** purple sprouting broccoli; brussels sprouts; autumn and winter cabbage; savoy; cauliflower and white sprouting broccoli; kale;	runner beans; tomatoes for outdoors; cucumbers and pumpkins. **Thin** Chinese cabbage; kohl rabi; salsify and scorzonera; summer spinach; New Zealand spinach; seakale beet and spinach beet. **Pinch out** growing tips of trailing marrows and pumpkins.	**Harvest** globe artichokes; summer cabbage; kohl rabi; beetroot; carrots; broad beans; dwarf and French beans; first-early peas; mange tout and petit pois; asparagus peas; early potatoes; asparagus; American cress; lettuce; radish; salad onions; summer spinach.
Sow in seed beds seeds of red cabbage. **Sow in permanent site** kohl rabi; globe varieties of beetroot; spinach beet; turnips; dwarf, French and haricot beans; salad and pickling onions; summer spinach. **Transplant to permanent site** purple sprouting broccoli; brussels	sprouts; autumn and winter cabbage; savoy; cauliflower and white sprouting broccoli; kale. **Thin** kale; kohl rabi; beetroot – all varieties; parsnips; salsify and scorzonera; chicory; summer spinach; New Zealand spinach; swedes. **Pinch out** growing tips of broad beans; tomatoes and New	Zealand spinach. **Pollinate** cucumbers. **Harvest** globe artichokes; summer cabbage; kohl rabi; beetroot; carrots; turnips; broad beans; dwarf, French and haricot beans; runner beans; first-early peas; second-early peas; maincrop peas; mange tout and petit pois; asparagus peas; early and	second-early potatoes; American cress; lettuce; radish; garlic; marrows and courgettes; salad and pickling onions; summer spinach and New Zealand spinach.
Sow in seed beds seeds of red cabbage and lettuce. **Sow in permanent site** seeds of kohl rabi; spinach beet; swedes; turnips; turnips for greens; corn salad; endive; lettuce; radish; winter radish; salad and pickling onions; onions from seed – overwintering varieties; summer	spinach; winter spinach. **Transplant to permanent site** cauliflower and white sprouting broccoli; summer cabbage. **Thin** Chinese cabbage (and tie up outer leaves to encourage inner growth); kohl rabi; chicory; endive; summer spinach; spinach beet.	**Blanch** celery. **Harvest** summer cabbage; kohl rabi; beetroot; carrots; seakale beet and spinach beet; swedes; turnips; broad beans; dwarf and French beans; runner beans; first-early peas; maincrop peas; late peas; mange tout and petit pois; asparagus peas; second-early	potatoes; outdoor tomatoes; American cress; lettuce; radish; garlic; marrows and courgettes; salad onions; shallots; okra; summer spinach; New Zealand spinach; sweetcorn.
Sow under glass or indoors seeds of cauliflower, lettuce – overwintering and forcing varieties; radish. **Sow in permanent site** seeds of corn salad; American cress and	winter spinach. **Thin** corn salad; lettuce and winter radish. **Harvest** calabrese; early brussels sprouts; Chinese cabbage; summer cabbage; savoy; red	cabbage; cauliflower and white sprouting broccoli; kohl rabi; beetroot; carrots; parsnips; seakale beet and spinach beet; swedes; turnips; dwarf, French and haricot beans; runner beans;	first-early peas; late peas; mange tout and petit pois; lettuce; radish; celery; courgettes and pumpkins; okra; summer spinach New Zealand spinach; salad onions; sweetcorn.
Sow under glass or indoors seeds of lettuce – overwintering and forcing varieties. **Sow in permanent site** seeds of broad beans – longpod varieties; garlic. **Thin** corn salad and lettuce.	**Blanch** endive and force chicory. **Protect** red cabbage with cloches; cauliflower curds by bending over the outside leaves. **Cut back** asparagus foliage. **Harvest** calabrese; brussels sprouts; Chinese cabbage; first	autumn and winter cabbage; savoy; red cabbage; cauliflower and white sprouting broccoli; kohl rabi; beetroot; carrots; parsnips; salsify and scorzonera; seakale beet and spinach beet; swedes; turnips; American cress;	lettuce; winter radish; garlic; celery; celeriac; leeks; summer spinach; salad onions.
Force chicory. **Blanch** endive. **Protect** first-early peas and winter spinach with cloches.	**Harvest** Jerusalem artichokes; brussels sprouts (and tops); autumn and winter cabbage; savoy; red cabbage; parsnips;	swedes; turnips; salsify and scorzonera; spinach beet; chicory; American cress; lettuce; winter radish; celery; celeriac;	leeks; onions; winter spinach, seakale beet.
Sow under glass or indoors seeds of cauliflower. **Harvest** Jerusalem artichokes;	brussels sprouts; autumn and winter cabbage; savoy; red cabbage; kale; parsnips; swedes;	spinach beet; chicory; corn salad; American cress; endive; winter radish; celery; celeriac; leeks and	winter spinach.
Sow under glass or indoors seeds of brussels sprouts; summer cabbage; cauliflower and white sprouting broccoli; early varieties	of carrots; turnips; lettuce; radish and onions from seed. **Prepare** seed potatoes for planting (chitting).	**Harvest** Jerusalem artichokes; brussels sprouts; autumn and winter cabbage; savoy; red cabbage; kale; parsnips; swedes;	spinach beet; chicory; corn salad; lettuce; celery; leeks; winter spinach.

Growing Vegetables

GROWING YOUR OWN vegetables is among the most money-saving of all garden activities and is obviously a must for all those who would like to think of themselves as becoming more self-sufficient. Even a small plot of land can generally yield sufficient vegetables to make it unnecessary for a family of four or five to have to buy any through the year. Some vegetables lend themselves to quick and easy methods of storage (see page 186), so that they can still be eaten fresh or in their natural state for most of the year. Others may be dried or salted, and nearly all will freeze successfully. Your own frozen produce will taste better than shop-bought equivalents and not just because it represents the sweat of your brow!

Most vegetables are not difficult to grow; if you do find something particularly hard, abandon it in favour of others that appear to suit your methods and your land better. The instructions given on the following pages must always be mixed with a lot of common-sense, and will often have to be adapted to suit your soil and your habits. Few vegetables are so rigid in their requirements that they cannot be made to accommodate such changes.

The weather is always a considerable controlling factor in any growing activity. It will often mean sowing, planting-out, transplanting and later, harvesting, have to be delayed because conditions are not right. Do not rigorously follow times given in this (or any other) book or on seed packets. Far better to delay sowing, for example, for a month or two than to put the seed in wet, cold soil where it will not germinate.

In the same way, planting distances between rows and plants, or distances to which to thin out seedlings, are always approximate. Any vegetable-grower will judge these by eye, using experience to adapt them to suit the garden. The only accurate measuring that is really necessary is when you are planning exactly what and how much to grow in the plot.

The pests and diseases outlined at the end of each of the different groups of vegetables are seldom the severe problem they might appear. Very rarely is it necessary not to grow a crop because of its possible problems, and few crops fail entirely because of disease or insect infestation, or at least they will not if you tackle the problem as it arises.

In this book the groups are as follows:

Brassicas: broccoli and calabrese, brussels sprouts, cabbages, cauliflowers, kale and kohl rabi.

Root crops: beetroots, carrots, parsnips, salsify and scorzonera, seakale and spinach beet, swedes (rutabagas) and turnips.

Legumes: beans and peas.

Potatoes

Salad crops: chicory, cress, endives, cucumbers, lettuces and radishes.

Other outdoor crops: globe and Jerusalem artichokes, asparagus, celery, celeriac, leeks, marrows and courgettes (zucchini), pumpkins and gourds, okra, onions, spinach and sweet corn.

Greenhouse crops: aubergines (eggplants), peppers and chillies, indoor tomatoes and cucumbers.

Raising Vegetable Seedlings

NEARLY ALL THE VEGETABLES outlined in the following pages can be raised from seed (a few exceptions being asparagus, globe and Jerusalem artichokes, which are more usually raised from crowns, suckers and tubers respectively, and potatoes which are grown from seed potatoes). Seeds can be raised outdoors in seed beds or in the vegetable plot in their intended growing, or cropping, spots; or indoors in pots, pans or trays. Which method is used will depend on a number of factors; among them the prevailing weather conditions, amount of space, type of seed and the desired time of harvesting.

Sowing outdoors

Most vegetable seeds can be raised outdoors, the chief disadvantage being that this often makes it harder to produce early crops. Most seeds will state a planting month on the packet, but be guided by the weather and the state of the soil. Seeds need moisture and warmth to germinate (as well as air), so the ground should be just damp (crumbly on the surface), not wet and cold.

Most sowing will take place in spring, with regulated sowing continuing through the summer, and sometimes the autumn, to give a succession of crops.

Sowing seeds in pots, pans or trays

This is done to bring crops on early, for those vegetables that take a long time to mature (thus leaving valuable space in the soil for quicker-growing crops), or for those crops that respond better to being raised individually, usually because they belong to the more tender plants that need rather higher temperatures to germinate.

Seeds grown this way must be planted in one of the special soil-based or soil-less seed or potting composts available at all garden shops. These have been specially prepared to provide the seeds with exactly the right growing medium; garden soil will not do – it contains too many weed seeds and is usually not a suitable texture for using in small containers. It is possible to make your own seed and potting composts using loam (if you can get it), sterilized peat and sand; but by and large, it makes more sense to buy it.

Plastic containers are generally better than those made of wood or clay. Whenever possible, use fairly shallow ones as they will use less compost.

Thinning and pricking-out

When the seedlings begin to appear in the rows outside in the plot, or indoors in the boxes, they need to be thinned or pricked-out to avoid overcrowding.

Outside, careful sowing should mean the minimum of thinning and thus the minimum of disturbance to the growing seedlings. Some, however, will be necessary and it is generally best to thin two or three times. The first time will be as soon as the seedlings are large enough to handle, and they should be thinned to a distance of about 5 cm (2 in) apart. The second thinning will be to

Sowing outside: 1 Knock down the soil with a cultivator, rake it over and remove any large stones. Add top dressing and rake again.

2 Draw up a sowing plan for the vegetable plot. Mark the correct planting distances along the plot and position a garden line along the first row.

3 Make out a drill the required depth, using the draw hoe. Pull it down the soil in a succession of strokes, rather than dragging it the entire length of the row.

4 If the ground shows any signs of being dry, water the bottom of the drill well throughout. Put in any fertilizer dressings you wish to use.

5 Using a dibber, sow the seed thinly. Even small seeds are best planted about two to each 2.5 cm (1 in). Use wooden stakes as guides to the distances.

6 Cover the seed by pulling the soil back and firming it gently with the back of the rake. Put labelled pieces of wood at both ends of the row.

SOWING SEEDS IN A PROPAGATOR

1 Check the moisture of the compost by squeezing it into a ball. Compost is wet enough if it cracks, but soil-less types should give moisture.

2 Place the compost in a seed tray and firm it down with your fingers or a piece of wood, so it is about 2.5cm (1 in) from the top.

3 If the compost is too dry, soak the tray in water and drain. Sprinkle seeds over compost, keeping them 1cm ($\frac{1}{2}$ in) apart.

4 Cover the seeds with another thin layer of compost. Soil-based compost should be sieved over the seeds to give a light cover.

5 Cover the seed tray with clean glass or put in a polythene bag, tied to enclose moisture. Place in a well-lit windowsill or greenhouse.

6 Remove the glass or polythene bag when seedlings begin to show through the compost, and thin out when large enough to handle.

Left: these seedlings have been left under glass for too long. They have become too tall and straggly, because the conditions of the propagator are not suitable for growth once the seedling has become established. **Above:** as a contrast, these seedlings have been correctly grown, and the glass removed at the right time. The seedlings are then allowed to grow further before transplanting.

about 15 cm (6 in) apart and the third to the final, recommended, spacing.

Seedlings from the first thinning will generally be discarded; those from a second thinning can sometimes be transplanted if space permits; those from the final thinning may produce vegetables – tiny carrots and turnips, for example – that the patient cook could use.

Thin seedlings when the soil is damp as this reduces the disturbance to those left behind, and pull the seedlings up by the leaves, not the stem – if you crush a leaf it will not harm the plant as much as if the stem is damaged.

Seedlings planted in containers must be pricked-out when they begin to crowd each other. Do this by gently holding them by a leaf and loosening the roots with a thin stick. Plant them into further pots or containers giving them more room. Make a small hole with a stick and bury the plants up to their first seed leaves.

Transplanting

This involves removing seedlings from their containers or spot in the ground and planting them in the final place where they are to grow and crop. It should be done carefully and sympathetically in order to lessen the shock. Make sure each plant has a growing point in the centre before you plant it.

Thinning: as soon as the seedlings are big enough to be handled, they must be thinned out to avoid overcrowding, whether they are in the ground **(top)** or in seed boxes **(above)**. The seedlings are generally thinned two or three times before they reach their correct spacing. You can often replant pricked out seedlings, unless they are very poor, and by the time of the third thinning, you may be able to eat the tiny vegetables which are pulled up **(left)**.

Transplanting: water the plant and new site well the day before. Choose a time when the weather is mild and damp, but not windy. **1** Dig up plants when about 10 cm (4 in) high, retaining some soil around their roots. **2** If in containers, either dig them out or, if planted in single pots, tip the pot upside down, supporting the plant carefully in your hand. **3** Make holes in the new site with a dibber, ensuring they are slightly larger than the roots with the soil attached, and are set the correct distance apart. **4** Carefully set the roots in the hole and fill in the sides with soil. The plant should be set slightly deeper in the ground than before. Pull at a leaf to see if the plant is firm in the ground. **5** Water in well.

Growing Brassicas

ALTHOUGH ONLY seven different vegetables fall under this heading – broccoli, brussels sprouts, cabbage, cauliflower, calabrese, kale and kohl rabi – the different variety, in terms of shape, size and taste they offer, is enormous. There are so many types of cabbage, for example, that it is quite possible to produce some form of it in the garden the whole year round. Most are very easy to grow.

Broccoli comes in two basic types – purple-sprouting or white-headed. The latter is more commonly grouped with the cauliflowers it closely resembles and is often known as the winter cauliflower. Purple-sprouting broccoli, with its abundance of purple-headed spears, is also easy to grow (provided you keep the pigeons away). It is ready for picking in the late winter/early spring – a time when fresh produce from the garden can be in short supply. Its close relation, calabrese, yields large heads of tightly packed green flower buds in the late summer/early autumn. Some of the hybrid varieties will grow in a comparatively short time.

Cauliflowers can also be grown the whole year round, although it takes a gifted gardener to do this, because they are the most difficult of all the brassicas to produce. Different varieties are available, but they tend not to vary so much in appearance as the various cabbages. One noticeable exception is the purple cauliflower, the

Brassica types: as well as the different types of brassicas, each crop has a wealth of different varieties, which suit different soil conditions, weather, and timing. The best guide before buying is to read the seed packets, which will tell you the requirements of the particular variety you have chosen. The three types here are broccoli **(above)**, brussels sprouts **(top)** and curly kale **(right)**.

tightly packed curd of which is a dark purple colour as its name suggests.

Brussels sprouts are a traditional favourite and are certainly one of the mainstays of winter vegetables. Early spring sowings yield autumn crops; decide whether it is worth the time and land to do this. It may be better to freeze some of the winter crop (which they take to well) and use the precious land for a crop that is quicker to mature.

Kale is a crop that might be thought of as cattle food in the minds of many, but it has long since been grown for the table, and its strong, distinctive taste (even better after a frost) has much to offer. The different varieties

Unusual brassicas: two of the more unusual brassicas which you can grow are kohl rabi **(left)** and calabrese **(right)**. The different varieties of kohl rabi mean that it can be grown for most of the year, and is eaten raw in salads or cooked like a turnip. Calabrese is similar to broccoli and has a shorter growing season, but is less hardy. As a contrast, cauliflower **(below)** is very popular, but can be difficult to grow.

GROWING TIMES AND HARVESTING MONTHS

Many types of brassicas – cabbages in particular – can be produced in your garden all the year round. The cropping season of others can be extended either by making sowings in succession over a period of weeks or months or by choosing to grow varieties that take varying times to mature (some have been specially produced to mature quickly).

Below is a chart which gives the shortest time each type of brassica will take to reach full maturity and the months in which they can be harvested (subject, of course, to timed sowing).

Vegetable	Shortest Growing Time	Harvesting Months
Purple sprouting broccoli	11 months	March–May
Calabrese	3–4 months	August–October
Brussels sprouts	8 months	September–early March (best in November and December)
Cabbage		
Summer:	4 months	June–September
Autumn & winter:	At least 6 months	October–February
Savoy:	At least 5 months	September–May
Spring:	8 months	April–May
Red:	8 months	September–May
Chinese:	3 months	September – October
Cauliflower and white broccoli	At least 4 months (most varieties take longer)	Can be harvested the year round; easiest to produce for autumn and winter
Kale	8 months	December–April
Kohl rabi	2 months	May–October

Cabbages: There are so many different varieties of cabbage from red **(left)** to Chinese **(above)**, that it is possible to grow some form of it throughout the year. It is perhaps the most abused vegetable, often served swimming in water, but properly cooked, or grated raw in salads, it is delicious.

CULTIVATION OF BRASSICAS

Vegetable	Soil/Position	Sowing	Drill depth
Purple-sprouting broccoli and calabrese	**Soil:** firm, heavy, loamy soil that is well-dug and manured. **Position:** open and sunny, but with some shelter.	Sow in seed beds mid-April to May. Calabrese sowings can begin in late March.	1 cm ($\frac{1}{2}$ in).
Brussels sprouts	**Soil:** rich loam – a firm soil which has been well-manured. **Position:** prefer an open site, but do not mind partial shade.	Sow under glass in February for early crops. In seed beds from mid-March to April.	1 cm ($\frac{1}{2}$ in).
Cabbage	**Soil:** all types like well-drained, fertile, non-acid soil, preferably following a crop for which the ground was manured. They will grow successfully in most well-cultivated soils. **Position:** open and sunny.	**Summer cabbage:** sow under glass or in boxes from January to February. In seed beds from late March/April to May. **Autumn and winter cabbage:** sow in seed beds from April to May. **Spring cabbage:** sow in seed beds in summer. **Savoy:** see winter cabbage. **Red cabbage:** sow in seed beds from April to early September. **Chinese cabbage:** sow in ultimate cropping site mid-June/early July.	1 cm ($\frac{1}{2}$ in).
Cauliflower and white-sprouting broccoli	**Soil:** deep, well-drained, well-cultivated, rich soil. **Position:** open and sunny, but well-sheltered.	**Early varieties** *Cauliflower:* under glass in September, or in seed boxes in heated position in January. *Broccoli:* under glass late February to March. **Maincrop varieties:** sow in seed beds in regular succession from late spring to early summer.	2 cm ($\frac{3}{4}$ in).
Kale	**Soil:** rich loam but will grow in most well-cultivated soil. **Position:** any, but particularly likes a well-exposed site.	Sow outdoors in cropping site or in seed beds in April to May.	1 cm ($\frac{1}{2}$ in).
Kohl rabi	**Soil:** fertile, well-drained. **Position:** any, but not too shaded.	Sow outdoors in cropping site at monthly intervals from March to August.	1 cm ($\frac{1}{2}$ in).

Cultivation of brassicas: 1 because brassicas are not a quick-maturing crop, sow the seeds in a seed bed first.

2 Thin seedlings as they appear. Transplant them carefully when they are large enough to handle.

3 Plant out large crops in final cropping site on a mild, damp day, using a garden line as a guide.

4 Support tall plants, such as brussels sprouts and broccoli, with large stakes and tie them with twine.

Planting out/Transplanting	Planting Distances (between plants/rows)	Cultivation	Harvesting
Thin regularly; plant in cropping site when plants are 10–15 cm (4–6 in) tall (about six weeks after sowing).	**Broccoli:** 60×65 cm (2 ft×2 ft 6 in). **Calabrese:** 45×60 cm (1 ft 6 in×2 ft). (Calabrese plants can be planted closer together to give a large harvest of small spears.)	Hoe regularly between rows to eliminate weeds. Protect from birds by netting. Water well if at all dry. Stake plants, tie loosely to support if weather is windy, and draw soil up around the stems for extra support.	In both cases cut while flower buds are still tightly closed. Cut from the centre, taking central heads with 10–12.5 cm (4–5 in) of stem. Cut just above a side-shoot to encourage more growth. Harvest side shoots as they appear.
Thin regularly; plant in cropping site when plants are 10–15 cm (4–6 in) tall (about six weeks after sowing).	65×65 cm (2 ft 6 in×2 ft 6 in). Stagger the rows.	Pull soil around stems a month or so after planting to firm plants. Stake plants and tie loosely. Water freely. Break off the lower leaves as they turn yellow.	Pick while still small and tightly knotted, preferably after the first frost. Start at the bottom of the stem. Pick off top leaves and cook as greens. (This brings on sprouts at top of the plant.)
Summer cabbage: those sown under glass should be planted out in seed beds in March to harden off. **Other cabbage:** should be transplanted to cropping site when 10–15 cm (4–6 in) tall (about six weeks after sowing). **Red cabbage:** sown in September. Can be left in seed bed through winter, protected by cloches. **Chinese cabbage:** thin seedlings progressively, so they are correct distance apart when plants are 10 cm (4 in) tall.	**Summer cabbage:** 45×45 cm (1 ft 6 in×1 ft 6 in). **Autumn and winter:** *Cabbage and savoy:* 60×60 cm (2 ft×2 ft). *Spring cabbage:* 22×45 cm (9 in×1 ft 6 in). *Red cabbage:* 60×60 cm (2 ft×2 ft). *Chinese cabbage:* 30×45 cm (1 ft×1 ft 6 in).	**For all cabbages:** hoe regularly between rows to discourage weeds and keep plants well-watered. Remove any decaying leaves as they appear. **Chinese cabbage:** gently pull any drooping outside leaves up around inner ones and tie loosely to encourage thicker inside growth.	**For all cabbages:** cut when heads are firm and leave stumps in ground (except spring ones) to give a few extra subsequent greens. **Spring cabbage:** cut cabbages in March and use as spring greens.
Early varieties cauliflower: prick out those from heated boxes and put in cold frame to harden off. Plant all seedlings in cropping site when 10–15 cm (4–6 in) tall, using a dibber.	**Early varieties:** 45×45 cm (1 ft 6 in×1 ft 6 in). **Maincrop varieties:** 60×75 cm (2 ft×2 ft 6 in) in staggered rows.	Hoe between rows to discourage weeds. Water frequently if at all dry. When curds form, bend outside leaves over them. This protects from sun, frost or staining from soil – all of which discolour the curds.	Cut when curds are formed, but are tightly packed. Cauliflowers are nicest picked in the morning, when the dew is still on them. If more ripen at one time than you need, pull them up and hang by the roots in a cool, dry place. They will keep for up to three weeks.
Thin as seedlings appear. Transplant from seed bed when plants are about six weeks old. If sown in cropping site, thin to recommended distances.	60×60 cm (2 ft×2 ft).	Hoe between rows and plants to eliminate weeds. Tread round plants to firm ground. Stake and tie if necessary.	Cut from early January, taking from the plants' centre to encourage more growth.
Thin progressively until required planting distance is achieved.	22×38 cm (9×15 in).	Hoe between rows and keep plants well watered.	Pull out bulbs (which you can see on the ground) when about 7.5 cm (3 in) in diameter. If larger than this, they will be woody.

5 Cabbages growing in the winter may need to be protected from harsh weather with polythene cloches.

6 Harvest crops as soon as they are ready. Cut cabbages just above the ground when their hearts have firmed.

give crops with crinkly or smooth, but deeply serrated, leaves; again it can be harvested through the leaner months from December to April.

Kohl rabi is another unusual vegetable. The round purple or green growths, with their long, tough, leaf-bearing stems, rest on the surface of the ground, where they can remain until they are needed. Do not leave them too long, though, or they will turn fibrous; better to freeze them, which they take to well. They can be cooked like a turnip, the taste of which they somewhat resemble.

The different varieties of each type of brassica mentioned could take a lifetime to explore, but it is worth experimenting to see which suits both your garden and your palate best. Try early and late varieties, and even when you have found ones which suit you well, do not entirely neglect the new hybrids as they appear on the market.

Cultivation
Comprehensive instruction for sowing, growing and harvesting brassicas are given above in an easy-to-follow

chart. All brassicas like slightly alkaline, rather than acid, soil, so unless you know the soil to be alkaline, dress it with lime before planting. By and large, brassicas like good fertile soil too, but often do best if they follow another crop for which the soil was manured.

As most types take a number of months to reach maturity and become ready for harvesting, it is a good idea to sow them in seed beds, thus leaving room in the vegetable plot for some quicker-growing crops. Follow instructions on pages 46–47 for sowing, thinning and transplanting.

After harvesting, plants should be dug up and the roots of broccoli, cabbages and cauliflower burnt. The leaves and stems can be composted, but cut up or crush anything particularly woody first. If there is any hint of disease in the crop, burn the plants; if they are composted, the infecting bacteria will thrive and multiply, and therefore spread when the compost is dug into fresh soil.

Pests and diseases

Brassicas are susceptible to a number of pests and diseases which can kill the plants. In almost all cases, the problems can be controlled or eliminated by treating the soil with various proprietary sprays or preparations. There are some very good vegetable-based treatments available. However, many others contain toxic materials and you must decide whether the benefits they bring outweigh the harm they do to the soil, and insect and plant life. Damage from spraying, in which the leaves of the plant become scorched or distorted, is by no means uncommon and often makes the produce useless. If you feel some sort of chemical treatment is essential to bring

Winter brassicas: curly kale **(top)** is an extremely hardy crop which can be grown throughout the winter. It will withstand very cold conditions, and will provide you with fresh vegetables during the winter and early spring. Some vegetables **(above)** will need to be grown under cloches to survive.

the problem under control, consult your local garden shop on which preparation to use and make sure you follow the instructions carefully.

Brassica plants, broccoli in particular, are especially attractive to birds. Protect young seedlings by stretching black cotton along the length of the rows. It may be necessary to net broccoli plants later, in order to ensure your harvest. Slugs can often be a problem too, eating their way quickly through a line of seedlings. They can be controlled by scattering slug pellets on the ground. However, these pellets contain poison that can be harmful to domestic pets, so put them under a flowerpot

and prop up one side of it, so the slugs can enter, but the pets cannot.

Good garden hygiene will do much to keep disease at bay. This means ensuring that dead plants are removed from the ground and composted at once. Never leave them in the soil once they have yielded their full harvest. Equally, burn all infected or diseased plants and ensure all the tools and equipment you use are clean.

Below is a chart of some of the common pests and diseases that attack brassicas, with means of identification, and (where applicable) non-chemical forms of prevention or control.

PESTS AND DISEASES/BRASSICAS

Mealy cabbage aphis

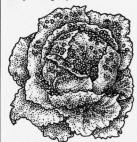

Identification: hordes of tiny round-bodied insects which cluster on leaves and stems, causing distortion to plant's growth.
Treatment: spray with soapy water.

Cabbage root fly

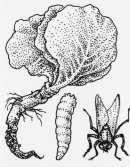

Identification: feeds on roots (particularly of recently transplanted seedlings), causing leaves to turn a blue-grey colour and plants to wilt and collapse.
Treatment: fly lays its eggs on soil surface and the hatched maggots burrow into the ground eating stems and roots. Prevent them doing so by fitting a plastic or rubber disc round the stem of the young plant and pushing it just below the surface.

Cabbage white butterfly

Identification: caterpillars eat through the leaves, making a

mass of holes.
Treatment: squash or pick off clusters of yellow eggs from the leaves and remove and destroy any caterpillars.

Flea beetle

Identification: eats through seedlings in particular, leaving small neat holes.
Treatment: evening watering discourages the pest.

Gall weevil

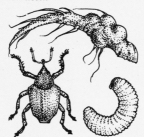

Identification: makes hollow swellings on the roots, stunting the plant's growth.
Treatment: pull up and burn infected plants.

Cabbage whitefly

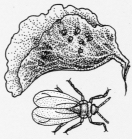

Identification: small whiteflies which feed on the underside of leaves leaving sticky discoloration. The growth of leaves is checked.
Treatment: spray with proprietary insecticide.

Club root

Identification: one of the commonest diseases of brassicas. Unpleasant-smelling swellings form on the root, stunting the plant's growth. The leaves turn yellow and wilt.
Treatment: always dig, rather than pull, roots up to ensure none are left in the ground. The disease can stay in the soil for years. Diseased plants must be burnt. Alternatively, lime the soil. If possible, leave land entirely dormant, growing nothing on it for a year or two.

Downy mildew

Identification: sometimes attacks young plants under glass. Yellow spots appear on top surface of leaves and a furry, greyish-brown growth forms

underneath.
Treatment: keep the atmosphere dry and pay more attention to garden hygiene.

Wire stem

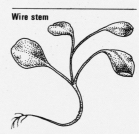

Identification: the stems of young plants turn brown and begin to shrink.
Treatment: raise seedlings in sterilized compost and treat the soil with a recommended top dressing.

Whiptail

Identification: attacks cauliflowers, broccoli and kohl rabi in particular. The leaves appear to shrink towards the central vein.
Treatment: make sure the soil is not too acid and if so, treat accordingly.

Growing Root Vegetables

THE MEMBERS of the root crops provide a wealth of vegetables, and once again the variety within each type is enormous. Included here are beetroot, carrots, parsnips, salsify and scorzonera, spinach beet, seakale beet, swedes (rutabagas) and turnips. The last two are, strictly speaking, members of the brassica group, but their growing habits and requirements have meant they are often grouped with root vegetables.

Beetroot, perhaps most frequently thought of as a salad vegetable (cooked and then eaten cold), is also delicious eaten hot. In addition, it can be grated and eaten raw (the young ones are the most palatable), in which form it is a particularly rich source of vitamin B. Among the many different-shaped varieties there are also those that are golden in colour, and the leaves of these can be harvested, and cooked and eaten like greens.

The carrot, with its rich supplies of vitamin A, may be grown in myriad shapes from round, or finger-shaped, to conical, or elongated. Like most roots, carrots store well (see page 186) and so can generally be eaten fresh all the year round. Their cooking possibilities are endless; even making an effective sweetener in some puddings. Parsnips, too, have culinary uses other than just as a vegetable accompaniment. They are one of the most common ingredients of home-made wine. New varieties, bred to yield small roots, have proved very useful for people who have only a small amount of land to devote to vegetable production.

Salsify and scorzonera are two more unusual root vegetables which are well worth growing for the tasty interest they can give to family meals. Both produce long, thin roots; salsify looks a little like an elongated parsnip, while scorzonera is similar in shape but has a black skin. A point that could be considered a disadvantage is that they take up a fair amount of land for a good six months or more, and this must be considered in

GROWING TIMES AND HARVESTING MONTHS

Continuous crops of roots can again be produced in the garden by regular sowings and experimenting with the various early- and late-maturing varieties. Many root crops are sown in two main stages; one planned to give the early, small, sweet crops, while the heavier sowing follows to give the maincrop through the winter.

Vegetable	Shortest Growing Time	Harvesting Months
Beetroot	4 months	June–October
Carrot	3–4 months	June–October
Parsnip	7–8 months	End September–February
Salsify and scorzonera	6–7 months	October–November
Seakale beet	3–4 months	August–November
Spinach beet	4 months	August–April
Swede (Rutabaga)	Early sowings take about three months. Later May/June sowings take about five months.	July/ August–April
Turnip	At least two months.	July–November (Greens: November–April)

Leafy root crops: although seakale beet **(far left)** and spinach beet **(left)** are root vegetables, they are both grown for their leaves. Seakale beet is a form of spinach beet, and has wider leaf stalks and midribs. Spinach beet is also known as perpetual spinach, and is one of the easiest vegetables to grow, having a heavier yield and being able to withstand dry conditions. It has a less acidic taste than true spinach.

Root crops: there are many different types of root vegetables, some of which are very common, such as carrots, swedes, turnips, parsnips and beetroot **(left)** and others which are less so, but are gaining in popularity, such as salsfiy and scorzonera **(above)**. As well as the more usual red beetroot you can grow white beetroot **(far left)**. This variety has globular roots, but you can also grow ones which taper.

the light of your overall vegetable garden plan. Seakale beet and spinach beet are perhaps a little more unusual too. Both are grown for their leaves rather than their roots. That of seakale beet has a dual purpose; the green leafy part may be torn from the stem to be cooked and eaten as greens, and the white midrib can then be cooked and served on its own. Spinach beet is often known as perpetual spinach and is the easiest of all spinaches to grow. As its name suggests, it can be harvested for most

of the year. These vegetables cannot be stored like other root crops, but they take very well to being frozen.

The swede has a delicate taste that is somehow surprising from such a hardy vegetable. It is a crop that suffers not at all from being left in the ground throughout the winter, so long as space permits. Equally it takes well to being stored. Turnips come in all manner of shapes and sizes as well as a variety of colours. They may be round like a ball or flattened on the top and bottom.

CULTIVATION OF ROOT CROPS

Vegetable	Soil/Position	Sowing	Drill Depth
Beetroot	Soil: light but deep loam that has been well-dug and cultivated. Position: will grow in most places, but avoid heavily shaded sites.	Globe varieties: sow under glass in March. Harden off before transplanting by leaving glass off cold frame. Sow in cropping site from April to July. Long-rooted varieties: sow in regular succession in cropping site from May to June. Beetroot grows from clusters of three or four seeds. Space these about 5 cm (2 in) apart.	1 cm ($\frac{1}{2}$ in). 2–2.5 cm ($\frac{3}{4}$–1 in).
Carrot	Soil: well-cultivated and deeply dug sandy loam, but will grow in any light soil, providing it is free of large clods of earth or big stones. Position: any which is not heavily shaded. Early crops like an open, sunny spot.	Early varieties: sow under glass in February. Maincrop: sow in regular succession in cropping site from late March to July. Sow two seeds to 2.5 cm (1 in).	0.5 cm ($\frac{1}{4}$ in).
Parsnip	Soil: deeply dug, light loam, free from large stones. Position: any which is not heavily shaded.	Sow in cropping site late February/March to April. The surface of the soil must be dry and fine.	2.5 cm (1 in).
Salsify and scorzonera	Soil: deeply dug, light loam. Position: open and sunny.	Sow in cropping site from March/April to May.	2 cm ($\frac{3}{4}$ in).
Seakale beet and spinach beet	Soil: any well-cultivated soil; these vegetables particularly dislike being waterlogged. Position: any which is not heavily shaded.	Spinach beet: sow in cropping site in April and again in July and August. Seakale beet: sow in cropping site in May.	2.5 cm (1 in)
Swede (Rutabaga)	Soil: light, fertile loam that is well-drained but not too dry. Does not like acid soil. Position: open and sunny. React badly to overshadowing.	For an early crop, sow in cropping site in early spring; otherwise sow in cropping site in May/June. Sow two seeds to 2.5 cm (1 in).	2 cm ($\frac{3}{4}$ in).
Turnip	Soil: well-cultivated, light loam. Position: see Swede (rutabaga).	Sow under glass in February. Then in cropping site in regular succession from March/April to July/August. (Late sowings provide winter maincrop.) Turnips for greens: sow in cropping site at end of August.	1 cm ($\frac{1}{2}$ in). 1 cm ($\frac{1}{2}$ in).

Colour-wise, they may be white or golden, or green-, red- or purple-topped. Their rapid growth means that they could be grown as a catch crop between rows of longer maturing vegetables, and they can also be grown for their leaves (harvested through the winter and early spring), which can be cooked in a similar way to, and make a pleasant change from, spring greens.

The cultivation details for the root crops included in this section are given below in the usual chart form. As will be seen, most root crops favour a similar type of soil and they should not generally be grown in soil that has been freshly manured. This encourages the roots to fork and split in all directions in search of the fresh riches in the soil. Similarly, excessive stony ground can cause forking of the roots.

Unlike most brassicas, it is more usual to sow seeds of root crops straight into the cropping site. Make sure the soil is well prepared for sowing and is dry and crumbly;

Thinning/Transplanting	Planting Distances (between plants/rows)	Cultivation	Harvesting
Thin seedlings under glass to 15 cm (6 in) apart. Plant out in cropping site end April. Thin seedlings initially when about 2.5 cm (1 in) high. Thin to final recommended spacing when roots are about 2.5 cm (1 in) in diameter.	**Globe:** 12.5 × 30 cm (5 × 12 in). **Long-rooted:** 20 × 45 cm (8 × 18 in).	Protect seedlings from birds and slugs (see pages 113 and 55). As they grow, hoe between rows and water plants well.	Begin harvesting by pulling out every other plant. Those that remain can be left in the ground until wanted, but globe varieties should not grow more than 7.5 cm (3 in) in diameter or they will turn woody. Lift in late autumn before any danger of frost. Twist (not cut) off the leaves just above the root, to seal in the juices.
Early varieties: thin to 2.5 cm (1 in) apart, then 7.5 cm (3 in) when first proper leaves appear. Thin to final recommended spacing when carrots are thickness of a finger. Never leave thinnings lying on the ground – they attract carrot fly.	**Early:** 7.5 × 22 cm (3 × 9 in). **Maincrop:** 15 × 30 cm (6 × 12 in).	Water after sowing to aid germination. After thinning draw soil up around base (top of carrot should not show through soil). Hoe between rows to check weeds.	**Early crops:** pull every other plant. Pull young carrots by hand. **Maincrop:** lift carefully with a fork no later than October. If storing (see page 186), trim off the top (and compost immediately), remove the soil from the carrots but do not wash them before they are stored, or they will rot.
Thin to 5 cm (2 in) apart, then to final recommended spacing. (It is not worth trying to transplant thinnings – it is not usually successful.)	15 × 38 cm (6 × 15 in).	Hoe between the rows to keep weeds in check. Water plants if they are at all dry.	Dig up parsnips as wanted – the flavour improves after the first frost. If you can spare the ground they can stay in their cropping site until spring; otherwise, dig them up and store them.
Thin twice to recommended distance.	**Salsify:** 22 × 30 cm (9 × 12 in). **Scorzonera:** 30 × 30 cm (12 × 12 in).	Hoe between rows and water plants in dry spells to prevent them running to seed. Pull the soil up around the base of the plants.	Lift carefully from mid-October onwards. Although both are hardy and can be left in the ground, it is probably better to harvest all the roots you want and freeze them. If space permits, you can leave some salsify in the ground until the spring; the new green growth can be picked and cooked like spring greens.
Thin progressively to recommended distance, beginning as soon as the plants are large enough to handle. Later thinnings can be eaten.	15 × 22 cm (6 × 9 in).	Hoe to eliminate weeds. Water plants freely if there is any danger of them drying out.	Pick the early sowings in summer and the later sowing through autumn and winter. Do not pick autumn plants too heavily if you want a good supply through the winter months. To harvest, take the outer leaves gently away from the root, leaving the young, central leaves to encourage more growth.
Thin regularly to recommended distance.	30 × 45 cm (12 × 18 in).	Hoe in the early stages to control weeds; this will not be necessary when the luxuriant leaves cover the ground and so smother the weeds.	If you want some very small, sweet-tasting swedes for immediate use, you can begin harvesting two to three months after the first sowing. Most will be allowed to grow bigger and can be harvested as needed. Leave in the ground through the winter or pull up and store (see page 186).
Seedlings under glass: thin when large enough to handle and transplant – about 10 cm (4 in) high. **Other sowings:** thin to 10 cm (4 in) apart when first true leaves appear. Thin to 20 cm (8 in) when turnips are just large enough to make cooking worthwhile. **Turnips for greens:** no need to thin, just leave plants to grow.	20 × 30 cm (8 × 12 in). **Greens:** rows 22 cm (9 in) apart. (See Transplanting.)	Hoe to eliminate weeds.	Pull early sowings when turnips are 5–7.5 cm (2–3 in) in diameter (check by pulling foliage aside; top of turnip is just visible). Lift maincrop in mid-October to November. Twist off tops and store (see page 186). **Greens:** cut leaves when they are about 20 cm (8 in) long. They can be picked end October/early November but are more usually left until spring.

Root cultivation: 1 Prepare the land, raking in a general fertilizer. Sow seed.

2 Water young plants well and to prevent the roots forking in search of water.

3 Regularly weed between rows of growing plants. Take care not to damage the roots.

4 Thin plants progressively. The third thinning may produce tiny vegetables.

it is better to delay planting than to sow seeds in wet, sticky, cold soil. Most root crops take less time to mature than the brassicas; a catch crop of quicker-maturing vegetables such as lettuce can be sown between the rows of the longer-maturing varieties in the early stages of growth. Another way of making the land yield twice is to sow radish seed together with parsnip along the same rows. The radish seeds germinate much quicker; thus indicating where the parsnip seedlings will later emerge, as well as giving an extra crop of radishes.

All root crops should be watered freely if there is any danger of their drying out. Those deprived of water will be woody and fibrous as a result and they may also fork if

Increasing productivity: you can increase the size of your vegetable yield by sowing seeds of quick-maturing lettuces between the rows of root vegetables. The quick-maturing

vegetables are known as catch crops. Parsnips **(right)** can be left in the ground until needed, and their flavour will be improved by frost.

PESTS AND DISEASES/ROOT VEGETABLES

Carrot fly

Identification: maggots eat into roots. Leaves turn a reddish colour then yellow and wilt.
Treatment: sow seed as thinly as possible, so later thinning is kept to a minimum. Avoid handling plants. Early and late sowings may escape attack.

Beet fly

Identification: maggots hatch on beetroot leaves, tunnelling through them.
Treatment: check leaves frequently and pick off and destroy damaged ones.

Wireworm

Identification: larvae eat into developing roots. The small worm-like creatures may be seen in abundance around the roots as you dig or hoe between rows.
Treatment: make traps by sticking a short length of stick

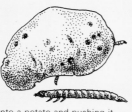

into a potato and pushing it into the ground. The larvae will eat into this. Pull it out and destroy it.

Black slugs

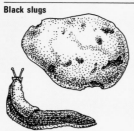

Identification: eat into developing roots.
Treatment: hard to control as they live beneath the ground, so are difficult to detect. Try setting traps as above.

Celery leaf fly

Identification: attacks parsnips –

the maggots burrow into leaves, leaving trails of brown blisters. Growth becomes checked and plant will ultimately die.
Treatment: check leaves and crush blisters as soon as you see them. Pick off badly infected leaves, burning them to help prevent pest spreading.

Cutworm

Identification: eats through the stems at ground-level. The greenish-grey caterpillars may be visible around the plants.
Treatment: make sure weed growth is controlled.

Canker

Identification: attacks parsnips, causing rusty brown

discolorations near the top.
Treatment: sow varieties bred to be disease-resistant and follow strict crop rotation plans (see page 35). Discourage carrot fly as this helps to spread the disease.

Rust

Identification: brownish spots on leaves of beetroot, spinach beet and seakale beet.
Treatment: pull off leaves and destroy them.

White blister

Identification: one of the few problems to beset salsify and scorzonera. Leaves become covered with white blisters.
Treatment: remove and destroy leaves. Caught in its early stages it should not affect plants adversely.

allowed to dry out and are then subjected to a heavy rainfall. Hoeing between the rows is necessary to keep down the weed population, but take extra care not to chop through the developing vegetables.

Most roots can be harvested over a fairly long period, the early pullings providing small, but delicious, sweet-tasting vegetables. Pull these by hand and then lift later crops with a fork, being very careful not to damage and thus bruise the roots. Some, such as parsnip and swede can be left in the ground until they are wanted (provided you do not want the land for anything else) and their flavour is improved by frost. Others, such as turnips, do not take so kindly to this treatment and should be lifted and stored (see page 186). Roots, incidentally, are among the best types of vegetables for storing, although they also freeze well.

Pests and diseases

Root crops are prone to pests and diseases, which again can often be controlled with proprietary mixtures.

Consult your local garden centre if this is the method of control you favour.

The rules of paying attention to garden hygiene and destroying infected plants immediately (see page 49) also apply. One of the most virulent pests is the carrot fly (which, despite its name, may also attack parsnips). Early crops of carrots are likely to escape attack as they may be harvested before the maggots hatch and burrow into the ground in search of the tasty roots. Carrot fly are attracted by the smell given off by leaves when handled, so avoid touching the plants as much as possible. For the same reason, destroy any thinnings, or remove them from the ground immediately.

Swedes and turnips will be affected by those pests and diseases that beset brassicas (see page 49) – flea beetle being the greatest danger. Avoid growing these crops on land which you know is still harbouring club root, because the vegetables will be swollen, distorted and inedible. Both beetroots and carrots can suffer from violet root rot (see page 87).

Growing Pulses

ALTHOUGH THIS SECTION includes only two main groups of vegetables – peas and beans – they are of vital importance in the average home garden production and there is also considerable variety within the two groups. They are useful components of the vegetable garden because, by and large, they are quick to mature, and their roots manufacture valuable nitrogen which they release into the soil. They yield their main harvest through the summer and autumn, but both peas and beans can be produced especially for drying, and all types also freeze well so they can be enjoyed the year round.

Among the bean group are broad, French, dwarf, haricot and runner beans. The large, kidney-shaped broad beans sometimes have an ill-deserved reputation for being tough among those who have never eaten them straight from the garden when they are young and mouth-wateringly tender. Another little-known fact about broad beans is that the top foliage can be picked and cooked like spinach. There are endless varieties of broad beans, suitable for sowing at different times of the year. They also include dwarf varieties, whose diminutive growth makes them suitable for small vegetable plots. Most types are hardy and will yield heavy crops.

French and dwarf beans are virtually the same species, dwarf ones generally being a little hardier and producing very heavy yields. Both these beans are available in many varieties, from those with a waxy finish and yellow pods to those that are flat- or round-podded. Haricot beans are a type of French bean grown specifically for drying. The white-seeded varieties are best for this.

The harvest from runner beans generally follows on from dwarf beans (although they can be grown to be harvested simultaneously) and is usually very heavy.

Runner beans are easy to grow and pretty enough to be incorporated into a flower garden on a wigwam system (see page 60). Dwarf varieties are also staked.

Peas also produce endless varieties and different types will grow to different heights. They are generally divided into four main groups – first early, second early, maincrop and late. These have slightly different qualities; some, for example, are hardier than others so as to be able to withstand earlier sowing, but a succession of planting can produce harvests of succulent young peas right through the summer and into autumn. Wrinkle-seeded varieties, known as marrowfat, are

GROWING TIMES AND HARVESTING MONTHS		
Peas and beans are largely a summer and autumn crop, but there is no reason why all types should not yield heavy harvests throughout these seasons. Many different varieties are		available – both early and late maturing. Sow a good selection for maximum cropping, but make sure you sow the right variety at the right time.

Vegetable	Shortest Growing Time	Harvesting Months
Broad beans	5 months	Late May/June–August
Dwarf and French beans	2–3 months	June–October
Runner beans	3 months	July–September
Peas:		
First early	$2\frac{1}{2}$ months	End May–June and September–October
Second early	$3\frac{1}{2}$ months	July
Maincrop	3 months	July–August
Late	3 months	August–September
Mange tout and petit pois	$2\frac{1}{2}$ months	June–September
Asparagus peas	3 months	June–August

Growing pulses: this well stocked vegetable garden illustrates the principle of crop rotation. The pulses which the gardener is tending will be rotated next year to grow in a different cropping site, and the brassicas and roots moved accordingly.

Peas: these are the other half of the pulse family and are equally easy to grow, and quick to mature. As well as some varieties which are shelled before they are cooked, there are types which are cooked whole, such as mange tout **(below)**. The asparagus pea **(left)** has crinkly, rather than smooth, pods.

Beans: there are several types of beans—climbing **(above)**, runner **(top)**, dwarf **(right)**, and haricot **(centre right)** and broad **(far right)**. Experiment by growing as many different varieties as possible.

CULTIVATION OF PULSES

Vegetable	Soil/Position	Sowing	Drill Depth
Broad beans	**Soil:** good rich loam, but will grow in any well-cultivated, well-drained soil. **Position:** prefer a well-sheltered site.	Sow in cropping site in October/early November (choose a longpod variety) at recommended planting distances. In cropping site February/April (for summer crops) and again in May (for autumn crops). In cold, exposed gardens sow indoors in boxes or singly in peat pots late January/early February. (Sow beans 5 cm (2 in) apart in boxes.)	5 cm (2 in).
Dwarf, French and haricot beans	**Soil:** light, well-drained, non-acid loam. **Position:** open and sunny, but sheltered.	Sow indoors in boxes or under glass March to April. In cropping site in May (or slightly earlier if protecting with cloches), then regularly until early July. Put seeds in pairs 2.5 cm (1 in) apart or sow singly 7.5 cm (3 in) apart.	4–5 cm (1½–2 in).
Runner beans	**Soil:** rich, well-cultivated, well-drained, deep soil. **Position:** open and sunny, but sheltered.	In cropping site in late April (if well protected with cloches). To be safe, plant in early May; in cold districts, mid- to late May. Seed will not survive frosts. If worried about outdoor conditions, sow indoors in April.	5 cm (2 in).
Peas	**Soil:** most medium loam that is well-cultivated, well-drained and non-acid. **Position:** open and sunny.	Flood drills with water if dry and sow when water has soaked through. Sow seeds 5–7.5 cm (2–3 in) apart or make a V-shaped drill, 7.5 cm (3 in) deep and sow in a single row along this. **First early:** sow in cropping site in late October/early November, but protect with cloches through the winter. Or sow in cropping site in March/April and again in June. **Second early:** sow in cropping site in March/April. **Maincrop:** sow in cropping site in May. **Late:** sow in cropping site in May.	5 cm (2 in).
Mange tout (Snow peas) and petit pois	**Soil:** see Peas. **Position:** see Peas.	In cropping site in March–June (follow general instructions above for sowing).	5 cm (2 in).
Asparagus peas	**Soil:** see other peas, but soil must be really well-drained. **Position:** see Peas.	Under glass in cropping site in late March/early April or in May/June. Sow two seeds together every 25 cm (10 in).	5 cm (2 in).

Cultivating pulses: 1 Sow seeds in evenly dug rows in their cropping sites. Make sure the ground is watered.

2 Protect the emerging seedlings against birds by covering them with chicken wire, or polythene cloches.

3 If you planted two or three seeds at each station, you will have to thin the seedlings.

4 Most peas and beans will need to be supported as they grow to stop them straggling. Train them up poles.

Thinning/Transplanting	Planting Distances (between plants/rows)	Cultivation	Harvest
Those sown in cropping site need no thinning; fill in any gaps with the extra plants sown. Those sown indoors should be hardened off by putting outside at the end of March and then planted in cropping site as soon as soil conditions allow (usually in April). Stand peat pots in water first and plant so the rim is beneath soil surface.	**Tall varieties:** double rows 20 cm (8 in) apart with 20 cm (8 in) between plants. Stagger seeds in the two rows. Leave 60 cm (2 ft) between double rows. **Dwarf varieties:** single rows, 22 cm (9 in) between plants. 45 cm (18 in) between rows.	Protect seedlings from birds with tunnels or rows of cotton. Support growing plants with stakes (see page 60). Hoe between rows to control weeds. Pinch out growing tips either when plants are in full flower, when the first pods are showing or when the first black fly appears (see page 61). This helps to control black fly as well as keeping plant bushy.	Begin as soon as beans are big enough to cook (or sooner, before beans are properly formed, if you like to eat the pods too). Pick the bottom clusters first and continue regular picking as beans become ready. Old beans will be tough, but can be used for next year's seed.
Harden off those in boxes or under glass by putting outside or removing glass in early May. Plant out at the end of May. If sown outdoors, pull out the weaker seedlings as soon as germination has occurred, or thin to recommended distance.	**Smaller varieties:** 15×38 cm (6×15 in). **Larger varieties:** 22×45 cm (9×18 in).	Hoe to eliminate weeds and draw the soil up around the stem of the plants to firm them. Water plants freely and mulch with peat, compost or farmyard manure if ground is prone to drying out. Support larger plants (see page 60).	Begin harvesting when beans are about 10 cm (4 in) long and pick regularly to get tender beans and to encourage more to grow. **Haricot beans:** leave to ripen fully on plant. In late summer pull up entire plant and hang upside down in dry, airy place to finish drying. Pod beans and store them when quite dried.
Indoor sowings: harden off by putting outside in May. Plant out in June. Those sown in cropping site need no thinning; fill in any gaps with extra plants.	Depends on method of support (see page 60). **For crossed poles:** two staggered rows, plants 25 cm (10 in) apart; rows 75 cm (2 ft 6 in) apart. If more than two rows, allow 1.5 metres (5 ft) between them. **Vertical supports:** single rows 30×75 cm (12 in×2 ft 6 in). **Wigwam:** six plants spaced round 90 cm (3 ft) diameter circle.	Supports can be erected either before seeds are sown, or when seedlings emerge (method will have been decided before sowing). Most common are crossed poles, vertical supports of wigwams. They should be 2.4–3 metres (8–10 ft) high. Encourage plants to grow up them by entwining tendrils around supports as soon as they appear. Hoe between rows to eliminate weeds, and water freely, mulching ground if it tends to dry. Spray foliage to help to set flowers and pinch out top growing tips as growth progresses to encourage side growth.	Pick regularly while pods are young and tender – freeze or salt the inevitable surplus rather than leaving them to get tough on the plant. As soon as beans swell in the pod, they will make tough eating.
Seedlings are not thinned but allowed to grow thickly as sown. Fill in any gaps as seedlings appear with the extra seeds sown.	Leave 5–7.5 cm (2–3 in) between plants. Distance between rows depends on height of plants (consult packet of variety chosen). Generally, the distance between rows should be approximately the same as the height of the plant.	Protect seedlings from birds with black cotton, tunnels of wire mesh, or polythene cloches (which must be removed as plants grow). Hoe between rows initially; later growth will smother the ground, making this unnecessary. Water plants freely and mulch if soil tends to dry. Push twiggy supports into the soil when you sow. They should not be too thick, so tendrils can entwine round them easily.	Pick as soon as peas are swollen in the pod and use or freeze at once. Leave some peas on the plant to ripen fully for drying. Treat in the same way as for haricot beans.
No need to thin. Fill in gaps with extra plants.	5–7.5 cm×90 cm (2–3 in×3 ft).	See Peas.	**Mange tout:** pick when pods are about 5 cm (2 in) long, before peas have formed properly. Use at once. **Petit pois:** harvest as other peas.
Those under glass: harden off ready for planting out in May. **In cropping site:** pull out weaker seedlings as they emerge.	25×45 cm (10×18 in).	General cultivation is similar as for other peas. Support emerging seedlings in the same way, or if you prefer, leave to grow bushy over the ground.	Gather when pods are about 2.5–5 cm (1–2 in) long.

5 Pinch out the tips of the broad bean plants to discourage the pest black fly. Destroy any infected leaves.

6 Most peas and beans are best when picked young and tender. This will also encourage the plants to grow.

considered to be better flavoured, but they are less hardy than the round-seeded types.

In addition to the peas mentioned above, mange tout (snow peas) and petit pois are very popular. Mange tout are harvested while the peas are barely formed, and are eaten – pods and all. Petit pois are very small, sweet-tasting peas, which can be cooked in the pod and shelled afterwards, or shelled first like other peas. Less well-known is the asparagus pea, which is a member of the pea family, but differs markedly from its relatives in appearance. Known also as the winged pea because of the crinkly, double pods, asparagus peas are also cooked whole and are said to taste like asparagus.

Cultivation

Here are the comprehensive cultural details for peas and beans. All legumes like soil that has been heavily

SUPPORTING PULSES

1 2 3 4

5

Practically all varieties of peas and beans need to be supported as they grow, with the exception of dwarf varieties. **1** The most common way of staking peas is to push pea sticks into the ground by the growing plants. The wispy tendrils will wrap around the sticks. **2** To support broad beans, tie string between poles which are staked at the ends of each row. The plants are then loosely tied to the strings. **3 & 4** Runner beans can be grown in wigwam supports consisting of four poles which are positioned on the ground as shown and tied at the top. **5 & 6** Runner beans can be grown along crossed poles. By the time of harvesting the runner beans will have reached the top of their supports. Search carefully through the leaves of the plants for any concealed beans. If left, they will grow too large and become tough.

6

manured for a previous crop. Failing this, for peas and runner beans in particular, dig some well-rotted manure at least one spit deep into the ground a month or two before sowing. The roots will quickly grow down in search of this, thus giving the plants a firm anchorage.

Peas and beans are sown deeper into the soil than most other crops, the drills for sowing being a good 5 cm (2 in) deep. When sowing, the soil should be forked over again to a depth of at least 10 cm (4 in), making it crumbly, with no big clods or stones, throughout this depth. Take out wide drills of 15–20 cm (6–8 in), using the width of the draw hoe blade, and rake the soil loosely back over the seeds.

Mice are very partial to these seeds; discourage them by sprinkling some holly leaves in the drill, dousing the seed in paraffin, setting traps along the rows or keeping a good, hungry, garden cat! Seeds are usually placed the correct distance apart at sowing time (ie no thinning is required) but to ensure a full crop, either two seeds can be sown at each station and the weakest pulled out as the seedlings emerge, or some extra seeds can be sown at the ends of the rows and the resulting seedlings used to fill in any gaps as the others germinate.

By and large, legumes need some sort of support.

(Dwarf varieties can be left to grow straggly and bushy with no supports. However, not only will the pods become very mud-splashed, but they are not always easy to find in the tangle.) Various ways of supporting them are shown on the facing pages.

All peas and beans should be harvested when young for the best culinary results (except for those varieties grown for drying). The more you pick a plant, the more pods it will produce, so pick heavily and regularly, freezing any surplus vegetables.

Legume roots make valuable nitrogen, so they can be left in the soil after the plant has yielded its full harvest. Cut off stems and compost the leaves.

Pests and diseases

Mice have already been mentioned as one of the greatest enemies of peas and beans. Slugs will similarly attack seeds and seedlings. Letting the plants dry out will generally have disastrous effects on all peas and beans, causing them to wilt and die very quickly. If the plants are not well-watered (including their foliage), the flowers fail to set, so pods do not form. Conversely, though, in wet weather, particularly if it is cold too, downy mildew (see page 49) may attack peas.

PESTS AND DISEASES/PULSES

Pea and bean weevil

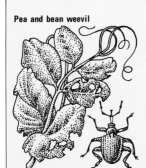

Identification: small, light brown beetle which is active at night when it eats the leaves of these plants.
Treatment: hoe between rows to disturb sleeping insects and make them good prey for birds.

Pea moth

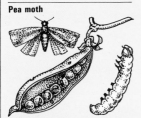

Identification: eggs laid on the leaves hatch into maggots which tunnel into the pods to feed on the developing peas. Can often be detected by the tiny holes which appear in the pods.
Treatment: eggs are laid in June and July, so early and late crops should escape attack. Control by spraying with proprietary mixtures.

Red spider mite

Identification: tiny creatures which feed on the leaves, turning them a dusty red colour. Spin very fine webs between the leaves.
Treatment: usually only attack plants under glass or in a hot, dry atmosphere. Spray regularly with water.

Pea thrips

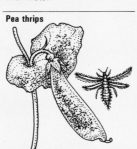

Identification: tiny, winged insects which eat pea leaves. If not controlled, they can cause stunted growth and poor flower development.
Treatment: keep plants well-watered and spray them well, too.

Black fly

Identification: infestations of tiny

black flies which cling to the stems and suck the sap, causing the plant to wither and growth to become distorted. Eventually the plant dies. Attacks broad beans in particular but also French and runner beans.
Treatment: early crops usually escape as the pods are harvested before black flies are active. Pinch out growing tips of plants as soon as you notice black fly and pick off and destroy any infected leaves. Spraying with proprietary mixtures will help to control them.

Bean seed fly

Identification: maggots in the soil eat the freshly-sown seeds.
Treatment: dress drills with proprietary mixtures.

Footrot

Identification: root shrivels, causing foliage to turn yellow and stems to turn a browny-red colour before rotting.
Treatment: follow strict crop rotation (see page 35) and avoid replanting on infected ground.

Chocolate spot

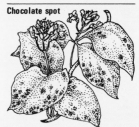

Identification: dark-brown spots which appear on broad bean leaves in particular.
Treatment: disease is not usually serious, but prevent it by making sure the soil is well limed and has had applications of potash. Pick off and destroy the infected leaves before sowing.

Growing Potatoes

POTATOES ARE AMONG the most widely eaten of all vegetables and, although they do take up quite a lot of space in the vegetable plot, it is worthwhile trying to allocate some space to them. They are often said to clean the land, particularly in a new vegetable plot. The cleaning operation is actually brought about by the thorough digging that is advisable for a potato crop, and the earthing-up process which helps to check weed growth.

The various varieties of potato produce types that are round, oval or kidney-shaped. The skins may be yellow, pale brown, red or white and the flesh may be floury or waxy. Even if you have a strong preference, it is wise to consult a local supplier to find which is most suitable for your land.

Potatoes are divided into earlies, second earlies and maincrop.

Soil
They like fertile, well-drained, well-cultivated soil and, unlike most other vegetables, favour acid conditions (they grow best in a pH of 5.5 – see page 35). Ideally the ground should be double dug and a good supply of well-rotted manure added especially on light, sandy soils. Bonemeal added to the soil of the top spit is beneficial.

Position
Choose an open site. Heavy overshading can lead to light top growth and a small crop.

Planting
Potatoes are grown from seed potatoes. Although these are from the previous year's crop, it is advisable to buy them from a good dealer rather than to try growing your own, which are quite likely to harbour disease. For the same reason, do not use potatoes sold for eating. Instead, buy those that are certified disease-free. The end of January is the time to buy them.

Seed potatoes are generally egg-sized, and they

GOOD VARIETIES

FIRST EARLIES:
Sutton's Foremost heavy crop of white-skinned oval tubers
Epicure excellent flavour

SECOND EARLIES:
Pentland Dell long oval-shaped tubers with white to cream flesh

MAINCROP:
Desirée pink-skinned tubers of varying shapes. Good for cooking
King Edward pink and white skinned tubers of high quality

should never be much larger. For earlies, put the potatoes in shallow wooden boxes, plastic washing-up bowls or similar containers, with the eye pointing upwards. Leave in a light, warm place for a few weeks until the shoots appear. Two or three will probably grow close together. Leave two shoots and rub off any others; alternatively, if possible, cut the potatoes in half to give two pieces with two shoots, but cut just before planting. Potatoes that are put in too warm or dark a place may develop long, spindly shoots. These will not be so healthy and will be difficult to plant.

Drills for seed potatoes can be taken out with a draw hoe (using the entire width) or the potatoes may be planted individually with a trowel (see below for planting depths and times). Put the emerging shoot uppermost and pull the soil loosely over the potato; do not pack it tightly because you might damage the shoots.

Planting times, depths and distances
Earlies: 7.5 cm (3 in) deep; 25 cm (10 in) between tubers; 60 cm (2 ft) between rows. Plant mid-March/early April.
Second earlies: 10 cm (4 in) deep; 30 cm (12 in) between tubers; 70 cm (2 ft 4 in) between rows. Plant mid-April.
Maincrop: 12.5 cm (5 in) deep; 38 cm (15 in) between tubers; 75 cm (2 ft 6 in) between rows. Plant late April.

Cultivation
Immediately after planting, hoe between the lines and draw the soil up over the tubers very slightly. This will protect them from any late frost. When the first leaves appear, either cover the plants with straw or dried bracken or draw some more soil lightly over them, allowing the tips of the shoots to peep through the surface.

When the stems are 20–22 cm (8–9 in) high, start earthing-up. This process is done by gently drawing up

Chitting potatoes: before planting early and seond-early potatoes, the seed potatoes must be prepared for the soil. This is done by chitting. The potatoes are placed in wooden boxes or plastic bowls with their eyes pointing upwards, and are left in the light until they begin to sprout shoots. When these are large and healthy, leave two shoots on each potato or split the potatoes in half, each with two shoots, and plant them immediately.

CULTIVATION OF POTATOES

Cultivation of potatoes: 1 Plant individual potatoes in holes and gently cover with soil.

2 Alternatively, make drills with a draw hoe and plant rows of potatoes with shoots uppermost.

3 When first leaves appear, cover bases of the potatoes with more soil and water the growing plants well.

4 When stems are large enough, begin to earth up the potatoes at 2-3 week intervals.

5 Harvest first earlies by hand, leaving the smaller crops in the soil to grow more. Lift tubers carefully.

6 Harvest maincrop when tops have died down. Leave crops on the ground to dry out before storing.

the soil either side of the rows around the stems. It is designed to encourage the plant to develop more roots and thus more potatoes, as well as to keep the developing potatoes well covered in soil so the light does not turn them green. About 15 cm (6 in) of leafy growth should show above the ridge, the top of which should be kept broad rather than narrow, and tapering. A pointed ridge gives a greater likelihood of the potatoes being exposed. Repeat the earthing-up process every few weeks so that deep trenches develop between the rows. This process also helps to control weeds and improves drainage in the soil.

A general-purpose fertilizer can be added to the soil at the first earthing-up with advantage. In dry spring weather, make sure the potato plants are kept well-watered.

Harvesting

Start harvesting the first early potatoes at the end of June. The very first harvests can be done by hand, taking the largest potatoes (even these will be very small) and leaving the others to grow larger. Make sure those left behind are well covered with soil. Later earlies can be dug up, using a broad-tined fork. Push this into the ground well clear of the plant, so as not to spear the potatoes. Turn the plant into the trench, then collect all the potatoes by hand.

When the earlies have run out towards the end of July, start harvesting the second earlies. They should yield good-sized potatoes until early September.

The maincrop should be lifted between mid-September and early October on a fine, dry day. Leave them on the surface of the ground for several hours to dry off, particularly if they are wanted for storing. Then rub off any large clods of earth and store the potatoes.

After-care

Compost the old plants, unless they were diseased, in

GROWING UNDER POLYTHENE

An alternative to the traditional method of growing potatoes is to place them on the ground and cover with black polythene. Anchor the edges with stones or earth.

Make small slits in the polythene directly above each growing plant. Watch for slugs which thrive in these conditions. Roll back sheeting for harvesting.

which case they should be burnt. Avoid using this compost on ground in which potatoes or tomatoes will be grown the following year, because it might still harbour harmful bacteria common to these vegetables. Make sure you have removed all the potatoes from the ground. It can then be used straightaway for another vegetable crop.

Pests and diseases

Potatoes are subject to a fair number of pests and diseases. The latter in particular can be greatly reduced by using certified, disease-free seeds. Observing a strict crop rotation will also help to reduce the likelihood of disease hitting your potato crop.

Apart from those mentioned below, wireworm (see pests page 55) can be a nuisance to potatoes.

PESTS AND DISEASES/POTATOES

Potato blight

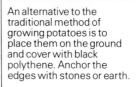

Identification: occurs in damp autumn conditions, so early varieties should not generally be affected. The leaves become blotched with brown marks and the lower ones turn yellow. The tubers develop similar brown marks and turn rotten.
Treatment: spray with proprietary mixes.

Potato cyst eelworm

Identification: small cysts develop on roots. The crop is vastly reduced and plants may wilt and die. Earlies may escape attack as the eelworm is not usually active until July.
Treatment: use certified, disease-free varieties and follow strict crop rotation.

Potato scab

Identification: occurs in soil which has been heavily limed or does not contain sufficient organic matter. Scabby patches occur on the skin of the potatoes.
Treatment: if caught in the early stages, scabs can be removed before cooking. Later, too much of the crop will be affected. Dig up and destroy if the attack is very severe.

Wart disease

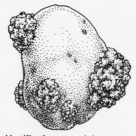

Identification: one of the most serious, but now less common, diseases. Large, warty growths appear over the surface of the potato. Areas in which the disease is prevalent are required by law to grow disease-free potatoes, labelled 'immune'.
Treatment: dig up and burn diseased potatoes and inform local authorities.

Black leaf

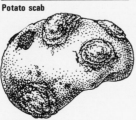

Identification: occurs in cold, wet soils. The bottom of the stem begins to rot, the roots shrivel, the whole stem softens and the plant becomes stunted with yellow growth. The tubers are wet, soft and slimy.
Treatment: follow strict crop rotation, but destroy any affected plants immediately

Growing Salad Vegetables

SALAD CROPS are a delight of the summer and early autumn months, although it is possible to grow many of them in winter and spring too. Of course, many vegetables could be classed as salad crops, but those included here are chicory, corn salad, American cress, cucumber, endive, lettuces and radishes.

Chicory is a useful winter salad vegetable that may be eaten raw or cooked. It is grown in two stages, the first taking up space in the plot, and the second requiring just a couple of large flowerpots. This second stage is known as forcing and it is at this time that the light-green, spear-shaped heads or chicons are produced.

Corn salad and endives also provide fresh leaves for winter salads, although both can be produced through the summer too. Corn salad has small, dark-green leaves and is a small plant; endive is much larger and may either have deeply crinkled and curly leaves or ones that are waxy and indented. Endive is blanched during growth to reduce its otherwise rather bitter taste.

Watercress ideally needs to be grown in a running

Salad vegetables: these crops do not have to be grown just in the summer, as differing varieties allow them to be grown now for most of the year. **Above:** winter varieties of radishes mean that this crop can be harvested until December. **Left:** cucumbers grow in the summer, outdoors.

Lettuces: the many different varieties of lettuce which are available mean that you can always find some to grow which will suit your palate and soil conditions. They can vary from having very soft or crinkly leaves and little heart to those which are very crisp.

GROWING TIMES AND HARVESTING MONTHS

It is certainly possible to produce some salad crops in your garden throughout the year, although undoubtedly summer and autumn are the principal seasons. Lettuces can be grown the year round, but winter and spring crops are harder to produce successfully.

Choose lettuce varieties according to your taste and those you find easiest to produce. The different types all include varieties suitable for sowing variously throughout the year.

The chart below shows the quickest time in which it takes these crops to reach maturity (remember this will vary according to the month of sowing) and the months in which they may be harvested.

Vegetable	Shortest Growing Time	Harvesting Months
Chicory	*To lifting:* 5 months *Forcing to harvesting:* 1 month	November–March
Corn salad	4 months	December and January
Cress, American	2 months	March–December
Cucumber	4 months	Late July/August–September
Endive	*To blanching:* 3 months *Blanching to harvesting:* 2–4 weeks	October–November December
Lettuce	2½ months	April–November and January–March
Radish Ordinary Winter	1 month 4 months	April–November October–December

Corn salad: this crop will grow during the winter when other types of lettuce are not growing in such abundance. They may need to be protected against harsh winter conditions with cloches, and must be kept weed-free. Two or three leaves are picked at a time.

GROWING CRESS

Watercress is not easy to grow without a stream or running water, so mustard and cress is a good alternative. It is grown indoors, ideally on a kitchen windowsill, and is ready for cutting in two to three weeks. You can also grow sprouting seeds.

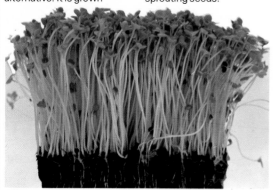

Other salad crops: less well known salad crops include endive **(top)** and chicory **(above).** Both these crops have to be blanched before they are harvested. Land or American cress **(left)** can be grown as an alternative to watercress and does not require a source of running water.

CULTIVATION OF SALAD CROPS

Vegetable	Soil/Position	Sowing	Drill Depth
Chicory	**Soil:** deep and well-cultivated. Appreciates some well-rotted manure or compost dug-in deeply before sowing. **Position:** any, but does not like to be heavily overshadowed.	Sow thinly in cropping position from April to June.	0.5 cm ($\frac{1}{4}$ in).
Corn salad	**Soil:** any well-cultivated soil. **Position:** open and sunny.	Sow thinly in August/September.	1 cm ($\frac{1}{2}$ in).
Cress, American	**Soil:** damp, full of well-rotted manure. **Position:** moist and shady.	Water the drills well and sow seed thinly in March; then again in September.	0.5 cm ($\frac{1}{4}$ in).
Cucumber	**Soil:** good soil which has been well enriched with manure or compost shortly before planting. **Position:** sunny and sheltered.	Sow indoors in individual peat pots in late April. Keep in warm place. Sow under glass in cropping site in mid-May, or unprotected in cropping site from the end of May. Sow three seeds in a 10–15 cm (4–6 in) group, every 60 cm (2 ft).	1–2.5 cm ($\frac{1}{2}$–1 in).
Endive	**Soil:** light, well-drained and fertile soil. **Position:** any, but prefers a well-sheltered spot.	Sow in cropping site late June to early August, or in a seed bed if more convenient.	1 cm ($\frac{1}{2}$ in).
Lettuce	**Soil:** fertile, well-drained light soil. Crisp varieties like soil with lots of organic matter incorporated to help make them water-retentive. **Position:** open and sunny. Will not generally grow well if trees are shading the site.	**Required harvesting time:** *May to November:* outdoors in cropping site, thinly, every two weeks from March to early August. *May to July:* indoors in boxes January/February. *April to May:* choose hardy over-wintering varieties and sow under cloches end September/early October. *November to December:* choose forcing varieties and sow in well-prepared seed bed early August. Sow thinly in rows 15 cm (6 in) apart. *March to April:* choose a forcing variety and sow in a cold frame or under cloches in October.	All drills 1 cm ($\frac{1}{2}$ in).
Radish	**Soil:** any fertile, well-cultivated soil, preferably containing well-rotted organic matter. This is particularly necessary if soil is light and sandy. **Position: for spring sowing:** open and sunny, but sheltered. Over-shadowing may result in radishes that are woody and hot. **For summer sowing:** cool, shady site.	**Ordinary radish:** sow in cropping site in succession from March; sow very thinly every two weeks until August/September. If you want radishes even earlier (for late March), sow under cloches in January/February. Put cloches in place a fortnight before sowing to warm ground. **Winter radishes:** sow in cropping site in July/August. If grond is dry, water base of drill before sowing.	1 cm ($\frac{1}{2}$ in). 0.5 cm ($\frac{1}{4}$ in). 2 cm ($\frac{3}{4}$ in).

Thinning/Transplanting	Planting Distance (between plants/rows)	Cultivation	Harvest
Thin progressively to recommended spacing.	20×38 cm (8×15 in).	Hoe between rows and water well if plants show any signs of drying. In October/November, when the narrow green leaves have turned yellow and died down, dig up the long, parsnip-shaped roots. Cut off leaves about 2.5 cm (1 in) above roots and rub off all the lower end of the root to make it about 20 cm (8 in) long. Either force at once (see under Harvest) or store in boxes covered in dry,fine soil in a dark place,until wanted.	**To force:** plant roots in soil- or peat-filled flower pots, so there is 2.5–5 cm (1–2 in) between them and the tops are visible above the soil. Water the soil and cover pot with another pot the same size, inverted. Put in a warm place and leave for about four weeks. The heads are ready when they are 12.5–15 cm (5–6 in) high. Cut as required and then compost the roots.
Thin to recommended spacing.	10×15 cm (4×6 in).	Water plants freely and hoe between rows to eliminate weeds. Protect from frost by packing straw or dried bracken round plants. Alternatively, place cloches on top.	Begin to harvest when at least six leaves have formed on the plant. Pick older leaves first or pull up the whole plant. Usually ready by the end of December.
Thin progressively to recommended spacing.	20×30 cm (8×12 in). One row is probably sufficient.	Water freely. Mulch the ground if there is any likelihood of it drying out.	Begin picking outer leaves about two months after sowing. More will grow from the centre. As plants get older, the outer leaves become tough. Pick the centre ones.
Harden off those grown indoors in May by putting outside. Plant out in early June, spacing as recommended. Can be planted together with the peat pot, but make sure surface is beneath soil. If they are planted outside, pull out the weaker seedlings as they emerge, leaving one strong plant at each station.	60×90 cm (2×3 ft).	Water the plants freely. It helps to encourage side shoots to grow if you pinch out the growing tips when four or five leaves have formed. Pollinate female flowers by pushing pollen-bearing male flowers into their centres (see photograph). Alternatively, transfer pollen from male flowers onto females with small brush. As young cucumbers form, pinch out shoots that have no cucumbers beyond the seventh leaf.	Cut the cucumbers while they are still young. More will form.
Thin progressively to recommended spacing if sown in cropping site. If sown in seed bed, transplant to cropping site when seedlings are 5–7.5 cm (2–3 in) high.	30×38 cm (12×15 in).	Hoe to eliminate weeds and water freely. Growth should be rapid so give a liquid feed to encourage this if you think it necessary. Centre leaves must be blanched when plants are well formed and about three months old. To do this, first make sure they are dry (do not begin during a rainy spell) then either cover the plant with a flower pot or just cover the centre with a piece of flat wood or a slate. Alternatively, cover the row of endives with black polythene or white-painted cloches.	If harvesting in autumn, the plants will take about ten days to blanch. For later winter harvesting, leave them for twice this time. Harvest by pulling up the entire plant, and do this to all plants before any danger of frost. They will keep for a few weeks if placed in boxes of soil and put in a dark shed or cellar. However, they are at their best if used immediately.

Thinning/Transplanting		Cultivation	Harvest
Required harvesting time: *May to November:* thin to 7.5 cm (3 in) when plants are large enough to handle. Thin twice more to reach recommended distances. Second thinnings can be transplanted (but do not do this after April – plants are likely to bolt); third thinnings can be eaten. *May to July:* prick out seedlings as they appear. When about 10 cm (4 in) high plants out in cropping site under cloches or tunnels in March or in the open ground in April. *April to May:* thin to 7.5 cm (3 in) when plants are large enough to handle. Do not thin again until early spring. *November to December:*	transplant seedlings to 22 cm (9 in) apart to a cold frame. Alternatively, thin to this distance and then protect with cloches. *March to April:* thin to 7.5 cm (3 in) when plants are large enough to handle. Thin again in late February. If sown in seed bed, transplant to cropping site in mid-December but protect with cloches. **Planting Distance (between plants/rows)** Distances between plants vary from 15–30 cm (6–12 in) according to varieties. Check with packet when sowing. Distance between rows is usually 30cm (12 in).	Protect all seedlings from attack by birds, either with threads of black cotton or polythene tunnels. Those sown to grow during the summer need constant watering. If they are allowed to dry out, they are almost certain to bolt prematurely. Those sown to grow during the winter need little watering, but must therefore be sown in well-cultivated soil. To encourage a cos-type lettuce to form its centre heart, draw up the outer leaves and tie round the plant loosely.	Cabbage-type lettuces are ready when the heart is well formed. Feel it gently, but do not pinch it. Crisper varieties are ready when the centre leaves have curled over each other and this part feels hard and compact. Cos types are ready when the centre leaves are well developed. Cut all lettuces as they are wanted for the table, but do not leave in the ground for too long after they are ready; they soon go to seed.
Ordinary radish: little thinning will be necessary, providing seed was thinly sown. **Winter radish:** thin to recommended spacing as seedlings emerge.	2.5×22 cm (1×9 in). 20×30 cm (8×12 in).	**Ordinary radish:** water well – crisp and mild-tasting crops depend on rapid growth. In dry soils, or if plants are allowed to dry, radishes will be woody and very hot-tasting. Keep an eye on summer-sown radishes – they are prone to very rapid bolting. Provide shade with plastic tunnels in very hot weather. **Winter radish:** hoe between rows to eliminate weeds.	**Ordinary radish:** pull largest ones first (you can check by pushing aside leaves and stems), beginning the harvest when they are about 1 cm ($\frac{1}{2}$ in) in diameter. Pull up in succession quickly. Pull up and compost any excess rather than leave uselessly in the ground. **Winter radish:** start harvesting in November. They can be left in the ground through winter, but it is probably best to pull and store like other root crops (see page 186).

Catch crops: you can grow catch crops of lettuces between rows of the longer-maturing pulses in the summer in order to get the most produce from the soil. This is a good example of not wasting space in the vegetable garden.

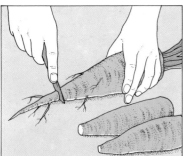

Chicory: 1 This crop requires two growing periods. When the long roots are dug up they are trimmed of any shoots, topped and tailed.

Endive: 1 Loosely tie raffia around the stems of fully grown plants. This keeps the lower tresses off the ground and reduces the risk of them rotting.

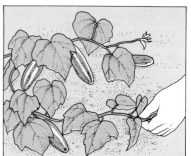

Cucumber: 1 Pinch out any growing shoots when enough cucumbers have formed on the plant, to prevent any further growth.

2 Replant in pots filled with peat, keeping the crowns just above the soil. Water and blanch with black polythene. Harvest chicons.

2 Cover the drainage holes of flower pots to exclude light and place pots over plants. Ensure there is ventilation around the base of the pot.

2 If necessary, hand pollinate the female cucumber flowers either with a brush or by pushing the male flowers into the centres of the female flowers.

stream, although it is possible to produce it in a heavily watered trench. I have abandoned it here in favour of American cress, which is easier to grow. This. has smaller, rather more symmetrically arranged leaves, but its flavour is not dissimilar to watercress. Mustard and cress has not been included as it is usually grown indoors. This you can do either by sprinkling the seed on saucers containing dampened blotting paper, sheets of kitchen paper, or in shallow, peat-filled containers. Keep these in a dark place until the seed has germinated, then move them to a light windowsill. Cut and use when the stems are about 4 cm (1½ in) high.

The two main types of lettuce – cabbage and cos – have countless sub-divisions and types. As well as normal-sized lettuces in all shades of green imaginable, there are dwarf varieties, those with very crisp leaves that curl over each other while growing, and those with soft leaves that form loose hearts in the centre. Choose according to the type you like and the time of year in which you want to grow them, by consulting the many packets of seeds found at any garden supplier.

Radishes are actually members of the brassica group but are included here as they are so essentially a salad crop. The ordinary radishes grown throughout the summer may be round, bomb-shaped or conical. They can be brilliant red, red and white or even pure white. Winter radishes, which can add a lot of interest to winter salads, are parsnip-shaped, black-skinned and can grow up to 15 cm (6 in) long.

Tomatoes, which are such an important salad crop and can be grown successfully out of doors in most districts, are discussed in more detail on pages 72–74.

Cultivation

On pages 68–69 are the comprehensive cultural details for the salad crops in this section. Nearly all these crops appreciate a fertile soil which is rich in organic material. This is particularly so for cucumbers, which can be successfully grown on a mound of well-rotted compost or farmyard manure covered with 7.5–10 cm (3–4 in) of good top soil. The roots of cucumber plants need to be kept very moist, but the crop will fail if they are waterlogged. Cucumber plants can be left to trail over the ground (but remember they take up quite a lot of space), or trained to grow up a vertical trellis.

Both endive and corn salad are usually thought of as autumn and winter vegetables but they can also be sown in early spring to produce summer crops. Decide whether this is worth it, bearing in mind that you should have an abundance of lettuce through the summer.

As most salad crops are quick to mature, they can be sown as catch crops – that is, between rows of slower-maturing vegetables. Alternatively, lettuces, in particular, can easily be grown in odd spots in a flower garden. Sow all types of salad crop very thinly and in rapid succession. As most crops are best eaten at once, it makes more sense to have a small, steady flow, rather than to be swamped with a glut of say, radishes and lettuce, all at once.

Salad crops need to be kept well watered whilst growing. Most must be grown rapidly both for the best taste and to stop them running to seed. Once harvested, pull up the roots quickly and compost them. The land can be used immediately for another crop.

Pests and diseases

Like all other vegetables, salad crops will be affected by some pests and diseases, although they are generally less troubled in this regard than some. Slugs are one of the main problems, chewing their way through leaves and plants. Control them in whichever way you find most effective – either by setting traps (see page 49) or by using proprietary mixes. Cutworms (see page 55) can be a problem, as can downy mildew (see page 49). Radishes, which are brassicas, will be subject to the brassica diseases (see page 49), although the only one that causes very much trouble is the flea beetle. Do not grow radishes in ground infected with club root.

PESTS AND DISEASES/SALAD CROPS

Botrytis (grey mould)

Identification: brown spots appear on the leaves and grey mould then forms on these. Lettuce grown through the winter is particularly susceptible to attack. The plants will wilt and die.
Treatment: do not grow plants in cold, damp conditions (check under glass or cloches). Also choose disease-resistant varieties of vegetables if growing them in winter.

lessened by making sure summer plants are kept well-watered.

Root aphis

Identification: yellow-coloured aphis which attack lettuce roots in summer. The plants become stunted and wilt.
Treatment: this is comparatively rare, but can generally be avoided altogether by growing resistant varieties.

Mosaic virus

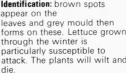

Identification: turns the leaves and fruits of plants – cucumber in particular – yellow and mottled. Eventually growth becomes stunted and the fruits do not develop properly.
Treatment: disease is spread by greenfly, so control these by paying attention to good garden hygiene.

Swift moth

Identification: whitish caterpillars which feed on plant roots and have been known to attack chicory. The caterpillars may be visible when digging or hoeing the soil.
Treatment: attention to garden hygiene. Control may be necessary with proprietary mixes.

Greenfly
Identification: clusters of these tiny insects may attack lettuces in summer. They will be noticeable on the leaves, and plants will eventually become stunted and die.
Treatment: attention to garden hygiene and prompt destruction of any greenfly-carrying crops. Likelihood of attack can be

Growing Tomatoes

THE MANY NEW HYBRID varieties of tomatoes available today have made it possible to grow tomatoes outdoors successfully in many areas. Failing this, a good-sized crop can often be produced on a small paved area on a windowsill in a garden room. The varieties of tomatoes are endless, from round ones of all sizes – those that are scarcely bigger than a sugar lump to those that are almost too big to hold in the hand – to plum- or pear-shaped ones that may be yellow, striped green and red, or yellow and red.

The most usual way of growing tomatoes outdoors is on a single-stemmed plant known as a cordon, but there are also bush and dwarf varieties, the latter growing to a height of no more than 15 cm (6 in) but sprawling extensively over the ground.

Soil
This should be well-cultivated and well-drained, into which a load of well-rotted organic matter (leaf mould is particularly acceptable) has been incorporated the previous autumn. If the ground is freshly manured just before planting tomatoes, the plants will be very leafy but bear few fruits. Tomatoes will grow successfully in

---

GOOD VARIETIES

OUTDOOR STANDARD:
Alicante early variety with thin-skinned fleshy fruits
Moneymaker very popular heavy cropper with medium-sized fruits
Sweet 100 long trusses of sweet cherry-sized fruits

OUTDOOR BUSH:
Amateur popular, with medium-sized fruits

Sigmabush excellent fruits and high yield

DWARF:
Tiny Tim very small sweet fruits ideal for pots

---

potting composts and fertilized peat bags, although they will need regular liquid feeding in later stages of growth.

Position
A warm, sunny and sheltered spot. Sunshine is the main requisite, so plant tomatoes in the sunniest spot of the garden. South-facing walls or fences generally make the best sites, because they also act as wind-breaks.

Sowing or planting
Tomatoes can be grown successfully from seed. Make sure you buy an outdoor variety and sow them in boxes or pots filled with seed compost in late March/early April. Sow seeds 2.5 cm (1 in) apart or sow two seeds to each 7.5 cm (3 in) pot. Damp the compost well and cover with newspaper until the seed has germinated. Put the containers in a warm, darkened place and, as soon as the seedlings emerge, remove the newspaper and put containers on a warm, south-facing windowsill in full light. When the first leaves appear, transplant strong seedlings from boxes to individual pots filled with potting compost, or just remove the weaker seedling of the two sown in individual pots.

Cultivation: 1 Sow the seeds in boxes filled with seed compost in late March/early April. Dampen the compost, cover the boxes with newspaper and leave them in a warm, dark place.

2 When the seedlings begin to grow, prick out the strongest and plant in individual flowerpots or peat pots, filled with potting compost. Water the seedlings lightly but regularly.

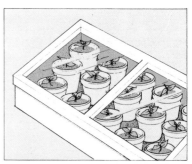

3 Harden the seedlings off either by placing them in cold frames in mid-April, or in cloches in May. If necessary, pot on any seedlings which are out-growing their pots.

4 Plant out the seedlings when they are about 20 cm (8 in) high. Tip them out of their pots, holding them carefully by their root balls, and plant them in the soil.

5 It is very important that the plants are watered regularly to prevent them wilting. Take care with plants in growing bags, as too much water can rot their roots.

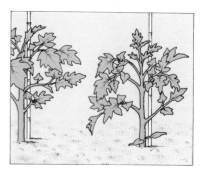

6 Space the plants about 45 cm (18 in) apart, to allow them room to grow. As they grow taller they will need to be supported with canes, loosely attached with soft garden string.

Above: a side shoot grows from an axil – the angle between the leaf and stem. If these are left to grow, they will use vital water and nutrients and must therefore be picked off when they are small.
Left: flower trusses grow from the main stem. After four trusses have formed, pinch out the growing tip to help the development of the trusses.

From about mid-April, begin to harden off the plants by putting them in cold frames. If these are not available, either put them under cloches in mid-May or keep indoors and plant out in the garden in early June. If necessary pot the seedlings on to bigger pots as they grow and before planting them out. Whilst in containers, the compost should be kept damp, but not waterlogged.

Many people prefer to buy plants from a nursery rather than raise their own from seed. Buy them when they are about 20 cm (8 in) high, making sure you buy sturdy-looking plants, bred to grow outdoors. They should be dark-green and short-jointed; avoid those that look weak or have large gaps between rather fern-like leaves.

Plant tomatoes out carefully (following planting distances given below). Tip them out of the pot and hold them by the root balls, not the stems. Plant them with all the compost still adhering to the roots, digging holes so the top of the root ball is a good 1 cm ($\frac{1}{2}$ in) below the surface of the soil. Plants should be about 45 cm (1 ft 6 in) apart. If growing more than one row, place them 75 cm (2 ft 6 in) apart.

Cultivation
Water the seedlings after planting. Sink a 10 cm (4 in) diameter flowerpot into the soil near the root and fill this to the top with water once a week thereafter. This allows water to get to the roots quickly and ensures the plant is

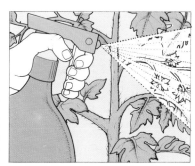

7 The plants should be given liquid feeds from about the end of July, once they begin to bear fruit. They must be fed regularly, otherwise the fruits may grow unevenly and split.

8 Remove any bottom leaves which turn yellow, and tie back any others which are shading tomatoes from the sun. Place straw on the ground to protect lower trusses from mud.

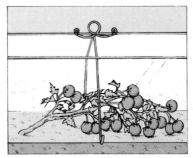

Harvesting tomatoes: 1 Pick tomatoes by supporting the fruit in the palm of the hand and gently snapping off the stem above the calyx.

2 If picking whole trusses of green tomatoes at the end of the season, leave them on a bed of straw and under cloches, outside, to ripen.

3 Alternatively, the trusses can be cut and hung up in a warm, sunny spot indoors, or ideally in the greenhouse, until they are ripe.

kept evenly moist. Irregular or over-watering can do as much damage as insufficient watering.

Push strong canes about 1.2–1.5 metres (4–5 ft) into the ground close to the plant, and as the plant grows, tie the stem loosely to the cane (giving the stem room to expand). As growth progresses, pinch out the side shoots that grow in the leaf axils – that is, the little shoots appearing between the leaves and the stem (see page 73). This helps to ensure that strong flower trusses (on which the fruits will form) develop, instead of a number of long, useless side shoots. The flower trusses grow from the main stem, not the leaf axils.

When the plant has developed about four trusses (usually towards the end of July), prevent further upward growth by pinching out the central growing tip. The plant's energies will then be directed into developing the trusses. Pinching out is not necessary on dwarf or bush varieties.

Tomatoes will benefit from regular liquid feeding from now on (you will need to begin earlier if growing in pots or peat bags). Spray or syringe the plants with water and liquid feed, as well as watering through the ground.

Remove any leaves that turn yellow and, as the fruits begin to form, tie back any lower leaves which are shaded from the sun. Tomatoes on lower trusses can be kept clean by putting a layer of straw beneath them.

Harvesting

Begin picking the tomatoes as soon as they are ripe, supporting the fruits in the palm of your hand and pressing the stem just above the fruit. It will snap, leaving the calyx on the end of the tomato.

In September, any fruit still remaining should be picked even if it is green – early frosts will cause instant death. Pull up the plant and hang either the whole thing, or just the tomato-bearing trusses in a warm, preferably sunny, spot indoors, or in a greenhouse, to allow the tomatoes to ripen. Alternatively, if space permits, leave the plants in the ground, but untie them and lie them down gently on a bed of straw and cover with cloches until the tomatoes ripen.

Green tomatoes can also be picked off the plant entirely and put carefully into trays, placed in a cool, darkened place. They will ripen gradually over the next few months, and will be encouraged to do so if you include one red tomato with every batch.

Pests and diseases

The tomato is closely related to the potato and therefore is likely to suffer from many of the same problems. It may be affected by the potato cyst eelworm (see page 64) and is likely to get blight if you handle tomato plants after tending potatoes. Always wash your hands between the two operations. Apart from those diseases mentioned below, young plants put out too soon may show signs of distress. If growth is slow and plants look sickly shortly after planting, protect them with cloches. Tomatoes grown outdoors, however, are usually far less susceptible to problems than their hot house relatives.

PESTS AND DISEASES/TOMATOES

Blossom and rot

Leaf mould

Identification: brown or black circular discolorations which appear on the bottom of the young, developing tomatoes. **Treatment:** keep plants evenly moist at all times.

Identification: the upper surfaces of the leaves display yellow spots and mould appears on the under surfaces. **Treatment:** a warm, humid atmosphere is the ideal condition for this disease, but control it with copper-based sprays. Plant disease-resistant varieties in future.

Buck eye rot

Splitting

Identification: brown rings appear on the tomatoes on the lower trusses. **Treatment:** take care not to splash the fruit when watering the plant.

Identification: the skin of the developing tomato splits either down, or around, the fruit. **Treatment:** water and feed the plant regularly.

Other Outdoor Vegetables

INCLUDED ON THE FOLLOWING PAGES, under this general heading of 'other outdoor crops' are globe and Jerusalem artichokes, asparagus, celery and celeriac, leeks, onions and garlic, marrows (large zucchini), courgettes (zucchini), pumpkins, okra, spinach and sweetcorn.

There are two main types of celery – that which must be blanched during growth and that which is self-blanching. Self-blanching is easier to grow and demands less work, but it will not survive the heavy frosts that the other types can withstand. Many people consider the taste of blanched celery to be better. Celeriac, known sometimes as the turnip-rooted celery because of the edible swollen bulb that grows at the bottom of the plant, is easier to grow than celery.

Globe artichokes are perennials, and their greeny-silvery leaves make them very ornamental. Each plant yields about six flower heads (the edible part) every year and will do so for about six years. However, it is advisable to renew the plants after three or four years, as thereafter the heads become smaller and rather tough. Jerusalem artichokes are grown for their tubers, which have a distinctly earthy taste. The plants resemble sunflowers (to which they are related), and they grow tall enough to form an effective screen, to hide a garden shed, or compost heap, for example.

Courgettes are actually young marrows, but their greatly increased popularity over recent years has led to the development of varieties specifically designed to produce heavy crops of these smaller fruits. If courgettes are wanted, it is better to grow these special varieties rather than to harvest small marrows. The cultivation of both vegetables is the same, as it is too for custard marrows and vegetable spaghetti. Marrows, in par-

1

2

3

4

5

Other outdoor crops: finding out more about vegetables will enhance and vary your diet. As well as spinach (**1**) and celery (**5**), there are other crops which you might not have considered growing yourself. Celeriac (**4**) is easier to grow than celery, and can be eaten raw or cooked. Jerusalem artichokes (**2**) will grow in almost any soil, and globe varieties (**3**) mean that you will be able to eat more often a vegetable which is considered to be a delicacy.

Squashes and sweetcorn:
courgettes **(1)** and marrows
(zucchini) **(3)** are very easy to
grow. Courgettes have
gained in popularity in recent
years and there are now
many different varieties
available. Pumpkins **(2)**
belong to the same family but
are less frequently grown.
Sweetcorn **(4)** also does not
need warm climates in which
to grow.

ticular, are available in bush and trailing varieties; the
latter can be trained to grow up vertical supports if space
is at a premium.

Also related to the marrow is the pumpkin and other
edible squashes, which are generally easy to grow, but
do take up a great deal of space. Gourds also belong to
the same family and may be grown in the same way, but
most types are purely ornamental and not edible. They
should be cut in late summer and put in a warm, sunny
place to dry.

Leeks, onions and garlic are all members of the same
family – leeks being the easiest to grow and the hardiest
as they will withstand heavy frosts. Growing them also
helps to break down heavy ground and improves its
texture. Onions can be produced the whole year round,
but they need careful attention if they are to survive the
winter. More usually they are harvested in the autumn
and then stored (see page 187), so they are available
through the winter.

Okra is a rather more unusual vegetable, but one that
may be used to flavour soups and stews as well as being
served as a vegetable accompaniment. Spinach is one of
the fastest growing of all leaf vegetables, making it a

GROWING TIMES AND HARVESTING MONTHS

The chart below gives the shortest time it takes for these other outdoor crops to reach maturity, and the months in which they are generally harvested. As with other vegetables, cropping seasons can be extended by regular sowings at intervals of a couple of weeks or a month, or by sowing different varieties that take varying times to reach maturity.

Vegetable	Shortest growing time	Harvesting months
Celery:		
Self-blanching	5½ months	End August– end October
Blanching	6½ months	End September–March
Celeriac	6½ months	October–November
Courgette (Small zucchini)	2½ months	July–September
Marrow (Large zucchini)	3 months	July–October
Pumpkin	3 months	July–October
Leek	8 months	Early October–April
Onion – salad	3 months	June–mid-November
Onion	6–10 months	September–November
Shallot	4 months	Late July–August
Okra	3 months	August–early October
Spinach:		
Summer	2 months	May–October
Winter	2½ months	November–April
New Zealand	1½ months	Mid-June–September
Sweetcorn	3 months	August–September

1

Onions: shallots **(1)**, spring onions **(2)**, garlic **(3)**, leeks **(4)**, and onions **(5)** all belong to the same family and are very easy to grow. Although they can be grown through the winter, onions may need to be protected during hard weather.

4

2

3

5

Okra: also known as ladies' fingers or gumbo, this is a more unusual vegetable. It may have to be grown under cloches.

good intercrop. The two main types are summer and winter spinach, but New Zealand spinach is usually grouped with them, although it is not a true member of the spinach family. It has smaller leaves which are less shiny, and it is not as hardy, being killed by frost. However, it will flourish in drier conditions.

Varieties of sweetcorn developed in recent years have made it possible to grow this essentially hot-weather vegetable in more temperate climates. Given a sheltered position, plants will give a reasonable yield, making them well worthwhile growing.

Cultivation

Instructions for sowing, growing and harvesting these are given on pages 82–83. Globe artichokes may be grown from seed, but it is more usual (as well as quicker and easier) to grow them from suckers. These may be cut off existing plants as they are produced, or bought from a garden centre. Jerusalem artichokes are grown from tubers. When harvesting, it is important to dig up all the tubers, and plant new ones the next year. This is not as wasteful as it sounds, because it leaves the ground free for other crops, reduces the chance of disease, and stops them taking over the land.

Celery that needs blanching is usually grown in

1

3

Cultivation of celery: 1 Plant out celery seedlings in trenches at the required distance and water well.
2 Before earthing up, wrap black polythene around the stems of each plant to keep them free from dirt, and to blanch if necessary.
3 Begin earthing up process, keeping the leaves exposed. Continue to water well.
4 Take care when harvesting celery not to damage the plants.

2

4

CULTIVATION OF MARROWS

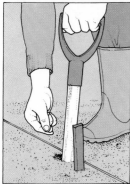

Planting: using a dibber to make holes in the soil, with a garden line as a guide, plant marrow seeds individually.

Pinching out: pinch out the growing tips of marrows to encourage the side shoots to grow, and the plant to spread.

Pollinating: marrows must be pollinated if they are to bear fruit. There are two methods of doing this yourself—either to transfer pollen from the male to the female flower on a paint brush, or to insert the male flower into the centre of the female. The pollen will fall into the female flower.

Protecting: place plants on pieces of wood, slate, or polythene to protect from mud. Harvest when tender.

Cultivation of onions:
onions are grown from onion sets **(left)** which are planted in the ground. When the leaves turn yellow, bend them over the bulbs **(right)** and leave the onions to finish ripening. Once they are harvested, they must be dried, preferably by hanging them in the sun **(above).**

deep trenches and the land between these can be used to grow intercrops of quick-maturing vegetables such as lettuce or radish. Self-blanching types of celery are usually grown in a block, which helps to blanch the stems – of the inner plants at least – naturally. A good alternative is to grow them in a cold frame with the top glass removed. The walls of the frame give shade to the outer plants, therefore blanching their stems, too. Sweetcorn is also grown in a block formation, because the chance of good pollination between the top flowers and those that form the cobs is increased where a lot of plants are grouped closely together. Pollination is necessary for the good production of cobs.

Onions may be grown from seeds or sets, the latter being tiny, immature onions which will each produce one large onion. The sets are easier to grow, but keep them in a cool, dry place if there is any delay between buying and planting them, in order to discourage premature sprouting. Shallots are also grown from sets, but in this case each bulb multiplies to produce about six new ones. After harvesting, keep some of the shallots to plant for the following year's crop. Their cultivation is the same as for onions from sets.

Pests and diseases

The common pests and diseases which attack other outdoor crops are outlined in the chart below. In addition to these, the celery leaf fly, which attacks parsnips (see page 55) is a major pest of celery and celeriac, and it inflicts similar damage. It should be dealt with as previously recommended. Any plants which are affected will recover more quickly if they are given a feed of liquid fertilizer.

Dry growing conditions and poor soil tend to make globe artichokes small, woody and generally unpalatable. Applying a general fertilizer to the soil and mulching the ground around the plants with well-rotted organic matter will help to improve conditions. Marrows and courgettes that are kept short of water, or spinach grown on land with poor drainage, may suffer attacks of mildew on their leaves. If this is not too severe, it will probably not affect the size of the marrow or courgette crop, and infected leaves can be picked off the spinach plants and discarded. Mildew is less likely to occur on spinach if the plants are thinned early, as recommended.

Marrows can also suffer from mosaic virus (see page 71) and slugs can be a problem with many of these crops – Jerusalem artichokes and earthed-up celery in particular. The problem can be alleviated to some extent in the latter by surrounding the plants with peat rather than soil.

PESTS AND DISEASES/OTHER OUTDOOR VEGETABLES

Leek moth

Identification: irregular white lines appear on the leaves. These are left by the maggots of the moth as they tunnel through the leaves. Leeks and onions are victims of this pest.
Treatment: spray with proprietary mixtures containing nicotine.

Frit fly

Identification: a pest of sweetcorn. Larvae eat into the growing plant, causing stunted growth and distorted and ragged leaves. Attack generally occurs in late May and early June.
Treatment: spray with a recommended proprietary mixture when the plants have produced just a few leaves. If attacks of this pest are known to abound in your locality, it is better to rear seed under glass, than to sow direct

into the ground. This way it is harder for the pests to reach them.

Onion fly

Identification: maggots hatch from eggs laid on the surface of the soil, and tunnel into the developing onion. It becomes soft and unpleasant. Attack can be detected by the grey-purple streaks which appear on the leaves.
Treatment: sets are not usually attacked, and the pest is most prevalent on dry soils. Dig up and burn infected plants. Attacks are less likely if the plants are handled as little as possible during development. Handling increases the smell which attracts the onion fly.

Eelworm

Identification: attacks onions, causing the leaves to become

swollen and distorted.
Treatment: make sure you buy good seed from a reputable dealer as this is generally treated against eelworm attack. Do not grow onions on ground you know to be infested for at least three years.

Petal blight fungus

Identification: large, dark spots appear on the heads of globe artichokes.
Treatment: spray with proprietary mixtures when buds develop, and repeat every two weeks.

Neck rot

Identification: this attacks onions in store (see page 187). It appears as a soft brown rot which will affect the whole onion, making it useless.
Treatment: make sure onions are dry before storing; if conditions are wet at harvest-time, bring

the onions indoors at once and dry them. Crops can be treated with proprietary mixtures which help to discourage the disease.

White rot

Identification: attacks onions and leeks, turning the leaves yellow. They wither and die, revealing the base of the plant which will be covered with a white mould.
Treatment: dig up and burn infected plants. Follow a strict crop rotation and sow seed very thinly. Seed drills can be treated with proprietary mixtures to help deter disease.

Celery leaf spot

Identification: brown spots with black centres appear on the leaves.
Treatment: spray with proprietary mixtures and buy only good seed (this is usually treated to safeguard against attack).

CULTIVATION OF OTHER OUTDOOR CROPS

Vegetable	Soil/Position	Sowing	Drill depth
Globe artichoke	**Soil:** rich, well-drained soil which was manured the previous spring. Apply lime about two months before planting if soil is acid. **Position:** open, sunny, but sheltered.	If raising from seed, sow outdoors in seed bed in March/April. If raising from suckers, plant them into a spare area in April.	1 cm ($\frac{1}{2}$ in).
Jerusalem artichoke	**Soil:** will grow in almost any soil, but the richer it is, the heavier the crop. If soil is poor, enrich with manure the winter before spring planting. **Position:** sunny, but will tolerate partial shade. Can be grown as a screen.	Plant tubers into the cropping site in February to March.	10–15 cm (4–6 in).
Celery	**Soil:** deeply dug, rich, well-drained soil with lots of well-rotted organic matter. Self-blanching types will grow in poorer soils. **Position:** open and sunny.	**Both types:** sow seeds under glass in mid-March and again in mid-April to stagger the crop. Keep in a warm place to germinate.	
Celeriac	**Soil:** richly cultivated and well-drained. It will grow in poorer soils than celery, but bigger vegetables are produced if the soil is rich. **Position:** sunny.	Sow under glass in mid-March and keep warm until germination.	
Garlic	**Soil:** see Onions. **Position:** see Onions.	Divide garlic bulbs into individual cloves and plant with the growing tip upwards just below the soil at regular intervals from March to May and again in October.	See Onions.
Leek	**Soil:** well-cultivated and well-drained soil, which has been manured the previous winter. Leeks are not as demanding as onions in their soil requirements. **Position:** any, but they dislike heavy shading.	Indoors in February/March or outdoors in a seed bed in March/April, sowing three seeds every 2.5 cm (1 in).	1 cm ($\frac{1}{2}$ in).

Thinning/Transplanting	Planting Distance (between plants/rows)	Cultivation	Harvesting
Thin seedlings as they appear, discarding the weaker ones. The following spring, transplant them into their cropping site at the recommended spacing. Transplant plants grown from suckers at this time, too.	75–105 cm (2 ft 6 in × 3 ft 6 in).	Mulch plants one month after planting out. Water them well in dry spells. Remove flower buds as they appear in the first year. In subsequent years, allow plant to develop four to six flower buds, picking off any extra ones. In early winter, cut main stems to ground level, leaving the small leaves at the centre which will protect the plant. Then either cover the plants with straw or draw soil up around them.	In the second and following years, pick the heads in the summer when they are plump, but green, and the petals are tightly grouped. There should be no brown tips to the scales. Use secateurs to cut them and begin with the central, largest, head. After harvesting, cut the stems back by half.
	38×75 cm (1 ft 3 in × 2 ft 6 in).	Hoe to control weeds and pinch out growing tips to prevent flowers forming. Stake plants if necessary and cut the stems down in early winter.	Lift tubers as required from October. You can leave the crop in the ground or dig them up and store. Save some tubers from the crop to plant out the following year.
When seedlings are large enough to handle, prick out into boxes or single pots. Harden off seedlings from early sowing in a cold frame in late April and plant out in May. Harden off later sowing in May and plant out in June. **Blanching types:** in April dig trenches 38 cm (15 in) wide and 30 cm (1 ft) deep. Make them 30 cm (1 ft) wide for a double row of celery. Dig manure into the bottom to leave trench 15 cm (6 in) deep. Plant seedlings in the trench at recommended spacings and times. **Self-blanching types:** plant out in a block formation rather than single rows, so the inner plants are blanched naturally.	**Blanching types:** 15 cm (6 in) between plants. If planting a double row in the trench (see under Thinning/ Transplanting) place plants in pairs, not staggered. **Self-blanching types:** 22×22 cm (9×9 in).	Water all plants liberally after planting them out. **Blanching types:** when plants are about 30 cm (1 ft) high, tie corrugated paper or black polythene around their stems, water them and then draw the earth up around the stems to exclude the light. Make sure soil does not enter between the stems and that the leaves remain exposed. Continue earthing-up process regularly over the next six to eight weeks, always keeping leaves exposed. **Self-blanching types:** remove the side growths as they appear and when plants are about 30 cm (1 ft) high, pack straw around the outer stems. Water all celery plants well during dry spells or they will go to seed.	**Blanching types:** will be ready to harvest from late September, but some people think flavour is improved after the first frost. Dig up plants from one end of the trench, shake off soil and cut off roots. Make sure those left for later harvest are well earthed-up. **Self-blanching types:** will be ready from the end of August and must all be harvested by the first frost. Pack straw around those exposed after digging up plants. Harvest in the same way as blanching types.
Treat in the same way as celery seedlings, pricking out and hardening off for planting out in late May/June. Plant directly into the cropping site with roots well buried so plants are firm in the soil.	30×20 cm (12×8 in).	Hoe to control weeds and keep plants well watered. Feed at fortnightly intervals with liquid manure to keep growth even. From August onwards, remove any side growths and yellowing leaves. This helps to ensure the roots develop to their full potential.	Begin lifting when roots are large enough (usually from the end of October), as required. Harvest the entire crop by the end of November and store any that are not required for immediate use.
No thinning necessary.	15×30 cm (6×12 in).	Hoe to control weeds and water well during dry spells. When flowers appear, feed the plants every fortnight with liquid fertilizer.	Harvest when leaves begin to turn yellow. Those planted in March will be ready from October. Those planted in October will be ready the following July/August.
Prick out indoor seedlings when large enough to handle and harden off in mid-March. Transplant into a seed bed when seedlings are 15–20 cm (6–8 in) high, in April. Thin those in the seed bed to about 5 cm (2 in) apart when large enough to handle. Transplant to cropping site in June/July. **To transplant all leeks:** trim off the top third of the leaves with a pair of scissors. Make holes in the ground with a dibber at the recommended spacing and drop leeks into them so the tips of the leaves just show. Do not firm the soil around them; instead just water them well. This will firm them into the ground sufficiently once the water drains away.	22×30 cm (9×12 in).	Hoe to control weeds and draw soil up around stem as plants grow. This helps to blanch the stems, but try not to let the soil go in between the leaves.	Dig up leeks as you need them from September to April, easing them gently out of the soil with a fork. Lift them in spring when you want the ground for some other crop, and put the leeks in a shallow trench in a patch of ground not wanted. Just cover the roots and stems with soil, with the leaves protruding. In this way, the leeks will not begin to grow again, which makes them go to seed. Use as required.

Continued from page 83

Vegetable	Soil/Position	Sowing	Drill Depth
Marrow and courgette (Zucchini)	**Soil:** rich and moisture-retentive. It should have lots of well-rotted manure added to it. **Position:** sunny or partial shade. These plants can be grown on a compost heap and trailing varieties can also be grown up and along a fence.	Indoors, sow two to a pot in early April. Outdoors, sow directly into the cropping site in mid-May, but protect with cloches or tunnels in cold areas. Sow seeds at 15 cm (6 in) intervals, the pointed end pushed down into the soil.	2.5 cm (1 in).
Onion No onion seed or seedlings should be sown or transplanted until the soil has really dried out after winter. If it sticks to your boots, it is still too wet. Firm the ground and rake it to a fine tilth.	**Soil:** well-cultivated, deeply dug soil which has been manured the previous autumn. Pickling onions are better grown in lighter, not so rich, soil or they will grow too big. **Position:** sunny and open.	**Salad and pickling:** sow in shallow drills directly into the cropping site at monthly intervals from March to September. **Onions from seed:** 1 sow under glass in January to February. 2 sow outdoors in seed bed or directly into cropping site from late February to early April (for early autumn crop). 3 sow overwintering varieties in seed bed in mid-August for harvesting the following June and July. **Onions from sets:** trim off the wispy growth from the tiny bulbs and push them into the soil at the recommended distance in March/April. Alternatively, sow in shallow drills.	1 cm ($\frac{1}{2}$ in). 0.5–1 cm ($\frac{1}{4}$–$\frac{1}{2}$ in).
Pumpkin	**Soil:** very rich with lots of well-rotted organic matter incorporated. **Position:** warm and sunny. Will grow in partial shade, but the vegetables will be smaller.	Indoors, sow two to a pot in early April. Outdoors, sow directly into the cropping site in late April/mid-May. Protect with cloches.	2.5 cm (1 in).
Okra	**Soil:** light, which has been well-cultivated to ensure good water retention. **Position:** warm and sheltered. A south-facing spot is ideal.	Sow indoors under glass in April. Sow direct into cropping site in mid-May, but protect with cloches or polythene tunnels.	1 cm ($\frac{1}{2}$ in).
Spinach	**Soil:** rich, moisture-retentive soil (this is particularly important for summer spinach). **Position: Summer spinach:** full sun or partial shade. **Winter spinach:** sheltered site.	**Summer spinach:** sow directly into the cropping site at fortnightly intervals from early March to July. **Winter spinach:** sow directly into the cropping site in August and again one month later.	2.5 cm (1 in).
New Zealand spinach	**Soil:** light and well-drained. **Position:** sunny.	Sow indoors in late March/early April. Sow directly into cropping site in early May. Sow two seeds together every 15 cm (6 in) along row.	2.5 cm (1 in).
Sweetcorn	**Soil:** well-cultivated, rich soil. Improve light soils by incorporating lots of well-rotted organic matter. **Position:** warm, sunny and sheltered, but not shaded.	Sow indoors in individual peat pots in late April/early May. Sow directly into cropping site in mid-May. Plant two or three seeds at each station (see Spacing).	1–2 cm ($\frac{1}{2}$–$\frac{3}{4}$ in).

Thinning/Transplanting	Planting Distances (between plants/rows)	Cultivation	Harvest
Pull out and compost the weaker seedlings of those grown in pots as they emerge. Harden off in cold frames during May and plant into cropping site at recommended distances at the end of May/early June. Pull out weaker seedlings as they emerge in the ground outdoors to achieve the recommended spacing.	**Marrows – bush varieties:** 90×90 cm (3 ft×3 ft). **Marrows – trailing varieties:** 90×120 cm (3 ft×4 ft). **Courgettes:** 60×60 cm (2 ft×2 ft).	Hoe to control weeds until leaves are big enough to smother weed growth. Water plants well, making sure the surrounding ground is well soaked. Protect young plants from slugs with pellets. Pinch out growing tips of trailing marrows when they have four or five leaves, to encourage side shoots to grow. Pollinate by hand to increase cropping (see page 79).	Cut courgettes when they are 10–12.5 cm (4–5 in) long and keep cutting to encourage more fruits to grow. Cut marrows when they are about 20 cm (8 in) long, and tender. Test this by pressing one of the ribs close to the stalk – it should yield slightly. Marrows are generally ready towards the end of July and are best if harvested young. In any event, harvest them all by mid-October, before any danger of frost. See page 194 for storing.
Salad and pickling: No need to thin. **Onions from seed:** 1 prick out seedlings when large enough to handle. Harden off in mid-March and plant in cropping site in mid-April, so that half the stem is underground. 2 thin to 5 cm (2 in) apart when seedlings are large enough to handle. Thin a month later to 10 cm (4 in), using thinnings for salads or small onions. Thin to final recommended distance a month later or transplant to cropping site. 3 do not thin, but transplant to cropping site the following March. Plant so that half the stem is underground. **Onions from sets:** need no thinning.	**Salad and pickling:** 22–30 cm (9–12 in) between rows. **All others:** 15×30 cm (6×12 in). If growing a large-bulbed variety, increase distance between bulbs to 22 cm (9 in).	**Salad and pickling:** hoe to control weeds and protect September sowings with cloches to give winter crops. **All others:** hoe to control weeds. Keep well watered, and if any plants produce flower heads, pull them up and use the onions straightaway. When plants are fully grown and leaves are beginning to turn yellow, bend the leaves over just above the bulbs.	**Salad and pickling:** pull onions from about March when they are about 15 cm (6 in) high. Leave some to get a little larger for pickling. Pull these when appropriate size and leave in the sun to ripen. **All others:** a week or two after bending over leaves, dig up onions gently to break their roots, but leave them in the ground for another two weeks. Then dig them up completely and leave in the sun to ripen. Store as described on page 187. Onions for winter storage should be lifted by late September.
Pull out and compost the weaker seedlings of those grown in pots as they emerge. Harden off in cold frames for planting out in late May/early June – ie when all danger of frost has gone. Thin outdoor seedlings to achieve final recommended spacings.	90×120 cm (3×4 ft).	Water the plants well and give fortnightly feeds of liquid manure when the fruits start to swell. Pinch out growing tips when three leaves have formed, to encourage growth of side shoots. Hand pollinate as marrows. Put young fruits on a slate or piece of wood to discourage slugs and keep them clean. Stop watering when pumpkins reach their maximum size, but leave on the plant to ripen.	Cut the pumpkins when they have fully ripened. This is usually in early autumn, although small-fruited varieties will be ready in late summer. If there is any danger of frost, cover the plants with a sack at night.
Prick out indoor seedlings into individual pots as they emerge. Harden off outdoors in a cold frame in early May and plant out into cropping site in late May. Thin those sown in the cropping site progressively until you reach the recommended spacing.	50×60 cm (1 ft 8 in×2 ft).	Hoe to control weeds and keep plants well watered, particularly during dry spells. Give plants feeds of liquid fertilizer at 14-day intervals when the flowers have appeared.	Cut fruits when they are 15–20 cm (6–8 in) long. Regular picking encourages more growth. Plants will be killed by the first frost, so harvest all the fruits by then. Freeze any surplus.
Both types: thin seedlings to 7.5 cm (3 in) apart when large enough to handle. Thin to final recommended spacing one month later. (These thinnings may be eaten.)	**Summer:** 30×30 cm (1 ft×1 ft). **Winter:** 15×30 cm (6×12 in).	Hoe to control weeds. **Summer spinach:** water well, particularly in dry weather. Plants will quickly run to seed in hot, dry conditions. **Winter spinach:** protect with cloches or straw from November onwards.	Pick leaves by pinching the base of the leaf stalk as soon as they are large enough. Summer spinach will be ready from May onwards and winter spinach from mid-November onwards. Take only half the leaves from a plant at one time, picking the largest first. Summer spinach can be picked harder than winter.
Prick out the indoor seedlings when large enough to handle. Harden off in early May and plant out in late May/June. Remove the weaker seedlings of the outdoor sowing to achieve recommended spacing.	45×60 cm (1 ft 6 in×2 ft).	Water plants constantly through any dry spells. Pinch out the plants' central growing tips. This encourages the growth of side shoots which bear more leaves.	Pinch off young shoots when they have two or three good-sized leaves. As with summer and winter spinach, do not strip the plant.
Harden off the indoor seedlings when they are 15 cm (6 in) tall. Plant them into the cropping site in late May and protect with cloches for a month or so (see Cultivation). Pull out weaker seedlings of the outdoor sowing as they emerge. Grow sweetcorn in a block rather than in long rows. This gives a better chance of good pollination.	45×60 cm (1 ft 6 in×2 ft).	Remove cloches when plants are well established. Hoe to control weeds, and at the same time, draw the soil up around the base of the stem to firm plants in the ground. Water well, and give weekly feeds of liquid fertilizer. Stake plants if necessary. Remove the side shoots that grow at the base of the stem as they appear. When three cobs have formed on the plant, remove any others that appear.	When the hairy tassels protruding from the top of the cobs turn dark brown, test the grains of the cob for ripeness. A milky liquid should ooze out when you press a grain with a fingernail. Grains should be a pale yellow colour. Snap off the cobs and use immediately or freeze.

Growing Asparagus

THERE IS NEVER a time when asparagus is inexpensive to buy and yet, growing your own, providing you have the space to devote to its long-term requirements, is comparatively cheap. Besides being one of the great gourmet treats, asparagus is also highly nutritious. It does take a while to get established – three years if you start from seed – but the same plants will then go on producing yields for up to twenty years.

Various types of asparagus are available. The French varieties tend to be whiter-stemmed than the English ones.

Soil

The most important requirement is that the soil is well-drained. Ideal conditions are a deep, rich, light sandy loam. As the site is so permanent, it should be well prepared by digging in lots of organic matter the autumn before planting (see below) and all perennial weeds must be removed. It also helps if the site is cleared of any large stones. If the soil is acid, lime it to give a pH of 6.5–7.

Position

An open and sunny site that is well sheltered from any strong winds. A south-facing site is usually the best.

Sowing and planting

If you want to raise your asparagus from seed, sow it in a seed bed, the surface of which should be fine, crumbly tilth, in April. Take out drills about 5 cm (2 in) deep and

GOOD VARIETIES

SEED:
Martha Washington very prolific strain producing shoots in May and June.

CROWNS:
Sutton Perfection two-year-old crowns. Cut stems from the second season after planting

30 cm (1 ft) apart. The seed is slow to germinate, so soak it in water for a day first to soften it.

Water the emerging seedlings well through the summer and thin them to 15 cm (6 in) apart when they are large enough to handle. The following spring, you can plant them out following the directions given below.

Asparagus is more usually grown from one- or two-year-old crowns, purchased from a reputable supplier. Two-year-old crowns may produce asparagus quicker, but one-year-old crowns are an all-round better bet. They are cheaper and less likely to suffer during transplanting. If you cannot plant them immediately you bring them home, cover the roots in damp peat or a damp sack – they must not be allowed to dry out.

To plant them, dig a trench about 20 cm (8 in) deep and 30 cm (1 ft) wide. If you have any coarse sand, you can scatter some at the base; it will help to improve the drainage. Put a little of the soil removed back into the trench to form a mound, the apex of which must be about 7.5 cm (3 in) from the bottom of the trench. Spread the crowns over this (see below for planting distances), so the roots are spread out either side of the ridge. Then cover them with about 7.5 cm (3 in) of soil.

Planting distances

Leave 45 cm (18 in) between plants; 1.2 metres (4 ft) between rows. (You can put the rows closer if space is a problem, without making too much difference.)

Cultivation of asparagus: 1 Plant crowns on top of mounds dug in trenches and carefully cover with soil.

2 For the first year, do not cut the foliage but continue to water the plants well. Control weeds by hoeing.

3 After the first frost, cut down the foliage before any berries begin dropping to the ground.

4 In the following spring apply fertilizer, and a mulch of compost or farmyard manure in the autumn.

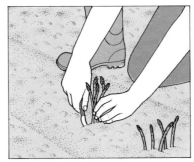

5 If growing two-year-old crowns, cut a few spears the following spring, but do not pick too many.

6 Established plants may need to be supported. When doing this, take care not to damage the crowns.

Harvesting asparagus: the plants are ready for picking when they form spears **(left)**. The best way to cut them is with a special knife **(right)** which allows you to cut just below the surface of the soil.

Cultivation

Fill in the trench gradually as growth progresses, always keeping the crowns just covered. Draw in the soil as you hoe between the rows. As the foliage grows in spring and summer, you may find it better to support it than to let it grow really wild and straggly. In fact, in the first year, this may not be necessary as the growth will be nothing like as prolific as in following years. Do not cut the foliage, as it reduces the crop.

Keep the bed well watered, particularly in dry spells; it must never dry out. For the first year, weeds can be controlled by hoeing; in subsequent years they are best pulled out by hand, because hoeing could damage the plants' delicate roots. Any perennial weeds that creep in are best eliminated with a weedkiller.

After the first frost, in about October, cut down the foliage to about 7.5 cm (3 in) from the soil. It should have turned yellow by now. Try to do this before any berries start dropping to the ground. If some have done so already, pick them up and destroy them; they should not be allowed to germinate, because they will spoil the layout of the site, and will crowd the plants already established.

If you like blanched stalks to your asparagus, pull the soil up around the crops in autumn and spring, making a mound of about 5 cm (2 in). Each spring, apply a general fertilizer to the soil, and each autumn a good mulch of rotted compost or farmyard manure. This will help to smother weeds as well as do good to the soil. Seaweed or sewage sludge make good dressings for the soil if they are available.

Harvesting

If you planted one-year crowns, do not cut any spears the first spring (one year after planting). Two-year-old crowns will give a small harvest the following year, but pick this sparingly – no more than one spear from each crown. When the plants are four years old, you can harvest the spears for four weeks, and in years thereafter, for six weeks. Cut the spears using a curved knife, about 7.5 cm (3 in) below the surface of the soil, when about 12.5 cm (5 in) should be showing above the ground if they are to be tender and succulent. If allowed to get much taller than this, they will be woody and stringy to eat.

Always stop cutting in the middle of June to allow the plants to build up their resources again. Contain the summer foliage if it gets unruly and cut it down each autumn as described above.

PESTS AND DISEASES/ASPARAGUS

Black slugs
These can eat asparagus plants. See pages 49 and 55.

to destroy the eggs. Dust or spray with recommended proprietary mixes.

Asparagus beetle

Violet root rot

Identification: orangey-coloured beetles and their grey grubs which feed voraciously on the foliage, turning it patchy brown and distorted.
Treatment: cut foliage in autumn

Identification: foliage turns yellow and the roots become covered with a purple-coloured fungus. Although the attack is usually on older plants, the disease will quickly spread to other crops.
Treatment: dig up affected plants and burn them.

Greenhouse Vegetables

A GREENHOUSE is by no means an essential item of equipment for those who want to grow their own garden produce and, indeed, the cost of buying the greenhouse (if this is necessary) and heating it (if you choose to do so) should be carefully weighed against the value of the crops you produce. A greenhouse has two main functions: it enables you to produce a variety of crops (lettuces and dwarf beans, for example) outside the usual growing season, or (and probably of more interest to those producing vegetables and fruit primarily for their own consumption) to produce some of the rather more delicate crops that grow less successfully out of doors.

There are three main types of greenhouse:

Span or ridge roof: the most popular and useful greenhouse for vegetable production. The walls can be made completely of glass, or can be solid (eg brick) for the lower 90 cm (3 ft) or so.

Lean-to: a simpler structure which has an advantage in that the wall absorbs heat during the day which it releases into the house during the night, and a disadvantage in that it has light coming from only one side. It must be constructed against a south-facing wall. This

1

2

3

sort of greenhouse is ideal for growing tree fruits such as peaches or nectarines, and also for grapes.

Dutch-light: the sloping sides are constructed of large panes of glass and attract the maximum amount of light.

Even among these three basic shapes there are numbers of different designs, and it is also possible to get circular or hexagonal-shaped greenhouses. These look attractive and are extremely practical in many ways, but they are generally not as good for vegetable and fruit production as the more conventional types.

The basic framework of a greenhouse may be con-

Types of greenhouse: although greenhouses are not essential to the cultivation of fruit and vegetables, they do mean that you are able to grow a wider variety of crops. You can build your own **(1),** using a basic framework of tubular steel over which thick polythene is stretched. Hexagonal greenhouses **(2)** are very attractive but not as practical as more conventional designs. A lean-to **(3)** has the added advantage of releasing heat into the house at night, but must be sited on a south-facing wall. Conventional ridge roofed greenhouses **(4)** are still considered by many to be the best shape of all.

4

Greenhouse staging: this can be made of slatted wood or plastic grilles **(right)** for drainage, or of other materials, such as aluminium **(above)**. In this model, the trays can be inverted to be used as seed boxes for propagation, or they can be turned over to be used as a flat surface.

structed of wood or metal – galvanized iron, steel or aluminium, for example. Wooden ones look attractive, but the wood must be of good quality or it will warp or rot. It must also be treated or painted fairly regularly. The metal greenhouses generally need very little maintenance and are easier to construct, but the material retains less warmth than wood.

Although the panes of a greenhouse are traditionally (and most successfully) glass, it is possible to use plastic or special polythene sheeting instead. This is cheaper than glass, but although it does not break, it scratches easily and heavily and needs renewing at regular intervals.

Siting the greenhouse
In most cases the greenhouse is likely to be sited where there is room for it, but it should obviously be in a sunny position and not heavily overshadowed by a line of overhanging trees. It is generally convenient if it is fairly close to the house and it should have solid paths leading to it if possible, to make it easier to reach with

wheelbarrows etc. Controversy rages as to whether it is better to site it with the roof ridge running east-west or north-south. East-west allows for more evenly distributed light to reach the whole house; north-south gives one warmer and one cooler side.

Heating, ventilating and shading
All the crops mentioned in the following pages can be grown in a cold greenhouse. The only heat they will need is to encourage germination from seed, and this can be supplied by a propagator (see page 41). If you want to grow crops out of season, it will generally be necessary to install some sort of heating, although this does not have to be the sophisticated equipment needed for growing orchids, for example.

Heating may be provided by gas, paraffin or electricity. Natural gas heaters are simple and efficient, but if they are to be run off the mains supply, the greenhouse must be close to the house, or the installation costs will be enormous. Paraffin heaters are perfectly acceptable, providing you burn high-grade fuel. Those with a

1

2

Heating: greenhouses do not have to be heated to be effective, although if they are, you will be able to grow crops out of season. Amongst the many systems available are fan heaters **(3)** which are plugged into an electrical point, and stoves which burn paraffin **(4)**.
Special windows which are controlled by a thermostat **(1)** will ensure the correct amount of ventilation in the greenhouse. Louvred windows **(2)** are operated by hand. All windows in a greenhouse must provide an upward flow of air so that the plants are never in a draught.

3

4

temperature control are the most satisfactory. Electricity is probably the most efficient form of heating and there are various types of heaters – fan, convector, tubular pipes or strips. Electric cables can also be buried in the soil to give it warmth, but they will not greatly affect the temperature of the greenhouse overall.

Ventilation is important, for while the growing plants will not want cold draughts, they will need fresh air. At least two panes in the roof should be hinged so they can be opened to provide ventilation, and ideally there should be one or two along the sides of the house as well. Some greenhouses are equipped with automatic openers which will open or close the panes according to the changes of temperature. During the summer, keep the windows open during the day and then close them at night.

Providing shading on very hot, sunny days is equally important, or young plants, in particular, could literally get burnt. Shading can be provided by some sort of roller blind which may be fitted in or outside the glass and which may be made of plastic, polythene, etc. An

alternative is to paint the glass with special shading paint, which can be washed off with soapy water as required.

Many prefabricated greenhouse kits are available and most are very easy to erect. One willing helper would be an asset. Although the floor of the greenhouse can consist of soil in which you can grow crops, the greenhouse must be erected on a solid foundation. The size of the greenhouse obviously depends on a number of factors, but you would be well advised to get the largest one you can afford, have room for, and will be able to manage.

Cold frames
Cold frames are invaluable for hardening off seedlings that have been raised indoors and would find the shock of going straight outdoors too great. If the frame has a base of good soil, it may be used as a protected seed bed or as a place to bring on an early crop of lettuces or cabbages, for example. Less hardy crops, like cucumbers or melons, can be grown in a cold frame. They come

Cloches: corrugated plastic cloches and tunnels **(above)** are a very easy way of providing ideal conditions for good plant growth. They are simple to make, one of the easiest being of polythene stretched over a shell of chicken wire **(above right)** and staked in the soil. A better system is that of polythene stretched over wire hoops, tied at each end and the whole cloche then being covered with netting as protection from birds **(right)**.

Cold frames: these are an ideal way of getting seedlings started, and there are many different types to choose from. If they are sited next to the greenhouse, they will absorb heat through the glass.

in just about as many different designs and sizes as greenhouses; they can be permanent structures attached to the side of the lower solid wall of a greenhouse (in which case they get heat from it), or they may be portable so you can put them virtually anywhere which is convenient.

The basic design of a cold frame is a square or rectangular box which is generally about 15 cm (6 in) higher at the back, the sides sloping down to the front. The frame itself may be constructed of wood, brick, concrete, breeze blocks or some sort of metal with glass or plastic sides. The top is glass or plastic to allow light to penetrate, and should ideally be hinged at the back so it can be propped open on sunny days.

Site cold frames so the sloping top is facing south, and keep the glass or plastic surface clean. Water plants sparingly so the atmosphere in the frame does not become too moist. You can keep the temperature pretty stable by opening the top to varying degrees according to the weather.

The size of the frame will again depend on how much space you have available and how great the use you have for it. As a rule, though, it should be at least 1.2 × 0.9 metres (4 ft × 3 ft).

Cloches

Cloches are the simplest of all devices used in the garden to speed plant growth by creating warmer, more humid conditions. They have evolved from a sort of glass dome that was placed over one or more plants, and are now most commonly used as tunnel structures that may be put over a row of germinating seeds, young seedlings or even mature plants such as strawberries, to bring them on quicker. Alternatively, they can merely be placed over the soil to warm it prior to sowing. The tunnels may be made of glass, moulded or corrugated plastic, or polythene sheeting. The latter are probably the cheapest and are easily constructed at home. Glass cloches

are still deemed by many to be the best; they let in the maximum amount of light and do not cause condensation (as polythene does), but they are expensive, very likely to break and often in short supply at garden centres. Remember, whatever type of cloche you elect to use, it must be closed at the ends if it is to be fully effective.

Growing crops

There is no mystique surrounding growing crops in a greenhouse and providing you keep them healthy, they should need little attention and give you very little trouble. The procedure for growing them will be similar whether you are growing in pots, peat-filled bags or in the border soil. All the crops outlined below can be raised from seed.

Aubergines (eggplants)

Sow the seeds in February and put them in a propagator to germinate, or sow in late March and raise in the greenhouse without a propagator, but put them on the side of the greenhouse which gets the most sun. When the seedlings are large enough to handle, prick them out into small pots filled with soil-less potting compost. When they are about 15 cm (6 in) high, put them into their permanent site – large pots, peat-filled bags or straight into the border soil, spacing them about 45 cm (18 in) apart.

When the plants are about 22 cm (9 in) high, pinch out the growing tips to encourage side, rather than top, growth. As the fruits begin to form, pinch out the tips of the branches so that there are no more than two or three fruits on each branch. Remove any side shoots, too. As the fruits begin to swell and become heavy, you may find it is necessary to support the plant with stakes to stop it drooping.

Water the plants well – they tend to dry out easily. The fruits will be better if you feed the plants each week

Greenhouse crops:
although peppers can be
grown outdoors, they will do
much better if they are grown
in a greenhouse **(right)**.
Unlike many vegetables, they
are eaten unripe, when they
are green. If left to ripen, they
will turn either red or yellow,
according to the variety
grown **(below)**. Watering is a
very important part of
growing crops, particularly
tomatoes, in a greenhouse
(bottom). The plants must
be watered, not only to
prevent them drying out and
the vegetables splitting, but
to discourage pests which
thrive in hot, dry conditions.

with a liquid fertilizer. Syringe the leaves with water in
warm weather as this discourages red spider mite – the
most frequent curse of the greenhouse.

Pick the fruits when they are swollen and a shiny, deep
purple colour (some varieties are mottled or have
creamy-white stripes, too). Cut them free of the plant
with scissors or a sharp knife, handling them carefully to
avoid bruising.

Cucumbers

If cucumbers develop from the male flowers on the
plant, they tend to be bitter, so the best idea is to plant
the special varieties which produce only female flowers.
These are self-pollinating. If you do not grow these,
remove the male flowers as they appear.

Raise seed in late February in a propagator and pot on
in the same way as the aubergine seedlings. Plant them
in their permanent site when the seedlings have begun to
develop their rough leaves, spacing them about 60 cm
(2 ft) apart. As the plants grow, you will need to support
them and this can be done in one of two ways. When the
plant is about 22 cm (9 in) high, tie a string very loosely
round its base and take this up to the top of the wall of
the greenhouse, attaching it to another string running up
the roof. As the plant grows, pinch out the side shoots
and train the main stem up the string by twisting it

gently. In order to be able to do this, the string should not be too tight, and the plant will need very careful handling to ensure you do not break the stem. When it reaches the top of the wall of the greenhouse, you can continue taking it up the string that runs parallel with the sloping roof.

The other method is to put a stake into the ground alongside the plant and let it grow level with the top of this, tying the main stem loosely to the stake to support it. Fix horizontal wires or strings at intervals up the stakes, then pinch out the growing tip of the cucumber when it reaches the top of the stake. As the laterals grow, train them along the strings, twisting them carefully around them.

Keep plants well watered, and spray them if it is very hot in the greenhouse. Again, you will get better cucumbers if you feed the plant with liquid fertilizer when the fruits are beginning to swell, but it is only necessary to do this once a fortnight.

Cucumbers will be ready for harvesting from about the end of July, and it is best to pick them as soon as they are ready. This is when they have nice straight sides, not

Greenhouse cucumbers: most varieties of cucumber produce both male and female flowers. Tiny cucumbers form behind the flowers of the female, while the male flowers just have a simple stem. It is important to recognize any male flowers and to pinch them out. If they fertilize the female flowers, the resulting crops will taste very bitter.

when they have reached their maximum size. Picking cucumbers at this stage will also encourage the development of more fruits.

Peppers and chillies

The round sweet peppers and the thinner, longer and very much hotter chilli peppers can be grown successfully in a greenhouse and are treated in the same way as these other greenhouse crops. Sow the seeds in March and raise the seedlings in a propagator. Thereafter treat the young seedlings exactly the same as those of aubergines and cucumbers, planting them in their permanent site when they are about 10 cm (4 in) high. If growing in border soil, put them about 45 cm (18 in) apart and push a heavy stake into the soil alongside each plant. The fruits are very heavy and the plant needs considerable support to stop it drooping as the fruits develop.

These plants need very little attention; just water them regularly and feed them with liquid fertilizer every week or so when the fruits begin to appear. Support them by tying them loosely to the cane as this becomes necessary.

You can pick the peppers when they are green (in late July/early August) or you can leave them on the plant to ripen still further, in which event they will either turn red or yellow, depending on the variety. Cut the fruit off the plant using scissors or a sharp knife in the same way as aubergines.

Tomatoes

Tomato seedlings are raised from seed in exactly the same way as the other crops so far discussed and the seed should be sown in mid- to late March. They, too, can be set in their permanent site when they are about 10 cm (4 in) high; there should be about 45 cm (18 in) between the plants and 60 cm (2 ft) between the rows. Stagger the plants in the rows so they are not directly in line with one another.

The easiest and most efficient way of supporting tomatoes growing in a greenhouse is to tie strings loosely round their bases and take these up to a horizontal string hung across the greenhouse, level with the top of the walls. As the plants grow, gently twist the main stems around the strings, taking great care not to snap the plants. Nip out the side shoots that emerge from the leaf axils and pinch out the growing tips when the plants near the top of the horizontal strings.

Mulch the tomato plants and thereafter water them once a week. Even, regular watering is important with tomato plants; if you allow them to dry out and then give them a healthy drink to compensate, you are likely to get split fruit. Feed with liquid fertilizer every ten days or so when the tomatoes have begun to develop.

As the plant grows, the leaves at the base will begin to turn yellow and die back, at which point it is best to pick them off. This facilitates picking the fruit and watering the plants. However, do not make the mistake some people do of virtually stripping the plant of all its leaves. If you do this, the plant is left with no means of manufacturing foodstuffs for the growing tomatoes.

You can pick the tomatoes as they ripen, or you can take them green from the plant and ripen them on windowsills, etc. Harvest the tomatoes by supporting

HINTS ON GROWING GREENHOUSE CROPS

1 Sow the seeds thinly in seed boxes, pricking out later into individual pots.

2 Most greenhouse crops will need to be trained up some form of support to prevent the plants getting straggly.

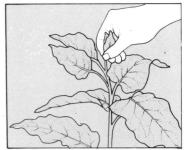

3 The growing tips of many greenhouse crops, tomatoes in particular, should be pinched out.

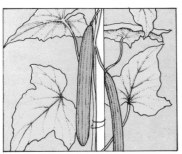

4 As soon as any of the crops in the greenhouse are ready, harvest them to make room for the remaining crops.

5 Continue to spray the plants with water to increase humidity and discourage pests. Give liquid feeds.

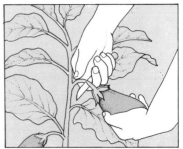

6 Do not leave crops until they have reached their maximum size before picking. Always cut them with a knife.

Growing systems:
peat-filled growing bags
(left) are very useful for
growing crops, particularly in
greenhouses. Raise the
plants in the usual way and
then transfer them to the
bags when they are large
enough to be moved.
Different types of these bags
are available. Besides
growing tomatoes in border
soil or peat-filled bags, they
can also be grown in a ring
culture **(above)**. This means
growing them in bottomless
pots or rings which are filled
with potting compost and
placed on a bed of gravel or
crushed stones. The roots
grow down into the gravel.
Water the plants well and
give liquid feeds when the
fruits form.

them in your hand and nipping off the stem just above
the calyx.

Greenhouse management
Crops may be grown in the greenhouse in the border
soil, in large pots or in fertilized peat-filled bags.
Tomatoes may be grown in a special system known as
ring culture, in which the plants are actually grown in
bottomless pots filled with growing compost and set on a
bed of gravel or sterile aggregate.

Probably the easiest method is to use the border soil
for growing, but if you mainly use the greenhouse for
growing tomatoes, you must either change the soil each
year or sterilize it before planting again. If you grow
tomatoes in the same soil in the greenhouse for two years
running, they are very prone to various diseases. You
can follow tomatoes with a different crop, such as
peppers or cucumbers, which will not be diseased in the
same way, but be prepared for little tomato seedlings to

crop up in the soil. The soil should be changed after
these crops have been harvested, and tomatoes can be
grown in the site the following year.

Change the soil in about February, merely swopping
that in the greenhouse for some in the garden. If you mix
in lots of farmyard manure at the same time, you are
likely to have even better tomatoes. You can put the old
soil back into the greenhouse the following year, after it
has been thoroughly exposed to the elements and has
had a chance to be washed through by the rain. If you
would rather sterilize the soil, sprinkle it with a solution
of formalin and covering with sheets of plastic, so the
fumes do not escape.

The warm, humid conditions you mean to encourage
in a greenhouse are ideal for the growth of bacteria and
disease as well as plants. To avoid disease therefore,
keep the inside of the greenhouse clean and tidy; if weeds
do appear in the border soil, pull them out straightaway
and check over all the crops each day.

Growing Herbs

ALTHOUGH GROWING HERBS may not always represent the same saving in cost as vegetables, they are so important in adding interest and flavour to great numbers of dishes that it is well worthwhile producing a selection. They are easy to grow, for although they mostly flourish best in rich, well-drained soils and sunny, sheltered positions, they will generally grow in almost any type of soil or garden site. In addition, of course, individual herbs take up only a small amount of space and they can be grown in any convenient spot.

Herbs are ideally sited close to the kitchen, so they are quickly to hand when wanted. If this is not possible, they can be grown at one end of the vegetable garden, or scattered individually around the flower beds. Many are quite decorative enough to grow in a border or bed and, besides adding colour, will also help pollination among the flowers, as they are particularly attractive to bees.

A formally planned and well laid out herb garden was once a common feature of many gardens. Lack of space has made them less common, but if there is room, they can be made extremely attractive. Traditionally they followed geometric shapes – triangles, circles, squares and so on. If you are planning a herb garden, bear in mind that the taller herbs should be placed at the back so they do not put others in perpetual shade. (Herbs that like partial shade can be planted close to them with good effect, however.)

In cases where the space in the garden is at a very great

CULTIVATION OF HERBS

Herb	Soil/Position	Sowing	Thinning/ Transplanting	Spacing
Balm (evergreen perennial)	**Soil:** any. **Position:** sunny, but will tolerate partial shade.	Indoors in pots or direct into cropping site April/May, in 1 cm ($\frac{1}{2}$ in) drills.	Plant out those grown in pots in early autumn. Thin those in cropping site to recommended spacing when large enough to handle.	45 cm (1 ft 6 in).
Basil (annual) Two varieties – bush and sweet. The taste is the same.	**Soil:** any that is well-drained. **Position:** sunny and sheltered. Bush basil may be grown in pots indoors to provide fresh leaves during the winter.	Indoors in pots or direct into the cropping site in May, in 0.5 cm ($\frac{1}{4}$ in) drills.	If those in pots are to be transplanted outdoors, harden them off in May and plant them out in early June. Thin those in cropping site to recommended spacing when large enough to handle.	30 cm (1 ft).
Bay (evergreen perennial)	**Soil:** any. **Position:** sunny and sheltered. Grows very successfully in a large tub or pot.	Buy a young plant or take 15 cm (6 in) cuttings about two months after the new spring shoots appear. Plant these in potting compost in a pot. Put a young plant straight into the growing site.		One tree is sufficient.
Borage (annual)	**Soil:** any that is well drained. **Position:** sunny.	Directly into cropping site in April and again in August (September in warm areas). Sow in 1 cm ($\frac{1}{2}$ in) drills.	Thin to recommended spacing when seedlings are large enough to handle.	30 cm (1 ft).
Chervil (biennial)	**Soil:** any that is moist and water-retentive. **Position:** sheltered, in partial sun.	Directly into growing site at regular intervals from March to August. Sow in 0.5 cm ($\frac{1}{4}$ in) drills.	Thin to recommended spacing as seedlings emerge.	30 cm (1 ft).
Chives (perennial)	**Soil:** any that is moist. **Position:** sunny or partial shade.	If raising from seed sow directly into cropping site in 0.5 cm ($\frac{1}{4}$ in) drills in March. Or buy young plants or obtain them by division and plant in growing site in spring.	Thin seedlings to recommended spacing as they emerge.	30 cm (1 ft).
Coriander (annual)	**Soil:** rich and well-drained. **Position:** sunny (grows particularly well near dill and chervil).	Directly into cropping site in April and August, in 0.5 cm ($\frac{1}{4}$ in) drills.	Thin when seedlings are large enough to handle.	30 cm (1 ft).

Cultivation	Harvesting
Water well in dry spells. The year after planting, cut back plants in early summer. In autumn, cut stems down to just above ground level.	Pick very sparingly the first summer. Thereafter, pick as required throughout late spring and summer. Pick leaves for drying in early summer
Water well in dry spells. Pinch out growing centres to encourage bushy, leafy growth and pinch out flowers as they form.	Pick leaves as required through the summer. The first frost will kill outdoor plants.
Bay may be left to grow naturally or pruned to a variety of shapes by cutting back new growth each summer. Trees grown in containers are best put in a light, airy shed in the winter. Very cold weather could kill young trees.	Pick leaves as required. For drying, cut branches on summer mornings.
They need no special attention except to keep weed growth around them in check. Borage grows very quickly and reseeds itself readily.	Pick as required. For drying, pick undamaged leaves in the morning after the dew has gone.
Water well in dry spells and pick off flowering stems as they appear.	Pick as required. For drying, pick sprays from mature plants on a sunny morning.
Water well in dry spells and pick off flower heads to help prevent early dying back of the plant. Plants may be dug up and divided in spring or autumn.	Pick as required, cutting leaves at the base. Picking encourages heavier growth.
Hoe to control weeds and water in dry spells.	Grown for its seeds, which are gathered by picking ripe flower heads when the smell becomes spicy and seeds have turned from green to beige. Dry heads in boxes, trays or racks, then shake out seeds.

Growing herbs: herbs are ideally grown in a separate garden, but if you are short of space they can easily be grown in a flower bed, where they blend in well with the other plants. Alternatively, they can be planted in pots and either used as a decorative feature or placed within easy reach of the kitchen.

Continued from page 99

Herb	Soil/Position	Sowing	Thinning/ Transplanting	Spacing
Dill (annual)	**Soil:** well-drained. **Position:** open and sunny.	Directly into growing site in March and April in 0.5 cm ($\frac{1}{4}$ in) drills.	Thin seedlings to recommended spacing when large enough to handle. Leaves from thinnings may be used.	25 cm (10 in).
Fennel (perennial)	**Soil:** rich and well-drained. Will grow on well-cultivated chalky soils. **Position:** warm and sunny. Does not flourish well if grown near coriander.	If raising from seed, sow at regular intervals from March to May in 1 cm ($\frac{1}{2}$ in) drills. New plants may also be obtained by division.	Thin seedlings to recommended spacing when large enough to handle.	30 cm (1 ft).
Horseradish (treat as an annual)	**Soil:** deeply dug light loam which is well-drained. **Position:** sunny or partial shade.	Plant roots or root cuttings which are about 12.5 cm (5 in) long in March so they are 5 cm (2 in) below the ground. (These can be dug up from wild plants.) Plant no more than three or four, because they spread.		45 cm (1 ft 6 in)
Lovage (perennial)	**Soil:** rich, moist and well-drained. **Position:** sunny or partial shade.	If raising from seed, sow into growing site or a seed bed in March or late August. Alternatively, obtain new plants by division (see diagram) in March and plant straightaway.	When seedlings are large enough to handle, either thin them or transplant them to their permanent growing site.	30 cm (1 ft).
Marjoram (treat as an annual)	**Soil:** light and well-drained. **Position:** sunny but sheltered.	Directly into cropping site in April and/or early September or raise from cuttings taken in spring (see diagram).	Thin seedlings to recommended spacing when large enough to handle.	25 cm (10 in).
Mint (perennial) There are many different kinds, but cultivation is the same for all. Applemint and spearmint are most widely grown.	**Soil:** almost any, but likes rich, moist soil best. **Position:** full sun tends to give enriched flavour.	Buy young plants or obtain young roots from a friend and plant into growing site in March. It is advisable to plant mint in an old bucket or similar container and sink this into the ground in order to contain the otherwise very pervasive roots. Mint is very hard to grow from seed.		15 cm (6 in).
Oregano (see Marjoram)				
Parsley (treat as an annual)	**Soil:** rich and well-drained, but moist. **Position:** sunny.	Sow directly into growing site at regular intervals through spring and early summer. Sow in 0.5 cm ($\frac{1}{4}$ in) drills and pour boiling water along the drills to aid germination (which is very slow). Alternatively, sow in pots for indoor cultivation.	Thin seedlings twice to achieve recommended spacings.	20 cm (8 in).
Rosemary (evergreen perennial)	**Soil:** light, sandy or chalky. Must be well drained. **Position:** sunny but sheltered. Grows well near sage.	Sow directly into growing site or seed bed in April, or raise from heel cuttings taken in early summer.	Gradually discard weaker seedlings and plants until one strong, healthy plant is left.	
Sage (biennial)	**Soil:** well-drained. **Position:** sunny, but sheltered.	Sow in seed bed at regular intervals from April to June in 0.5 cm ($\frac{1}{4}$ in) drills. Alternatively, raise from heel cuttings taken in summer (see diagram).	Thin seedlings as they emerge and finally plant into growing site in the autumn.	A maximum of two plants is all that is needed. Space them 30 cm (1 ft) apart.
Savoury (summer savoury is an annual; winter savoury is perennial)	**Soil:** fertile, well-drained soil. Winter savoury survives in poorer soils. **Position:** sunny.	**Summer:** sow directly into growing site at regular intervals from April to July, in 0.5 cm ($\frac{1}{4}$ in) drills. **Winter:** sow seed as above in spring or autumn or raise from cuttings taken in spring (see diagrams).	Thin seedlings as they emerge to achieve recommended spacing.	22 cm (9 in).
Tarragon (perennial)	**Soil:** well-drained. **Position:** sunny and warm.	Buy a young plant and plant in March or October, or raise from cuttings taken in spring or autumn (see diagrams) or from root division.		Only one plant is needed.
Thyme (perennial) The different types are all cultivated in the same way.	**Soil:** light, sandy, but well-drained. **Position:** sunny.	Sow directly in growing site from April to July in 0.5 cm ($\frac{1}{4}$ in) drills or sow indoors in trays. Alternatively, raise new plants from heel cuttings taken in May/June or by root division.	Thin seedlings to recommended spacing. For those grown in trays indoors, prick out to individual pots and plant out in the autumn when plants are well established.	22–30 cm (9–12 in)

Cultivation	Harvest
Hoe to control weeds and water in dry spells. Plants grow quite tall – stake them if blown about in windy weather.	Pick leaves as required before flowers appear, cutting shoots to the base to encourage more growth. Leave some plants to flower and produce seeds, which may be harvested in the same way as coriander.
Needs no special attention.	See Dill.
They need no special attention except for watering in dry spells. Dig up all plants each year and replant new ones.	Dig up roots from August until November. Then dig up all the plants and store roots as described on page 186.
Pick off flower heads as they appear.	Pick leaves as required during the summer and autumn. For drying, make sure leaves are unblemished.
Need no special attention.	Pick leaves as required before flowers form through summer and autumn. Leave the young central leaves.
Water well after planting. Dig up some roots in autumn and plant in pots to grow indoors to give winter supplies. Cut plants down to ground in October or November.	Pick as required through spring and summer. Young leaves have the most flavour. For drying, cut stalks as the first flower heads appear.
Water well in dry spells and protect plants with cloches in winter if trying to keep them until following spring. Giving liquid feeds of fertilizer helps to increase the production of leaves.	Cut out all flowering stems to encourage continuous leaf growth. Pick leaves sparingly until plants are well established, then pick them hard, leaving only the green centre. For drying, cut from mid-summer onwards.
No special attention.	Pick fresh as required all the year round (do not pick too heavily during winter). For drying, pick as plants come into flower.
Pinch out flower heads and growing tips to encourage more leaf growth and to make plants bushy. Cut back hard after flowering.	See Rosemary. The flavour tends to be at its best in mid-summer.
No special attention.	**Summer:** pick fresh leaves as required through summer and autumn. If drying, pick leaves in late summer and make sure all leaves are harvested by late autumn. **Winter:** pick leaves as required.
Water well in dry weather. Plant dies down in winter protect it in cold areas by covering with straw.	Pick fresh leaves as required through summer and autumn. For drying, pick leafy sprays from fully grown plants in the morning.
Water growing plants well and cut back after flowering. Pinch out growing shoots to encourage more leaf production and bushy growth.	As for Rosemary. Do not cut too heavily in the autumn or the plant may have difficulty in surviving the winter.

premium, herbs can be grown successfully in tubs, pots or other containers, placed anywhere that there is room, from patios and terraces to kitchen windowsills or the side of a flight of outdoor steps. Some herbs will even grow between paving stones in a path or terrace, but be careful not to tread on them.

The choice of herbs to grow is likely to depend on individual taste, although those most widely used in cooking are probably chives, parsley, thyme, rosemary, marjoram and sage. Try some of the more unusual ones as well though – by and large they are no more difficult to grow and will be of inestimable value in adding interest to the daily cuisine.

Herbs can be preserved for out-of-season use (see page 195). Many of them are perennial, although in some instances it is best to treat them as annuals and start them again each year. Few will withstand very heavy winter picking.

As a rule, herbs do not suffer too much from pests and diseases, and these will be kept to a minimum if normal garden hygiene is observed. In cases when they are affected, it is probably best to dig them up and burn them, planting fresh seeds or plants.

Cultivation

Cultural instructions for growing a variety of herbs are given left. The spacings refer to those between plants; in most domestic situations, it is not necessary to plant more than one row of any particular herb; indeed, one plant of each herb will provide sufficient leaves or seeds for most families. (Parsley is the most notable exception; as it is so widely used in the kitchen, most households will find they need several plants to fulfill their regular needs.) Sow herb seeds very sparingly, and then thin the seedlings progressively, discarding the weakest ones until you are left with the number you need. If sowing indoors, sow two or three seeds to a pot, and again discard the weaker seedlings as they emerge.

Many new herb plants can be raised by taking cuttings from existing plants or by digging up part of the plant or bush and dividing the roots. The procedure for both of these is explained in the diagrams.

Taking cuttings: you can increase your herb garden by taking cuttings from plants. Heel cuttings (1) can be obtained by removing side shoots from the main stem, and dipping the cut end in rooting powder (2), before planting in pots. An alternative is to divide a clump of roots into two (3), but be careful not to damage them.

Growing Fruit

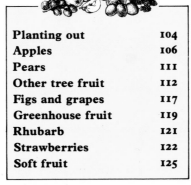

BY AND LARGE, fruit falls into two categories – tree or top fruit, and soft fruit. Tree fruit includes apples, pears, peaches, nectarines, plums, damsons, gages, apricots, cherries and figs. Soft fruit includes raspberries, loganberries, black-berries, blueberries, red, white and black currants, gooseberries and strawberries. Grapes, melons and rhubarb do not fit into either category – grapes grow on perennial vines, melons are annual plants and rhubarb grows from tubers. The last, once established, will last for many years with very little attention.

Almost all gardens will have room to grow fruit to some extent, and developments in recent years have made it possible to grow even top fruit in very small and confined areas. At one stage, just about all top fruits were grown only on standard or half-standard trees, these reaching heights and spreads of 6 metres (20 ft) and more which, apart from anything else, made picking difficult and possibly dangerous. Even if a garden is big enough to take a couple of these trees, it constitutes a great waste of space which would be far more pro-ductively used growing other fruit and vegetables or supporting livestock. Nowadays, most top fruit grown for domestic purposes is produced by grafting the different varieties onto special roots, which not only restricts the tree's growth in order to keep it manage-able, but also gives quicker fruit production. Where once it took ten years or so for trees to produce fruit, they

will now start to do so in their third year.

Make sure when purchasing top fruit, that the trees you buy are growing on dwarfing rootstocks, which are numbered according to their size. All apple varieties, for example, which are wanted for a confined area should be grafted onto M9, M26 or M106 rootstocks. Of these, M106 still produces trees that are quite large, growing to a maximum height of 4.5 metres (15 ft), so if you want to keep them smaller still, go for one of the other rootstocks.

Soft fruit has no such problems. The different types grow either on bushes (blueberries, red, white and blackcurrants and gooseberries), or canes (raspberries, loganberries and blackberries). Although these need pruning and training if they are to be fully productive, the procedures are considerably less complicated than for tree fruit.

Strawberries, incidentally, grow on neither bushes nor canes, but on low, spreading plants.

There are endless varieties of all types of tree and soft fruit. The best way to make a choice of what to grow is to consult a local nursery to see what grows best in your locality. You will find most nurseries stock a limited number of varieties, having established over the years which types are the most successful. Unless you have a real preference for some other specific variety, it is wisest to restrict your choice to the ones already stocked.

Planting Out

FRUIT TREES, bushes and canes should ideally be planted during the winter months when they are dormant, but not when the ground is frozen or waterlogged. The ideal time for planting is in early winter – late October/early November – but planting can be done any time through to the following spring. It is best to buy two- or three-year old top fruit trees and soft bushes, and one-year-old fruit canes.

If there is to be a few days' delay between buying the fruit and planting it, leave the roots encased in their protective wrapping and keep them in a cool shed. The day before planting, inspect the roots and if they are dry, soak them in water until planting.

Planting canes: fork well-rotted organic matter into the bottom of a trench. Plant canes, spreading out the roots. Pack with soil to firm into the ground. Replace remaining soil, firm it and cut back canes. Apply a mulch of peat, compost, straw or leaf mould around their bases. Drive stakes into both ends of the trench and stretch three evenly spaced strands of wire between them.

Planting a bush: dig a hole wide enough to take the roots of the bush and fork well-rotted organic matter into the bottom. Place the bush in the hole, spread out the roots, and cut off any which are growing upwards. Fill in around the roots with soil and peat and firm it down. When planted, the base of the bush should be just covered with soil. Apply a mulch of peat, compost, straw or leaf mould around the base.

PROTECTING PLANTS

Since the best time for planting trees, bushes, and canes is in the winter, the plants may need to be protected against the harsh weather, or birds in search of food. Wind breaks may help **(1)**, or the plant may need to be isolated in a polythene cage against frost or wind **(2)**. Soft fruit in particular will need to be protected from birds by being grown in cages. **(3)**.

Heeling in: do not plant a tree until the weather conditions are right. If they are not, you must heel the tree into the soil in a sheltered part of the garden by planting it in the soil at an angle, or leaving it in a garden shed. Keep the roots in damp straw until planting the tree in its proper site.

Planting a tree: 1 If the roots of the tree are dry, soak them in water the day before planting.

2 Place a layer of compost in a deep hole, and drive in a stake. Place the tree in the hole and spread out roots.

3 Mix soil with peat and fill soil around roots. Shake the tree to settle soil and eliminate air pockets.

4 Firm soil gently with feet and replace rest of soil, firming again. Apply fertilizer if necessary.

5 Water around the roots well and give the soil a mulch of peat, straw, compost or leaf mould.

6 Secure top of the main stem to the stake with a tree tie or plastic strap, which can be adjusted later.

Growing Apples

THESE ARE ONE of the most widely grown fruits of all and just about every garden, however small, will have room to support a few trees. Early-maturing varieties will be ready for picking in August and the late varieties in October, but they will keep well for eating through the winter until April and May. Therefore, it is possible to eat homegrown apples practically the whole year round.

Apples are not self-pollinating, so it is essential to grow at least two trees which blossom at the same time, unless, of course, you have a near neighbour who has a number of apple trees. An alternative, if you really feel you only have room for one tree, is to grow a family tree, which has two or more cross-pollinating varieties grafted onto a single rootstock.

Choose varieties according to your taste, their cross-pollination compatibility and what is known to grow well in your locality. Avoid growing Cox's Orange Pippins where the soil is poor or if you live in a cold area. The apple was developed in the South of England and is not able to withstand harsh weather conditions. Late-flowering varieties are best for gardens which are cold.

Soil and position
Apples like deep, fertile loam, but will grow in most well-cultivated soils providing they are not waterlogged or too acid. Choose an open sunny position that is well sheltered from prevailing cold winds and avoid planting in pockets or hollows where frost collects and lingers.

Planting and routine cultivation
Make sure the ground is completely free of weeds (particularly perennial ones) before planting (see previous page) and keep the area round a newly-planted tree weed-free, particularly through the first spring and summer. Remove weeds either with gentle hoeing or by hand, taking care not to damage the young roots. Also water very heavily in the first growing season, and thereafter water all trees in dry spells. Mulch the ground around the tree in spring until it is well established.

When you buy the apple trees, ask the nursery how far apart to plant them. This differs so much with the variety, the form in which the tree is to be grown, the type of soil and the rootstock on which it is grafted, that it is not practical to give any specific measurements here.

How many?
Four different forms of apple tree are recommended for the average garden (see pages 110–111). These will bear the following approximate yields when at their full bearing capacity. Remember, though, that the yield will depend on a number of factors, such as the weather, growing conditions, how they are pruned, and so on.
Cordon: up to 4.5 kg (10 lb), but with an average of 1.8 kg (4 lb).
Open centre bush tree with four main branches: up to 27 kg (60 lb), with an average yield of 13.5 kg (30 lb).
Espalier: the yield depends on the size of the tree, but expect it to yield about half the amount of a bush tree grown on the same rootstock.
Spindlebush: up to 13.5 kg (30 lb).

Apple varieties: there are myriad varieties of apples, which are divided into two basic types – cookers and dessert apples. Before buying trees, decide which type you want to grow, and then be guided according to the conditions in your garden and your own particular tastes.

Training and pruning

The eventual shape of any top fruit tree is established by the pruning and training done in the first four years of its life. A one-year-old tree, known as a maiden, comprises nothing more than a single stem, and it is from this that all the different shapes can be produced. By and large, it is most advisable to buy two- or three-year-old trees, the training of which will have been begun by the nursery. Trees which are much older than this are harder to get established.

The aim in pruning all apple trees is to maintain the shape you have established, to allow a good penetration of light to reach all parts of the tree and to maintain a constant good balance between growth and fruit. Enough new wood must be allowed to develop to turn into next year's fruiting growth and old wood should be cut out after its second or third season. Bear in mind that most people do not prune established trees hard enough – open centre bush trees and spindlebush trees in particular should be reduced by a third each winter. Winter pruning is invigorating – the harder you prune, the harder the tree will grow. Summer pruning is restricting as you are cutting out new growth as it forms.

Spur or tip bearing?

Apple trees are either spur or tip bearing – that is, the apples are borne on the spur wood that grows from the leaders and laterals, or on the end of the previous season's shoots.

When pruning spur-bearing varieties, the leaders should be cut back by half each year and all the laterals

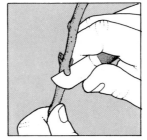

Pruning: 1 Always cut back to either a new growth bud or flush with the branch.

2 Always make a positive cut with sharp secateurs. Do not tear the wood.

3 Seal any cuts you make with wound-protecting paint to prevent disease entering.

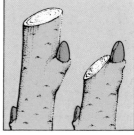

Mistakes: never cut between buds or cut so close that they might be damaged.

TERMS USED IN PRUNING

Leader

Lateral

Spur

Spur

Fruit buds

Growth buds

Growth and fruit bud

Leader: The leading shoot of a branch, main stem, or stem of the tree.
Lateral: Any growth which comes off leaders.

Spurs: Compressed shoots or fruit buds which grow on leaders or laterals.
Fruit buds: Round fat buds on two-year old wood or on

spurs on older wood.
Growth buds: Flatter buds produced on one-year old wood.

Harvesting and storing:
some varieties of apple can
be kept for many months,
providing they are stored
correctly. The storage of
apples is discussed more
fully later in the book, but the
most important rule is to only
use perfect fruit and to store
it in such a way that no apple
touches another.

cut back to three or four growth buds to induce the spurs
to grow. An alternative method to this is to operate a
three-year cycle, which works on the principle that the
second and third year wood produces the best fruit. For
this you need a framework of up to six strong branches
growing off a central trunk. The laterals which will bear
fruit in their second and third years grow from these
permanent branches. After their third year, cut out the
entire lateral, so that a new one will grow in its place.

In tip-bearing varieties, it is obviously important not
to cut off the shoots bearing the terminal buds which will
form the following year's fruit. The difficulty, therefore,
is how to keep the tree bushy and compact. This is best
done by sawing out big, old branches when they have
ceased to be productive. This will shape up the tree and
allow new branches to grow in their place. Do not snip at
the tree – make big cuts which will count!

Harvesting
If large clusters of apples are produced, these should be
thinned to ensure a good crop of reasonably-sized
apples. Do this in June/July, cutting out (with scissors)
any damaged or misshapen apples to leave one, or at the
most two, to a cluster. Ideally, the apples should be
about 15 cm (6 in) apart.

Test for ripeness by supporting the apple in your
hand and gently lifting it. If it is ripe it will come away
easily from the tree. Handle apples very gently, particularly if you want to store them (see page 196).

Pest control
Old-fashioned protection practices and remedies, such
as tying grease bands round the trunk of the tree in
summer and early autumn, can help to trap and therefore deter pests such as the codling moth, which climbs
up the trunk of the tree to lay its eggs. Some people still
recommend regular spraying with various chemical
preparations through the spring and summer, but in
most domestic situations (particularly if strict garden
hygiene is observed) this should not really be necessary.
If your trees are showing signs of disease, consult a local
grower on what action to take and remember that over-

spraying can do the tree as much harm as good.

If birds attack the crop the only remedy is to cover the
tree with netting.

Pests and diseases
There is a frighteningly long list of pests and diseases
that can affect apple trees, but the main ones to fear are
apple mildew, apple scab and canker.

PESTS AND DISEASES/APPLES

Apple mildew

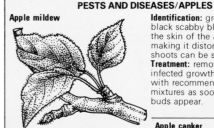

Identification: green, brown or
black scabby blisters form on
the skin of the apple, often
making it distorted. Leaves and
shoots can be similarly affected.
Treatment: remove and burn all
infected growth. Spray the tree
with recommended proprietary
mixtures as soon as the flower
buds appear.

Identification: new spring shoots
and leaves are covered with a
powdery, grey-white covering.
Treatment: spray with
recommended proprietary
mixtures to help keep the
disease at bay, but cut out and
burn badly affected growth.
Remove all diseased shoots the
following autumn. Make sure
the tree is well watered in dry
weather.

Apple canker

Apple scab

Identification: small hollows of
dead-looking wood appear on
the twigs and shoots. If left,
they get larger until the whole
branch dies.
Treatment: cut out diseased
wood and burn it. Seal the cuts
with canker paint. Proprietary
sprays are available for severe
cases. Trees grown on
waterlogged soil seem to be
more susceptible to attack.

Growing Pears

THE CULTIVATION OF pears is very similar to that of apples, although they are generally considered to be not quite as easy to grow. Varieties for garden cultivation are grafted onto dwarfing rootstocks of quinces, which produce larger trees than the smaller rootstocks of apples. They are not generally self-pollinating, although family trees of two or more varieties grafted onto the same rootstock are available. More satisfactory results are likely to be achieved, however, by growing two or more trees of different varieties. Varieties can be divided into those that mature early, mid-season or late.

Soil, position and cultivation

Pears like a deeply cultivated loam which is moisture-retentive, particularly in the summer. By and large, they need a more sheltered spot than apples, and it should be generally warm and sunny. As they come into blossom early, be sure not to plant them in a hollow or pocket where frost collects. Pear trees do not grow well with grass round their roots, and the soil around them should be kept well cultivated and perpetually free of weeds.

November is the ideal month to plant. If you are planting more than one tree, leave approximately 4 metres (13 ft) between them. Mulch the area round the roots in spring and make sure the trees are kept well watered in dry weather. They like more nitrogen than apples, and this should be supplied in a spring feed.

Pear trees of a similar size to apples generally yield rather less fruit. Yields will vary tremendously, however, according to variety.

Training and pruning

The four tree forms recommended for apples are also those most suitable for pears, and they are trained and pruned in the same way (see page 110–111).

Once established, pears can take harder pruning than apples without producing extremely vigorous growth.

Harvesting

Pears need some thinning; clusters should generally be reduced to one or two fruits as the fruitlets begin to turn downwards. Remove smaller fruits but check first that the larger ones have not been infested by the pear midge.

Early maturing varieties should be harvested while the pears are still hard (August to September). At this time they will not part easily from the tree if lifted and twisted gently, so cut stalks with secateurs. If left longer than this on the tree, the pears will ripen unevenly, going mushy in the centre before the outside is truly soft. Lay pears carefully in trays and boxes and keep in a cool place until ripening is almost complete. This is shown by the skins turning a slightly yellowish colour from the green they were when picked and, at this point, they should be brought indoors for a day or two to ripen properly before being eaten or stored.

Mid-season and later varieties should be picked when they part easily from the tree and then treated in the way outlined above until they are completely ripe.

Pear varieties: there are not as many varieties of pears as there are of apples. Some are ideal for eating while others are best bottled. Again, decide which type you want before buying. **Above:** the Doyenne du Comice is considered to be one of the finest tasting pears of all.

PESTS AND DISEASES/PEARS

Pear midge

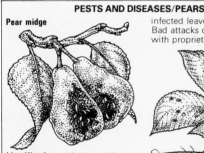

Identification: only occurs in certain places, but once it has attacked a tree, it will continue to do so until the tree has been thoroughly sprayed with a recommended proprietary mixture. The maggots of the pest bore through the skin and feed on the pears, slowing down the growth and making the fruit distorted. Infected pears will soon fall off the tree. **Treatment:** remove infected fruit and burn it. Keep the ground beneath the tree well-cultivated so that predators have a chance to eat the pests, before they climb up the tree.

Pear leaf blister mites
Identification: tiny insects which feed on the leaves and produce tiny browny-pink blisters.
Treatment: mites first appear in April, so pick off and burn

infected leaves after this time. Bad attacks can be controlled with proprietary mixtures.

Fire blight

Identification: causes flowers to blacken and shrivel, leaves to turn brown and wither, and shoots to die back.
Treatment: inform the local branch of the Ministry of Agriculture (Department of Agriculture), who will advise you of the action to take.

TRAINING AND PRUNING APPLES AND PEARS

There are four main ways of training and pruning apples and pears.

Cordon: allows trees to be planted close together, thereby making them easy to manage.

Espalier: often planted to indicate boundaries between different parts of the land, such as the fruit and vegetable gardens. An espalier is also a decorative feature.

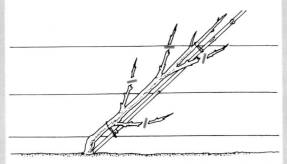

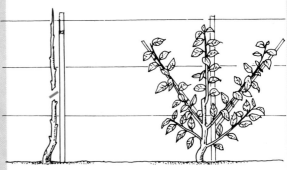

1 In winter, erect posts and wire system. Plant maiden tree at an angle of 45°, the union uppermost. Tie trunk of tree to a bamboo stake, and tie that to the wires. Cut any side shoots (feathers) back to three buds. Do not prune the leader unless it is a tip-bearing cultivar, which should be pruned back by half. It is best to buy a feathered maiden.

1 Erect stake and wire system. Plant maiden, preferably unfeathered, in early winter, and cut back to a good bud with two buds facing outward beneath it, about 30 cm (12 in) from the ground.

2 During the summer, train the centre shoot up the stake and tie the side shoots to bamboo poles set at an angle of 45° from the main stem. Secure the bamboo poles to the horizontal wires.

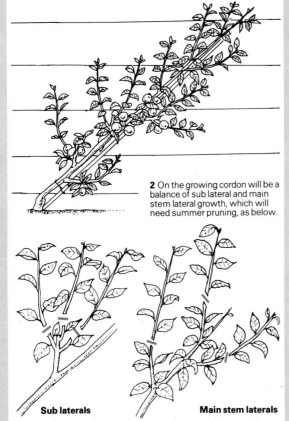

2 On the growing cordon will be a balance of sub lateral and main stem lateral growth, which will need summer pruning, as below.

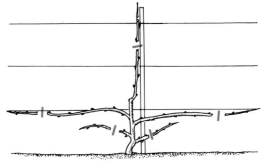

3 In the winter bend down the side growths and tie them to the horizontal wires. Prune them back by one third. Prune main stem back to three good buds, two of which should face in opposite outward directions. These will form the next tier, which should be about 30 cm (12 in) from the lower one. Cut side shoots down to three buds.

Sub laterals

Main stem laterals

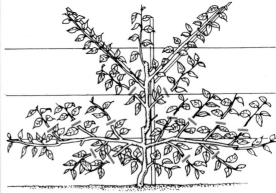

3 Start the system of summer pruning, in which sub laterals are pruned back to 2.5 cm (1 in) or one leaf, to encourage the formation of fruiting spurs. Prune laterals growing from main stem back to three leaves beyond the basal cluster. If the spur system becomes too crowded the spurs should be thinned in the winter, by removing some and cutting back others.

4 In the summer tie new tier to bamboo at an angle of 45° Continue until the required number of tiers is made. Start summer pruning on lower tiers by cutting back laterals on horizontals to three leaves to encourage formation of fruiting spurs and cut back sub laterals to 2.5 cm (1 in) or one leaf, in a similar way to the pruning of cordons. Cut off growths from the main stem to three leaves. On established espaliers cut back the main stem and growths from horizontals to ripe wood.

Open centre bush: this is used for growing apples, pears, peaches, plums and acid cherries.

However, it may take up to five years to train the tree into its required shape.

1 In winter plant maiden tree, and cut it back to 60 cm (2 ft) at a point where there are four buds well positioned around it.

2 Next winter, cut back the four primary leaders by a third, to an outward facing bud. Remove any other growths.

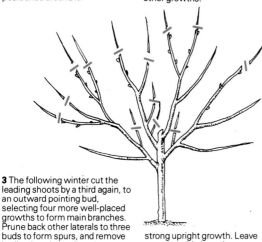

3 The following winter cut the leading shoots by a third again, to an outward pointing bud, selecting four more well-placed growths to form main branches. Prune back other laterals to three buds to form spurs, and remove badly-placed wood, such as

strong upright growth. Leave some outside laterals unpruned.

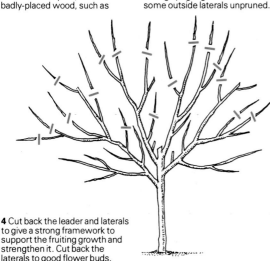

4 Cut back the leader and laterals to give a strong framework to support the fruiting growth and strengthen it. Cut back the laterals to good flower buds. Once the tree is established, aim to keep the centre of the tree open. Replace the leading shoots

by cutting them back to new laterals when they are about three years old.

Spindlebush: buy a feathered maiden if planning to train the tree in this way. The growth then

comes easily from the central leader, and forms a flat A-shape.

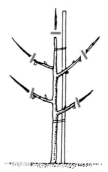

1 In winter, plant a feathered maiden. Prune back three or four laterals by one third to outward facing buds. Laterals should be

about 60 cm (2 ft) from the ground. Cut out other laterals, and cut back leader to two buds above the top lateral.

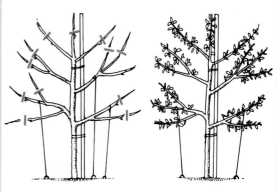

2 In summer, if growth of laterals has been good, tie them with soft string to 30° above the horizontal.

3 In winter, cut back main leader to an opposite growing bud. Remove any unright growth. Tip remaining laterals to a downward bud.

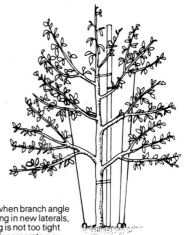

4 Remove ties when branch angle is set. Keep trying in new laterals, check that string is not too tight and restricting. Incorporate new horizontal laterals but keep those at the top of the tree short to allow penetration of sun to lower branches. When tree is 2-2.1 cm

(7-8 ft) high, cut back main leader to a weaker lateral, and tie it to the stake. To maintain A-shape remove vigourous upright growth.

Growing Other Tree Fruit

TREE FRUIT takes a longer time to become established in the garden than soft fruit and needs more room to grow. However, it has a longer fruiting season than soft fruit, and can also become a decorative feature of the garden.

DAMSONS, GAGES AND PLUMS

These all belong to the same family. Damsons are the smallest and are sour-tasting, so they are generally cooked in some way before eating. Gages may be eaten fresh, but are very often cooked. Plums have the greatest number of different varieties, which may be divided into dessert and cooking types. Some varieties are self-pollinating (but many are not!), so if you want to have only one tree of plums, make sure you choose one of these.

Soil, position and cultivation

All these trees will grow on most soil, but they like it to be well-drained. If it is wet and heavy, add lots of well-rotted organic material when preparing the ground for planting. Avoid planting in a spot where frost collects – particularly for plums and gages, which flower early. These trees will give their best crops if grown against a south-facing wall. Damsons can withstand more incle-

Other tree fruits: damsons **(top)**, gages **(above)** and plums **(right)** belong to the same family. Damsons and gages are usually cooked before eating, but plums can be eaten fresh as well as being cooked. Gages are more usually known as greengages, but can also be yellow in colour.

PESTS AND DISEASES/DAMSONS, GAGES AND PLUMS

Aphids

the inner wood of branches a purplish-brown colour. Eventually, the branches will die.
Treatment: cut out all infected wood to about 15 cm (6 in) beyond the discolored area and seal the wounds with protective paint. Make sure all pruning cuts are well sealed because the disease enters through cut or open spots on the wood.

Identification: affect plums in warm, dry spells and will settle in hordes on leaves, shoots and young fruit, causing distorted growth.
Treatment: spray with proprietary mixtures, either in December and January to kill eggs, or just before the blossom appears, to kill the insects.

Silver leaf
Identification: the disease most likely to attack plums. It turns the leaves a silvery colour and

Birds

Treatment: cover the entire tree with netting. A close mesh will also keep wasps away from the fruit.

ment weather conditions – ie a more exposed position and a heavier rainfall.

Plant all three fruits as early as possible in the planting period and if the soil is dry, soak it well 24 hours ahead of planting. If planting more than one tree, allow at least 4 metres (13 ft) between them and do not plant close to large trees which will exclude light and compete for soil moisture and nutrients. Keep the area around the tree free of weeds, but try not to disturb the roots of the trees while weeding, as this tends to encourage the tree to put out suckers. If they do form, tear them off from the root; cutting will only encourage further growth. Regular autumn mulches of well-rotted organic matter should give improved yields.

Unless you want a real glut of these fruits for jam-making, bottling or freezing, one tree of each type should be ample for the needs of most households. Yields per tree are impossible to give with any accuracy as they will depend on the individual variety as well as on the growing conditions.

Training and pruning
Damsons, gages and plums may be grown as open centre bush trees, pyramid (spindlebush) trees, or as fans against a wall. Once again, it is advisable to buy two- or three-year-old trees, in which the initial training will have been done already. The training for open centre bush trees and pyramid trees is the same as for apples (see page 111) and fan-shaped trees are trained as described for apricots on page 116.

Once established, these fruits need very little pruning and really, all that is necessary is to ensure that they do not become over-crowded. Also, remove very old, dead or badly placed wood. All pruning should be carried out in the spring or summer. This helps to lessen the likelihood of attack by silver leaf (see above), which enters the tree through open cuts and wounds and which is at its least active at this time of year.

Harvesting
Plums, in particular, should be thinned, as too heavy a crop could cause branches to snap, thereby leaving open wounds which will provide entry points for disease. Thin in two stages – first in early June and again at the end of June or early July. At this point, fruits should be about 5 cm (2 in) apart.

Pick all plums, damsons and gages carefully by the stalk to avoid bruising the fruit (the stalk should come away with the fruit as you pick). If you want plums for eating, leave them to ripen fully before picking, and pick over the tree several times. For cooking purposes, plums, gages and damsons can all be picked before they are fully ripe. If there is a lot of rain around harvesting time, the skins of gages are liable to split before they are fully ripe.

PEACHES AND NECTARINES
These are further examples of fruit which originated in the Mediterranean area, but which may be grown successfully in cooler climates. They can be reared from fruit stones, although if these were from varieties produced in a warmer climate the trees might well not bear fruit. The nectarine is a type of peach, differing only in that it has a smooth, rather than a velvety, skin. It is also less hardy. Both peaches and nectarines are self-pollinating, although it will help to ensure good pollination if you brush over the flowers with a soft paint-brush around noon on sunny days.

Soil, position and cultivation
Both trees like well-cultivated, well-drained soil, which will retain moisture in summer. Growing fan-trained trees against a south-facing wall is the surest key to success and it is the only place to grow nectarines. Peaches can also be grown as bush trees in warm, sheltered, sunny gardens.

Plant as early as possible in the recommended planting period (see page 104). Keep the ground round the roots free of weeds, but do not hoe too deeply in case you should accidentally damage the roots. Water well in dry weather and apply a mulch of well-rotted farmyard manure in the spring to help the moisture retention in

Other tree fruits: in warm climates peaches and nectarines **(right and opposite right)** will grow easily. In colder areas they must be grown against a south-facing wall or under glass. Sweet cherry trees are too large to be grown in most gardens, but sour varieites **(above)** can be grown as bushes or trees. Apricots **(opposite left)**, need a sheltered spot in which to grow, ideally against a south-facing wall. If the site is particularly sheltered, apricot bushes can also be grown.

the soil. It is particularly important to keep nectarines well-watered.

Pruning and training

As mentioned, peaches and nectarines are best grown as fan-trained trees against a wall, the training and pruning of which is outlined on page 116.

Once established, prune to get a constant, good supply of one-year-old wood, as peaches and nectarines only produce fruit on the previous year's wood.

Harvesting

The crops of both fruits must be thinned if decent-sized fruits are to be obtained. This should be done in two stages – the first when the fruits are marble-sized (in early June), reducing clusters to single fruits about 10 cm (4 in) apart, and the second when they are a little over walnut-sized. At this stage, reduce the crop by half so that they are about 23 cm (9 in) apart. Nectarines should also be thinned in two stages, but so that they are about 15 cm (6 in) apart. In both cases, at the first thinning remove all fruits that are growing towards the wall and will not have room to develop properly.

Test for ripeness by supporting the fruit in your hand and very gently pressing the flesh by the stalk. It should give under your fingers. The fruit will come away easily from the tree as you lift it. Handle peaches and nectarines very carefully; they bruise easily.

CHERRIES

There are two types of cherry – sweet and sour. As a rule, sweet cherries are not suitable for garden cultivation as, hitherto, it has not been possible to grow them on dwarfing rootstocks. Although experiments along these lines are proving successful, such trees are not yet widely available. It is possible to fan-train sweet cherries against a south- or west-facing wall, but they will grow up to 6 metres (20 ft) or more in all directions and, as they are not self-pollinating, it will be necessary to grow more than one tree. Also, unless they are very closely netted, the birds will take the entire crop before you get a chance.

Sour cherries, of which the variety Morello is the most popular, are suitable for garden cultivation and may be grown as bushes, trees or against a wall. They are self-pollinating, so only one need be grown and, although

birds certainly go for them, they are not subject to the same dedicated attack as sweet cherries.

Soil, position and cultivation
As cherries send their roots way down into the soil, they like ground that has been deeply dug and cultivated and is well-drained. They will grow virtually anywhere.

Plant at the times and in the way outlined on page 104, adding lots of well-rotted organic matter to the site whilst preparing it. If there is any danger of the soil drying out, mulch the area round the roots well in early spring. Keep the ground well-watered in dry periods.

Two trees will be sufficient for most households.

Training and pruning
As mentioned above, sour cherries may be grown as bush or fan-shaped trees, the training of which is outlined on pages 111 and 116 respectively.

Thereafter, prune to get a constant supply of new growth, as cherries fruit only on previous year's wood. Keep the trees under control by cutting out a selection of old wood (three years old and more), back to a new shoot. Like plums, cherries should be pruned in spring to lessen possible infestation by silver leaf.

Harvesting
There is no need to thin cherries. Harvest them when they are ripe (July to September) by cutting off the stalks, using scissors. If you harvest sour cherries by pulling them off the trees (as is the practice with sweet cherries), disease may enter any spot where the bark is torn.

APRICOTS
Apricots can be grown outside, but in very cold areas they will really only survive and produce decent yields of fruit if grown under glass.

Soil, position and cultivation
They like well-drained, fertile soil, preferably a fairly light loam. A warm, sunny position is essential, ideally against a sheltered, south-facing wall.

Apricots may be planted in autumn or spring. If planting in autumn, wait until the following spring to begin pruning. Water the site well before planting if it is at all dry, and mulch the ground round the roots in spring.

Apricots are self-pollinating, but as they flower so

PESTS AND DISEASES/PEACHES, NECTARINES, CHERRIES AND APRICOTS

Die back

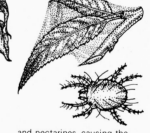

Identification: fungus which makes the young apricot branches and shoots wither and die suddenly.
Treatment: prevent the fungus entering breaks or cuts in the wood by sealing any pruning cuts with wound-sealing paint. Cut off affected branches and seal the cuts.

and nectarines, causing the leaves to become mottled before turning a yellowish bronze and dying. They are active during the summer and early autumn.
Treatment: spray with recommended proprietary mixtures. Keep leaves syringed with water, and dampen nearby paths.

Bacterial canker

Identification: disease spots appear on the cherry tree branches and ooze a sticky substance. These branches produce small, withered, discolored leaves and eventually die back.
Treatment: cut out all infected wood and seal cut surfaces with protective paint. Spray with proprietary mixtures in late summer/early autumn.

Glasshouse red spider mites
Identification: tiny insects which feed on the sap of peaches

Peach leaf curl

Identification: attacks the peach leaves, showing up first as large red blisters which turn white, then brown. The leaves become curled and crumpled before dying and falling off.
Treatment: spray with recommended proprietary mixtures in January and February as the buds begin to swell, repeating 10 to 14 days later and again in the autumn just before the leaves start to fall.

early in the year (February/March) before insects are very active, it is a good idea to help pollination by painting flowers with pollen using a fine paint-brush. Protect flower buds from frost by covering the tree with a thick layer of netting.

Generally, one tree will supply enough fruit for most average-sized households. The trees take up a fair amount of space, which would probably be better devoted to the production of other fruit rather than a second apricot tree.

Training and pruning

Apricots may be grown as an open centre bush tree, which is pruned and trained in the same way as an apple (see page 111). It is usual, however, to grow apricots against a wall and to train the tree in a fan shape (see below).

Harvesting

Thin the developing fruits if the tree is very heavily laden, so that they are 10–12.5 cm (4–5 in) apart. Most varieties ripen in August and, although they may feel soft before this, they will not be truly ripe. The skins should have turned completely yellow, with no trace of green remaining and they will come away easily from the tree. Pick them carefully – they bruise easily.

GROWING A FAN-SHAPED TREE

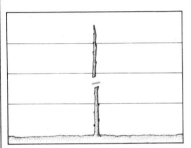

Training a fan: in winter erect wire support system. Plant maiden tree and prune to three buds 30-45 cm (12-18 in) above ground.

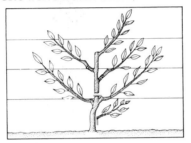

In summer: tie laterals to poles at 45° angles, which are attached to wires. Remove other side shoots and cut and seal main stem.

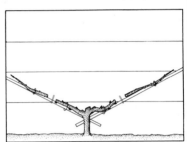

In winter: cut back the two laterals to give two good buds on the top, one at the end, and one underneath at the end.

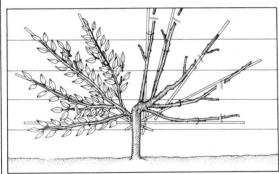

Next summer: train laterals to grow evenly-spaced. Tie each shoot to angled cane. Prune back sub laterals to 7.5-10 cm (3-4 in).

In winter: cut back all leaders by one third to suitable buds.

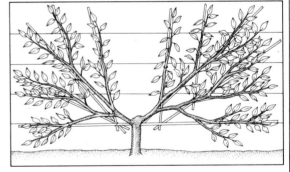

Established tree: the tree is considered to have covered the wall space when it has a good framework of branches, each rib having a fruit-bearing lateral at 10 cm (4 in) intervals, every fourth one being a fruit-bearing lateral.

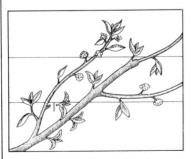

Pruning the fruiting fan: pinch back growth buds on fruiting laterals to two leaves, leaving a replacement and, if wanted, a reserve lateral.

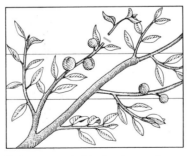

Next summer: pinch back replacement laterals to ten leaves, and pinch back fruiting ones to five, unless required for framework.

After harvesting: cut back fruited lateral to best replacement lateral unless required in framework. Cut out old or unwanted shoots, always maintaining a balance of young and fruiting wood.

Growing Figs and Grapes

FIGS are classified as a tree fruit, and grapes as a soft fruit, but both have characteristics which vary from other types of these fruits.

FIGS

Although figs are basically a Mediterranean fruit, they will grow in warm, sunny areas and can yield a reasonable crop. In colder districts, they will need to be grown under glass.

Soil and position

Figs grow best in poor soils – those which are light or sandy. Very rich soils tend to encourage too much leafy growth at the expense of the fruit. The ideal position is against a south-facing wall. Alternatively, they can be grown as a bush tree in a sunny corner, protected and sheltered by two tall walls.

Planting and routine care

Unlike other tree fruits, figs are grown on their own roots and these must be confined if the tree is to produce a good crop of fruit rather than a lot of fruitless leafy growth. There are various ways of confining the roots – either by lining the planting hole with stone, or concrete slabs, bricks or sheets of galvanized iron, or by planting a tree in a large tub or half an oil drum, with holes pierced in the bottom for drainage, and sinking this into the ground. If the first method is used, the bottom of the planting hole must be covered with a 30 cm (1 ft) layer of rubble which is packed down hard. Soil mixed with rubble and bonemeal is the ideal planting medium. Plant trees in spring – early March is generally the best time. If planting a young tree which has been raised in a pot, make sure the roots are evenly spread out in the hole and not tangled together. If planting more than one tree, allow 4.5–5.5 metres (15–18 ft) between them.

No mulching or manuring will be needed in the first few years of a fig tree's life as this will merely encourage over-vigorous growth. Once established, a mulch of well-rotted manure will be beneficial in dry conditions. Most people consider one tree is sufficient.

Training and pruning

A fan-shaped tree may be trained as outlined on the facing page and a bush tree as on page 111.

Once established, cut back side shoots each year in June to about 10 cm (4 in) long, or so that approximately five leaves remain. Remove suckers and unwanted growth in July and tie the new shoots in to keep the fan shape (if growing this way).

GRAPES

Grapes can be grown outdoors successfully in many areas, but reasonable crops will really only be obtained if they have lots of warm summer sun. Both dessert and wine varieties – either white or black – can be produced. Choose early ripening varieties for colder districts.

Soil, position and cultivation

Ideally they like sandy, stony or gravelly soil which is neutral or slightly alkaline and warms up quickly in sunny conditions. It must be well-drained. They need a sunny, sheltered position where there is no danger of frost collecting or lingering. If planning to plant a vineyard, it is best done on a south-facing slope. Easier and more practical for domestic situations is to grow a few vines on a south-facing wall or fence (this is the system described below).

Prepare the site by digging in some well-rotted compost, but not too much. If the soil is too rich, the vines tend to produce lots of luxurious leafy growth at the expense of fruit. Buy one-year-old vines and plant them in spring in the way outlined for a tree on page 105, setting them about 1.5 metres (5 ft) apart. If you have to plant in autumn, protect the vine with a covering of peat or leaf mould through its first winter. Keep the ground moist, but remember that the roots should be neither dry nor waterlogged. Mulching in summer will help.

The amount you grow is likely to be dictated by available space, as much as anything else. A garden will only have so much south-facing wall and there are a lot of competitors for it! An established cordon grown against a wall can produce up to 9 kg (20 lb) of fruit or even more. Again, growing conditions and variety of grape can vary this yield tremendously.

Harvesting

Fruits form in three layers along a fig branch. Those at

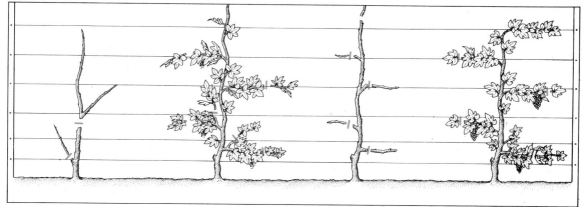

Training a vine: in winter erect wire supports and plant vine. Cut main stem by two-thirds. Cut laterals back to one bud.

In summer: remove flowers. Cut laterals back to five leaves and tie loosely to wires. Pinch out sub laterals to one leaf.

Next winter: after leaves have fallen, cut vine back by two-thirds, and prune laterals on the main stem back to a good bud. Repeat process next year.

Third summer: train leader to grow along top wire, Only allow two laterals to fruit, and pinch out to two leaves beyond fruit.

Figs and grapes: both these fruits grow best in hot climates but will grow well in cooler areas if trained against a south-facing wall. Grapes will thrive if grown in a greenhouse.

the bottom of the branch will ripen; those in the middle will not have a chance to do so before the frost hits them, and the ones near the top of the branch will be next year's fruit, so must remain on the branches through the winter.

Harvest the larger fruits as they ripen (August to October). Ripeness is indicated by the softening of the stem, the fruits turning brown and the skins starting to split. They are also soft to the touch. Remove the smaller fruits in the middle of the branch and discard them, and protect the following year's crop either by untying the branches and wrapping them in straw or by just tying straw or dried large foliage, such as ferns, round the end shoots. Remove this protection in spring, when the dangers of severe frost have passed.

Training and pruning

As mentioned above, I give instructions here for growing a single cordon or rod on a wall, this being easiest and generally the most suitable system for outdoor cultivation. Vines should not be allowed to bear fruit until they are three years old (do this by removing the flowers as they form) and thereafter they will bear their grapes on current season's growth.

Drive a stake into the ground near the wall and secure several horizontal strands of wire to the wall with special fastenings called vine eyes. After planting, cut out all but the strongest shoot and tie this to the stake. Pinch out the flowers as they appear in the summer, and cut back laterals to about five leaves. Tie these laterals to the wires. Rub out laterals that grow from the main rod between the wires.

Repeat this process the following year, stopping the fruits forming again. In the next year, allow the vine to produce three bunches, and in the next year four or five. Once established, prune the vine after the leaves have

fallen, taking the lead shoot back to ripe wood. When it has reached the top wire, train it along the wire in the summer, and then in the autumn cut it back to a bud which is growing level with the wire. Prune side shoots back to two buds, thereby cutting out the previous year's growth.

Harvesting

Remove any rotting berries as you spot them and cut the ripe branches off the vine with scissors. Providing they are not damaged, they will keep for a number of weeks in a cool place.

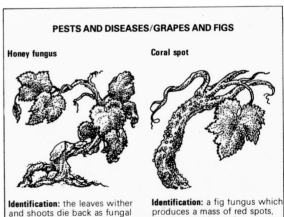

PESTS AND DISEASES/GRAPES AND FIGS

Honey fungus

Coral spot

Identification: the leaves wither and shoots die back as fungal growths appear on the vines, which die.
Treatment: dig up and burn dead vines, and change or sterilize the soil before attempting to replant vines in the same place.

Identification: a fig fungus which produces a mass of red spots, usually on old wood.
Treatment: cut back all affected areas to at least 15 cm (6 in) past the infection and burn. Seal all cuts with a wound-sealing paint.

Greenhouse Fruit

THE PRINCIPAL USE of the greenhouse for growing fruit is for melons, grapes and such tree fruits as peaches and nectarines.

Melons

Melons can be grown successfully in an unheated greenhouse, although care must be taken that they do not just produce a mass of greenery and very little fruit. Providing that you keep them well-watered and pinch out the side shoots as described below, however, there is no reason why you should not be able to enjoy your own home-grown melons. Help yourself still further by choosing those varieties recommended by seed merchants or growers as being suitable for growing in cold greenhouse conditions.

Raise the seed in a propagator, sowing it in April (earlier if your greenhouse is heated). Prick out the seedlings into small pots and then plant them in their permanent position in the border soil when they have four or five leaves. They will appreciate lots of well-rotted compost or farmyard manure incorporated into the soil. Put the plants about 60 cm (2 ft) apart and erect a similar framework to that described for cucumbers – a stake pushed into the soil close to the plant, to which a series of horizontal strings or wires are attached. Pinch out the growing tips almost as soon as you have put the plants into their permanent site – the main stem should have no more than about six large leaves. Train the side shoots along the horizontal wires and pinch out their growing tips when they are about 30 cm (1 ft) long. This should prevent them just producing a mass of leafy growth.

Melons will need pollinating by hand; either transfer pollen from the male flowers (those with no embryo fruit behind the petals) to the female flowers, using a fine paint-brush, or pick the male flowers, strip off the petals and press the stamen into the female flowers.

Keep the plants well watered and feed them regularly with liquid fertilizer as the fruits begin to develop. If the plant seems very heavily loaded with fruit, pick out any that are either very small or very large, so that the fruit left behind is of uniform size. Stop both watering and feeding the plant when the melons seem to have stopped swelling. Support the melons during the subsequent ripening either by placing them on a board or by putting them in a string bag which is suspended at a suitable height. If they are not thus supported they will fall off.

Pick the melons when they are ripe; they will feel just soft when you push them gently by the stalk. They will also smell wonderful.

Melons can also be grown under cloches or in cold frames. Pinch out the growing tip in the same way when the plant has about five leaves, then allow about four side shoots to develop (pinching out any others when you can see which is the strongest).

Grapes

Vines grown in even a cold greenhouse are likely to yield more grapes than those grown outdoors, particularly if they are planted in a south-facing position. If, for

Melons: these can be grown successfully in greenhouses or cold frames in cooler climates. Since the growing fruits are very heavy they will need to be supported. Either rest them on a board or suspend them from the roof of the greenhouse in string bags.

example, you have a lean-to greenhouse situated on a south-facing wall, you could grow vines on the side of the house furthest from the wall, reserving the actual wall for tree fruits. However, it is important in this instance to keep the vines under control, so that they do not fill the greenhouse with their foliage, thereby excluding most of the light. Vines can be planted either in the border soil of the greenhouse, or you can plant them just outside the greenhouse and train them through a small hole in the wall. The only real advantage of this is that watering is easier and, if you forget it in the winter the plant will still be watered by the rain.

Probably the simplest way to grow grapes in a greenhouse is on a single-stem cordon or rod – the same system as described for outdoor cultivation on page 117. Alternatively, you could allow two cordons to develop on the vine, but if you grow single cordons, you will be able to grow different varieties.

It is usual to plant one-year-old vines and this is best done in late October. Plant in fertile damp soil, enriched with well-rotted compost if necessary, placing vines at the same depth as they were growing at the nursery or previous site. If planning to grow single-stem cordons or rods, place the vines 1.2 to 1.5 metres (4 to 5 ft) apart.

To train a single stem, as it begins to grow during the spring following planting, tie the main stem to a stake and pinch out the growth of all laterals when they have five to six leaves. Ideally, these should be trained along strategically positioned wires or strings. Rub out any small side shoots that grow from the leaf axils. Stop the lead shoot when it has reached the height you want it (ie when it is level with the bottom of the greenhouse roof). As with vines grown out of doors, they should not be allowed to bear fruit until they are three years old, and it is always a good idea to restrict them to no more than two bunches per lateral. Vines are pruned back hard each winter, taking the laterals back to a new bud close to the main stem.

As the grapes develop, the patient grower will cut out the small grapes from each bunch. This allows for bigger ones to develop and also prevents the smaller ones turning mouldy as they get crushed by the bigger ones.

Do not forget to give the vine an occasional watering during the winter if it is planted inside the greenhouse, and also to top dress the soil with a fertilizer and some well-rotted compost in the spring.

Tree fruits

Peaches, nectarines, apricots and figs are the most successful tree fruits to grow under glass and all will thrive best if grown against a south-facing wall. Although these fruits can be grown out of doors as has previously been described, peaches and nectarines, in particular, will generally not bear fruit in cold areas.

The general cultivation and care of these trees is the same as that described for those growing out of doors, but there are some considerations to bear in mind when growing them under glass. They must be planted in very well-drained soil which is fertile to a fair depth – peaches, for example, extend their roots down into the soil for about 60 cm (2 ft). The trees must be kept well watered throughout the year, even in winter when there appears to be little or no growth. Give them a good mulch of well-rotted farmyard manure each spring.

In the winter, make sure you shut all ventilation windows quite early in the afternoon as this will help to trap any warmth that there is in the greenhouse. Open the windows in the morning, because it is important to let fresh air into the greenhouse for part of the day. As the weather warms up, probably in about May, it is important to shade the greenhouse with blinds or by painting or spraying the roof with the recommended paint, in order to prevent the trees becoming scorched.

Pollination is far less likely to occur in the greenhouse than it is outside, so do it by hand. Brush over the flowers with a light paint-brush, transferring the pollen from flower to flower. This is best done about noon, before you have sprayed the plants.

Tree fruit grown indoors needs constant gentle spraying or syringing with water to discourage the rampant red spider mite and to encourage the flowers to set fruit. Spray once a day when the flowers are out and ideally twice a day when the fruit buds have begun to emerge. Never spray the plants when they are in direct sun.

The training, pruning, thinning of indoor fruit, harvesting and so on, is the same as for trees grown out of doors. The usual shape for trees grown under glass against a wall is fan-shape, and be fairly severe with spring pruning so that the developing fruit is not completely obscured by foliage. If the foliage is still quite prolific, tie it back to allow the light to get to the ripening fruit. As the fruit begins to ripen, incidentally, it is better to stop the spraying or syringing.

GREENHOUSE TIPS

1 It is just as important to provide greenhouse crops with shade as it is with sun. They could easily scorch otherwise.

2 Many greenhouse crops are not self-pollinating and will need to be pollinated by hand, using the flowers or a brush.

3 Greenhouse crops should be given regular liquid feeds. Also spray them to deter pests, such as the red spider mite.

4 Regular and even watering of crops is essential if they are to grow properly, but not when they are in direct sun.

Growing Rhubarb

RHUBARB IS NOT A SOFT FRUIT, but it is undoubtedly a dessert fruit. It is ready for picking from February/March onwards (earlier if it is forced) – a time when virtually no other fresh fruit is available in the garden. It can be used in a variety of puddings.

Soil and position
Rhubarb will grow in just about all garden soils and sites. However, it does best in an open, sunny position.

Planting and routine care
As rhubarb is a perennial and can stay in the same place for five years or more, it is worthwhile taking trouble over the preparation of the bed. Dig it over well and make sure all perennial weeds have been removed. Incorporate some well-rotted organic matter into the soil, digging it deep, as rhubarb sends down long roots.

Buy rhubarb crowns from a nursery (or see if a neighbour is dividing up some plants and therefore has some to spare) and plant them in February or March so there is about 90 cm (3 ft) between plants. Planting holes should be wide enough to take the entire rootstock and deep enough to allow small shoots to protrude from the surface of the soil. Firm the soil around the rootstock and water the ground if it is at all dry.

Water well in dry spells and mulch the plants annually each spring. Feed them in summer with liquid fertilizer. Cut out flower stems if they develop and do not pick any rhubarb in the first year.

How many?
An established rhubarb plant should yield about 4.5 kg (10 lb) of fruit in a year, but remember this is spread over a period of nearly six months.

Harvesting
Pull stalks from the plant when they are turning pink. Hold them near the bottom and pull them from the plant with a gentle twisting movement. You should be able to gather rhubarb from February to August, but do not pick too heavily in the second year and always leave a few good stems and leaves on the plant to help it gather its resources.

Raising new plants
New rhubarb plants can be obtained by digging up a plant and dividing up the roots into pieces that must each have a growing bud. Do this in February or March, using two- or three-year-old plants.

Pests and diseases
Rhubarb is beset by very few problems.

Forcing rhubarb: rhubarb is generally ready for harvesting in spring, but it can be forced so as to be ready for picking earlier. To do this, cover the emerging leaves with a bucket or large pot, making sure no light can enter. Plants may also be dug up and brought indoors in early winter, so they are ready for harvesting in mid-winter. They are then planted out again, and covered with a bucket or pot to encourage further growth. This will give you two harvests from one plant.

Growing Strawberries

STRAWBERRIES differ from other soft fruit in that they grow as small bedding plants, rather than on bushes or canes. Although considered to be one of the greatest fruit treats of all, they are not difficult to grow and it is perfectly possible to produce them in the garden from May, right through the summer up to the first frosts. If space is a problem they can be grown in tubs, boxes, barrels, special strawberry pots or among the flowers in a bed or border.

There are three types of strawberries: single crop varieties which produce one heavy crop – usually in June and July; the perpetual or remontant types which produce a number of crops from July and August to October; and alpine strawberries, which bear their tiny, highly succulent fruits from June to September or October. They are all good sources of vitamin C.

Although strawberry plants are perennials, they should be scrapped after two or three years. Thereafter, they produce increasingly poor crops and are also more susceptible to disease. They are very easy to propagate (see below). Alpines are best treated as annuals and reared from seed sown in the spring or grown from young nursery-bought plants.

Soil and position
Strawberries grow in all well-cultivated garden soils,

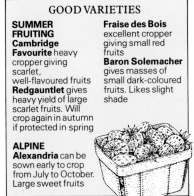

GOOD VARIETIES

SUMMER FRUITING
Cambridge Favourite heavy cropper giving scarlet, well-flavoured fruits
Redgauntlet gives heavy yield of large scarlet fruits. Will crop again in autumn if protected in spring

ALPINE
Alexandria can be sown early to crop from July to October. Large sweet fruits

Fraise des Bois excellent cropper giving small red fruits
Baron Solemacher gives masses of small dark-coloured fruits. Likes slight shade

but they do best in those that are well-drained and very rich in humus. Dig in lots of well-rotted organic matter about a month before planting. An open, sunny position will produce the heaviest crops, although they will grow successfully in some shade.

Planting and routine care
If buying new strawberry plants, buy only those certified disease-free. They can be planted any time from mid-July to early September, to fruit the following summer, and the earlier in this time, the better. If planting has to be delayed until the following spring, pinch off the flowers as they appear in May to allow the plant to direct its resources into becoming established before fruiting the following year.

Water plants well immediately after planting and for the next few weeks. Thereafter make sure they do not dry out. Keep weeds under control by shallow hoeing, but take care not to disturb the plants' roots.

When the fruit begins to appear, put a 5 cm (2 in) layer of clean straw between rows and tuck it well under and around each plant. This helps to protect the fruit from soil splashing up and rotting it. Alternative methods of protection are to use the special strawberry mats sold at garden centres, to lay black polythene on the ground, or to fit jam jars over the fruits and rest them on the ground. Make sure the soil is moist if using polythene.

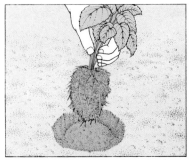

Cultivation of strawberries: 1 Make a hole in the soil with a low mound of soil at the bottom. Spread out roots.

2 Protect growing plants from mud which rots them, by growing them on special strawberry mats.

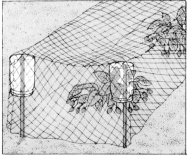

3 When fruits form, cover plants with cages of netting to deter birds from eating the strawberries.

Raising new plants: 1 Select one or two healthy runners from plants in June, and pinch out others.

2 Sink pot of potting compost into ground and pin runner into it. Pinch out any more growth of runner.

3 Cut runner from the parent plant when it is well-rooted and plant it out in the new site.

Protecting strawberries: one of the best methods of protecting growing fruits is to raise them on beds of straw. Not only will it prevent the fruits from rotting on soggy ground in wet weather, but when the season is over, the straw can be pulled up, taking any strawberry pests with it.

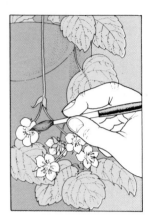

Left: any variety of strawberry can be grown in attractive strawberry pots. Most have holes in the bottom for good drainage, with a layer of large pebbles. Fill in the pots with potting compost to ensure a rich growing medium. Plant the strawberries in the cups provided. **Right:** if growing plants in a heated greenhouse, the flowers will have to be pollinated by hand, daily, as soon as they open, using a small brush.

row of strawberry plants every one or two years very easily. To raise alpine strawberries, sow the seeds in potting compost indoors in late summer and prick out at the end of October, or raise under glass from February to April. Plant out the seedlings in April and May, setting them 30 cm (12 in) apart, with the same distance between each row. Thereafter, treat them as for other strawberries.

Harvesting
Pick fruits on a dry day when they are fully ripe, pinching them off by the stalk so as to avoid handling and thus bruising. Pick alpine strawberries throughout the season – regular picking encourages more fruiting.

Pests and diseases
Aphids can be a problem (see page 113). Slugs and snails are fairly partial to young strawberry fruits and are best protected against by putting down slug pellets. Do this before putting down the layer of straw or polythene to protect the fruit.

Protect developing fruit from attack by birds by covering the plants with netting supported on low stakes driven into the ground, and give feeds of liquid fertilizer to increase the size of the fruits once they begin to swell. Pinch off runners as they appear unless you want to raise new plants.

If you want early crops, protect the plant with polythene or glass cloches in February, and if you want late crops from perpetual varieties, cover with cloches in early October. You should get crops at least until the end of October.

After harvesting, strawberry plants may be treated in a number of ways. With single-crop plants, loosen the straw around the plants and burn it (if the siting of the plants makes this a safe operation). This burns off old leaves as well as destroying pests and other rubbish which has collected in the straw, but it does not kill the plant. An alternative, however, and one that should be done with perpetual varieties that would be killed by the former method, is to cut off all the foliage to about 10 cm (4 in) above the crown of the plant, leaving the young growth to come through. Fork up the straw, cut stems and burn them.

Yet another alternative is to take one runner from each plant, and root them (see previous page) to form a new row. Then dig the old crop into the soil, or dig up the plants and burn them. This way you can produce a new

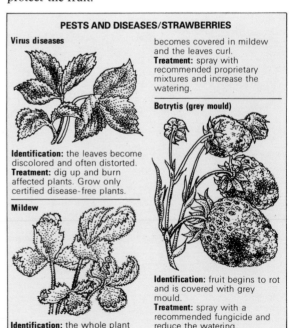

PESTS AND DISEASES/STRAWBERRIES

Virus diseases

Identification: the leaves become discolored and often distorted.
Treatment: dig up and burn affected plants. Grow only certified disease-free plants.

Mildew

Identification: the whole plant

becomes covered in mildew and the leaves curl.
Treatment: spray with recommended proprietary mixtures and increase the watering.

Botrytis (grey mould)

Identification: fruit begins to rot and is covered with grey mould.
Treatment: spray with a recommended fungicide and reduce the watering.

Growing Soft Fruit

NOT ALL soft fruit belongs to the same family, but can be divided into two types – that belonging to the gooseberry family, such as currants and gooseberries, and that of the rose family, such as blackberries, strawberries and raspberries.

GOOSEBERRIES

The different varieties of gooseberry make it possible to produce crops in the garden right through the summer, beginning in May. They may be dessert types, or those suitable only for cooking in some way. Gooseberries are excellent for making jams, chutneys and wine as well as many puddings. Although usually grown on a bush, they can be grown on single, double or treble cordons, which means they can be trained to grow against a wall or fence.

Soil and position

They will grow in almost all soils, but prefer those which are well-drained but moist, and enriched by the addition of lots of well-rotted organic material. They like a sunny site, and should never be planted in a place where frost collects as they flower early in the year, in March and it will damage them.

Planting and routine care

Make sure the ground is completely free from all perennial weeds and apply a general fertilizer (preferably one that is rich in potash) to the site before planting. Plant two- or three-year-old bushes in the autumn, leaving 1.5 metres (5 ft) between bushes. The lowest branches should be about 22 cm (9 in) above the ground. Single cordons should be 30 cm (1 ft) apart, double cordons 60 cm (2 ft) apart and triple cordons 90 cm (3 ft) apart. They will need wire supports along which to train the branches.

Keep the ground free of weeds by shallow hoeing (so as not to disturb the roots), or with a weed killer. Water the plants in very dry weather and apply an annual spring mulch of well-rotted compost, together with a sprinkling of sulphate of potash.

Protect plants from birds, either by covering them completely with netting or by weaving black cotton round the branches. If any shoots appear at ground level, tear them out.

How many?

Mature bushes will yield an average of about 3.5 kg (8 lb) of fruit annually.

Training and pruning

The aim with bush cultivation is to keep a cup-shaped form to the bush with a good open centre. In the winter, cut summer growth shoots back by about half to two-thirds to a bud (leave the pruning until the buds start to swell if the bush has been attacked by birds – then you can be sure of pruning back to a healthy bud). If the bush is of a variety that has drooping growth, cut to an upward-pointing bud; cut upright varieties to an outward-pointing bud. Leave about eight branches well-spaced round the bush and cut the others right out to one bud from the base.

Thereafter, keep cutting the new growth back by half each winter and cut back lateral shoots to about 7.5 cm (3 in) to encourage the formation of spurs. When the bush is really established, cut out old wood to maintain the shape and to allow light to penetrate evenly. Cut back leading shoots to about 2.5 cm (1 in) each year. Remove weak new shoots.

In summer, prune back side shoots to about five leaves (do this on all types of gooseberry bushes, cordons included). This encourages the fruit buds to form.

Cordons can be created from cuttings. For a single cordon, cut off all shoots close to the main stem, leaving the strongest one. Tie it to a stake and thereafter cut it back by half the current season's growth each year. Shorten side shoots to form fruiting spurs. Train and support double and triple cordons in a similar way but select two or three shoots initially. In a double cordon, these should be trained horizontally and then cut off an an upward-pointing bud so they grow vertically. In a triple cordon, train two shoots as for a double cordon and treat the centre one like a single cordon.

Harvesting

If the crop is very heavy, thin the fruits when they are big enough to use, so they are about 2.5 cm (1 in) apart. If you like, you can thin them again to leave them 5–7.5 cm (2–3 in) apart, in which case you should get large gooseberries for the final harvest. Gooseberries wanted for cooking do not have to be completely ripe

PRUNING GOOSEBERRIES

1 In the winter, cut summer shoots back to a bud, always maintaining a good cup shape to the bush.

2 In the summer, thin the fruits by removing every other one. Prune back side shoots to five leaves.

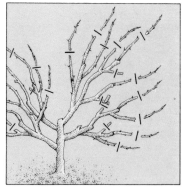

3 In winter prune mature bush to keep cup shape. Cut leaders back by half, and laterals to 7.5 cm (3 in).

Left: harvest gooseberries when they are about 2.5 cm (1 in) long. They can be picked early for cooking, but should be left to ripen on the bush if they are to be eaten raw.
Right: spread straw under raspberries if the crop is particularly good, as the weight of the fruits will drag the branches down toward the ground. The fruits would otherwise rot on damp soil.

PESTS AND DISEASES/GOOSEBERRIES

American gooseberry mildew

Identification: a white, powdery coating forms on the leaves, shoots and fruits. The growth at the tips of the shoots becomes distorted.
Treatment: cut out and destroy diseased shoots, and spray with recommended proprietary mixtures, or a weak solution of washing soda. Keep well pruned to ensure good light penetration to the bush.

Gooseberry sawfly

Identification: caterpillars eat the leaves, reducing them to skeletons.
Treatment: from May onwards pick off and destroy any caterpillars (green, with black spots). Spray with recommended proprietary mixtures.

before harvesting – those wanted for eating fresh should be, if they are not to be too sharp.

Raising new plants

New plants can be raised from cuttings in the same way as blackcurrants (see page 130), but they do not root as easily. Take cuttings in the autumn, about 38 cm (15 in) long, from the current season's growth while there is still some leafy growth. Cut off the top 7.5 cm (3 in) of soft wood and rub out all the buds from the lower end, leaving three or four near the top. Thereafter, treat as blackcurrant cuttings.

RASPERRIES

Raspberries are among the most popular of all soft fruits and are easy to grow. There are two types – summer-fruiting, which generally crop in July and August, bearing their fruit on the canes produced in the previous year, and autumn-fruiting, which produce a smaller crop from September to November on the current season's growth.

Soil and position

Raspberries will grow in almost all well-cultivated soils, but they prefer those which are slightly acid and well-

drained but moisture-retentive. They will grow in partial shade, but do best in a sunny site which is sheltered from strong winds.

Planting and routine care
Dig lots of well-rotted manure into the ground a month or two before planting, and make sure the site is completely free of perennial weeds. The canes can stay in the same site for eight years or so, so it is worthwhile taking care over its preparation. Plant, preferably in November, as outlined on page 104, leaving 45 cm (1 ft 6 in) between plants and 1.5–1.8 metres (5–6 ft) between rows. Buy only certified disease-free stock – anything else may well be harbouring virus disease (see page 124).

Water the canes well during summer and apply an annual spring mulch. Keep weeds under control by shallow hoeing, but be careful not to disturb the canes' roots. A weedkiller or a thick mulch might prove to be a more effective way of dealing with weeds. Protect the plants from birds by covering them with netting or by growing the raspberry canes in a fruit cage.

Established canes bear approximately 450 g (1 lb) of fruit annually so you can calculate how many you need to grow from this figure.

SUPPORTING RASPBERRY CANES

1 Drive stakes into the ground at either end of the canes and string parallel lengths of wire between the posts, the lowest being about 30 cm (12 in) from the ground. As the canes grow, tie them to the wires.

2 Drive stakes into the middle of each group of canes. Loosely tie them to the stakes at intervals as they grow.

3 Make a box structure to support the canes by driving one stake into either end of each row. Attach two cross struts to each stake and string wire between these along the rows, enclosing the canes within them.

Do not allow canes to bear fruit in their first season. Stop them doing so by cutting out any flowers as they appear. Provide supports from horizontal wires secured to posts at either end of the row and tie the canes loosely to these.

After harvesting the second season, cut out the fruiting canes on summer-fruiting varieties just above the soil. Tie the eight strongest canes to the wires, cutting out all weaker ones. Remove unwanted suckers which have sprung up between the rows at the same time. In very early spring, cut canes back to a bud that is no more than 15 cm (6 in) above the wire. Cut some canes a little shorter, so that you have fruit at all levels. In autumn-fruiting varieties, cut the canes back the following February.

Harvesting
Pull the fruits off the canes gently as soon as they are ripe, leaving the stalk and core behind. They should be used immediately.

Raising new plants
New canes are easily produced from the suckers put out by existing plants, but only take these from canes that were certified virus-free. Dig them up and transplant in November. It is generally best to buy in new stock every eight years or so.

Pests and diseases
Raspberries suffer from raspberry beetle (see page 135), cane spot (see page 135), spur blight (see page 135), honey fungus (see page 118) and virus diseases (see page 124).

BLUEBERRIES
Blueberries are a mountain and moorland fruit, widely grown in the United States of America. They are closely related to bilberries or whortleberries which grow in the United Kingdom. They make good jams and jellies.

Soil and position
They like an acid soil and will not grow on those which are alkaline. Peaty soils which are moisture-retentive will produce the best crops. Although these bushes can withstand cold conditions, they need sheltering from strong, cold winds. An open, sunny site gives the best crops.

Planting and routine care
Dig some peat into the site a month before planting if the soil is not peaty, and plant as outlined on page 104. Bushes are best started as three-year-old plants bought from a local nursery, and they should be planted 1.8 metres (6 ft) apart. They will appreciate an annual mulch in early summer.

You should grow at least two bushes to ensure good cross-pollination. They will produce anything up to 4.5 kg (10 lb) fruit per bush, depending on weather and growing conditions.

Blueberries need no pruning until they are four years old. After that, cut out old wood regularly each winter, taking it back to the ground or a strong new shoot. Cut out any suckers which emerge at the base of the plant.

Harvesting
Pick berries when they are entirely ripe – that is, when they have a blue bloom and come away easily from the bush. The ripening season is from the end of July to September, so you will need to pick over the bushes several times during this period.

Pests and diseases
Blueberries are remarkably free from problems.

BLACKCURRANTS
Blackcurrants are rich in vitamin C and have a wide culinary use – for making drinks (including wine), puddings, jams and jellies. Again, there are several different varieties and these will produce varying yields. If buying new plants, get them from a reputable source and make sure they are two-year-old certified bushes. These are less likely to succumb to disease.

Soil, position and cultivation
They will flourish in most soils, but do best on those which are well-cultivated, rich and well-drained. Ideally, they like a sunny position, but although they will tolerate partial shade, they do need to be in a

PRUNING AND TRAINING RASPBERRIES

Left and above: after harvesting, cut back canes which have just fruited to slightly above the surface of the soil. **Right:** choose the strongest new canes, which are to bear fruit the following year, and tie them to wires at 7.5-10 cm (3-4 in) intervals. Cut out the remaining new canes and any suckers. In February, prune each new cane back to a good bud above the top of the wire.

sheltered spot which is protected from cold winds and away from frost pockets.

Dig lots of well-rotted manure into the ground a month or so before planting – which is best done in the autumn. Follow instructions for planting outlined on page 104 and space plants about 1.5 metres (5 ft) apart. Cut all stems down to 5 cm (2 in) from the ground straightaway and apply a mulch around the roots.

Water plants well in dry periods and apply an annual mulch each spring. Keep the ground around them free of weeds by shallow hoeing. If necessary, control weeds by mulching, rather than digging, which would disturb the root system.

The number of plants to grow depends on the variety grown, but an average-sized mature bush yields approximately 4.5 kg (10 lb) of fruit a year.

Training and pruning

Blackcurrants fruit on new wood each year, but as the new wood grows on old wood, pruning should be done to maintain a good balance of new wood, whilst keeping the plant bushy and allowing light to penetrate to all parts. In the following autumn after planting, cut out the weakest shoots at ground level – the remainder will fruit the following summer. Thereafter, prune the bush by removing a quarter to a third of the old wood. Take the oldest wood first – it will be very dark. Cut back this wood to one or two growth buds from the ground so new shoots grow.

Harvesting

Pick blackcurrants when they are fully ripe – this is at least a week after they have turned black. If clusters of fruit have both ripe and non-ripe fruit, the berries should be picked individually, which is a tedious task. Those picked on sprigs or trusses will keep marginally longer before use, but they should all be used fairly quickly after picking.

Raising new plants

Take cuttings in the autumn from healthy shoots of that year's growth. Cut off either end just beyond a bud so

Left: blackcurrants are green before they ripen. Once they turn black, leave them for a week before picking them. If you are not sure about their ripeness, pick a few currants and eat them **(above)**. You can then either leave them to ripen further or harvest the whole truss. **Right:** the soil under this abundant red currant bush has been covered with straw to protect the fruit from mud and the damp earth, and also to act as a mulch.

the cutting is about 25 cm (10 in) long. Push it into the soil. If the soil is very heavy, dig a trench about 15 cm (6 in) deep and sprinkle sand in the bottom. The cuttings should be about 15 cm (6 in) deep in the soil with two growth buds showing above the surface, and there should be 22 cm (9 in) between cuttings. They will have rooted by the following autumn and may be transplanted to their permanent site.

RED AND WHITE CURRANTS

Although related to the blackcurrant, these fruits are cultivated differently. Their training bears closer resemblance to that of the gooseberry and, like it, they may be grown on open centre bushes or single, double or treble cordons. White currants are a variety of red currant and may be eaten fresh as a dessert. Red currants are more often used for jam- and jelly-making, although they too can be eaten fresh.

Soil and position

They like well-drained, but moisture-retentive soils which are generally lighter than those favoured by blackcurrants. A sunny position, sheltered from cold winds, and where there is no danger of frost collecting to damage the early flowers, is the ideal site.

Planting and routine care

Dig plenty of well-rotted organic matter into the soil

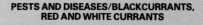

PESTS AND DISEASES/BLACKCURRANTS, RED AND WHITE CURRANTS

Aphids
These can affect red and white currants
Control as outlined on page 113.

Coral spot
This is the chief disease to affect red and white currants and is dealt with as outlined on page 118.

Big bud

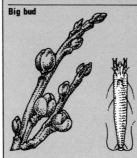

Identification: a serious condition caused by the blackcurrant gall mite. It makes buds swell and fail to develop further.

Treatment: pick off infected buds and spray bushes with recommended proprietary mixtures.

Reversion

Identification: a serious virus disease caused by big bud. The leaves become distorted and there is a poor crop, if any.
Treatment: pull up and burn infected plants. Avoid the disease by buying only certified disease-free plants.

Cultivation of blackcurrants: 1 Plant canes in a sunny, sheltered position and mulch well.

2 Prune young bushes by cutting back weakest shoots. Prune older plants by cutting back old wood.

3 Take cuttings in autumn. Rub all buds from lower end and push cane into v-shaped trench. Leave to root.

Red and white currant cultivation: 1 Plant bushes in a sunny, sheltered spot Stake and prune each year.

2 As fruit begin to form, protect them from birds by covering bushes with netting. Water in dry weather.

3 Cut out suckers as they appear near the roots of the main stems. Keep down weeds with gentle hoeing or by hand.

some weeks before planting and apply a general fertilizer containing potash to the soil. Buy two-year-old bushes and plant them as outlined on page 104 as early as possible in the recommended planting period. Plant bushes 1.5 metres (5 ft) apart, single cordons 38 cm (15 in) apart, double cordons 75 cm (2 ft 6 in) apart and treble cordons 1.05 metres (3 ft 6 in) apart. If more than one row of cordons is being grown, leave 1.2 metres (4 ft) between them. Drive stakes into the ground next to the cordons to support them and secure horizontal wires between these. Branches on bush trees should be no more than 22 cm (9 in) above the ground.

Water in very dry weather and protect plants from birds. Pull out any suckers that appear from the plants' roots or main stems. Control weeds by weedkiller or mulching rather than hoeing, which could damage the plants' roots. Apply annual winter mulches and feed with sulphate of potash at the same time.

How many?
The average yield from an established bush is 1.8–2.2 kg (4–5 lb), although in ideal growing conditions some bushes will give twice this amount. Cordons, of course, yield less.

Pruning and training
After planting, cut back branches so each has only four shoots. The second winter, cut each branch back by half to an outward-facing bud and cut lateral shoots back to

two buds. The aim is to produce an open centre bush where light can easily penetrate, and to produce spur wood which will bear the fruit. When established, cut the current year's growth back to about 2.5 cm (1 in) and cut out old wood regularly to make room for new shoots. In the summer, cut out lateral growths beyond five leaves.

Currants are trained and pruned in the same way as gooseberries (see page 125–126).

Harvesting
Pick the fruits as soon as they are ripe, harvesting whole trusses whenever possible. If they are not ripe, pick the currants individually before they spoil. Use immediately.

BLACKBERRIES/LOGANBERRIES
Many people think of blackberries as essentially fruits which grow wild in the hedgerows and, being so freely available, are not worthy of garden space. In fact, cultivated blackberries are far bigger, juicier and tastier than their wild-growing cousins and they have such a wide use in cooking and jam, jelly and wine-making that it is well-worth finding space for a few canes. There are many different varieties of blackberry.

Loganberries are apparently the result of an accidental cross between a blackberry and a raspberry that occurred in California in the late nineteenth century in the garden of a Judge Logan. The resulting berries are a dark red colour and may be eaten raw or used for cooking

Harvesting currants: it is far less painstaking, and better for storage, if you pick whole currant trusses at one time **(left)**. The berries can be picked individually **(above)** if only half the fruits on the trusses are ripe.

Harvesting berries: blackberries **(top)** are very soft and so should be handled carefully when they are picked. The trusses can be cut, or the berries can be picked individually. Always use them quickly before they become too damaged. Loganberries **(right)** are ripe when they have turned a dark red. They are harvested in the same way as blackberries.

purposes. They are cultivated, trained and propagated in exactly the same way as blackberries.

Soil and position
Blackberries will grow in any soil, although those that are slightly acid and rich in humus will produce the largest crops. Similarly, they will grow just about anywhere, even in a north-facing site, and they can be trained over the walls of a shed or along a fence to form a hedge. The largest yields, however, will come from those grown in an open, sunny position.

Planting and routine care
Plant blackberry canes as outlined on page 104, preferably in late autumn. Dig lots of well-rotted organic matter into the soil a month or so before planting. It is worthwhile preparing the site well, because blackberries

Weaving sytem: as current season's canes grow, train them to weave in and out of rows of wires. As the new canes appear, train them to grow along the top wire.

134

PESTS AND DISEASES/BLACKBERRIES AND LOGANBERRIES

Raspberry beetle

Identification: maggots tunnel into the fruits, making them distorted and useless.
Treatment: spray with recommended proprietary mixtures as the fruits begin to change colour.

Cane spot

Identification: a fungus which causes purple spots to appear on the canes. These later change to white and the cane eventually splits.
Treatment: cut out and burn badly infected canes and spray with recommended proprietary mixtures.

Spur blight

Identification: another fungus disease which also causes purple spots on canes. The leaves wither and canes snap in bad cases.
Treatment: cut out and burn canes and spray others with recommended proprietary mixtures.

can remain in the same place for ten years or more. Place canes about 2 metres (6 ft) apart (slightly less for smaller canes; more for the more vigorous varieties) and provide supports in the form of horizontal wires stretched behind them.

Water well in dry weather and keep the ground around the roots free of weeds. Mulch each spring with well-rotted manure or compost.

The number you grow depends on the varieties you choose – one cane of a vigorous variety can produce over 9 kg (20 lb) of fruit in a year. Smaller varieties will yield only half this amount.

Training and pruning
As the canes grow, tie them into the wire in whatever shape you like (see diagram). It is the one-year-old canes which produce fruit each year, so as these grow during the spring and summer, tie them into the wires to keep them separate from the current season's fruiting canes. After harvesting, cut out all that year's fruiting canes at ground level. If necessary, retie the new growth.

Harvesting
Blackberries ripen any time from late July to October, depending on the variety. Pick them when they are ripe, handling them carefully so as not to crush them. Use them in whatever way you have planned straightaway, as they will quickly turn soft and mushy.

Raising new plants
Bend over a new shoot in July or August and bury the tip in about 10–15 cm (4–6 in) of soil, holding it in place with a stone. Cut it away from the parent plant in early winter, when it has rooted, and replant it in its permanent site the following spring.

Alternative sides: train current season's canes to grow along one side of the wires, in a fan shape. Train the new canes, as they form, to grow along the other side.

Keeping Animals

KEEPING LIVESTOCK can be a delight that provides you with marvellous, highly nutritious and tasty produce as well as a number of animal friends, or it can be a nightmare of worry and grief that could well turn out to cost you infinitely more money than any you might make or save. Your attitude and how you tackle individual problems as they arise will determine which of these two situations apply.

The first thing to remember is

that keeping any livestock is a responsibility. The happiness and welfare of the animals is in your hands and even if you eventually mean to put them on the table in a tasty casserole, it is inexcusable not to give them a happy existence while they are alive. Although many people with smallholdings believe that they are saving their animals from living in battery, or highly intensive, conditions, they may be inflicting just as much cruelty through sheer ignorance of their animals' habits. In every case of livestock discussed in the following pages, from bees to pigs, always ensure that you have the necessary conditions, including housing, ready before they arrive.

On the subject of housing and living requirements, it is worthwhile pointing out that there are ideal hen houses, pig sties or rabbit hutches, and others that are perfectly adequate. If you live in a house which has a number of outbuildings or farmyard sheds and barns, always adapt these for the livestock you want to keep. .

Your animals will be happiest if you can keep them in conditions that emulate their natural life as closely as possible. Happy animals are good, healthy animals, and ones that give you the least trouble. But, remember, it is your animals that should fit in with you, not the other way round.

The feeding of animals is a subject on which it is always difficult to give hard and fast rules, mainly because animals are as individual as people. They have their likes and dislikes in food, as well as differences in appetite and individual feeding habits. The answer is to spend time watching your animals; see what they do and do not like and then pander to them whenever you are able. Whilst watching them, observe whether they seem to be losing or gaining weight and let this guide you, too,

towards how much to feed. Remember that they appreciate some variety in their diet.

The subject of illness and disease has scarcely been touched upon in this section. This is for two reasons: firstly, because any disease in animals is best dealt with by practical advice from a vet; secondly, because animals kept on a small scale in clean, healthy surroundings should seldom succumb to disease. You will generally find sunshine, fresh air and good food to be the best antidotes to disease. The rule is that if you notice anything wrong with your livestock isolate them to stop the problem spreading to the others and call the vet.

The economics of keeping animals to produce cheap, or free, food can come under heavy questioning. For example, few people would claim that their eggs or their honey cost them nothing, or that their pork was vastly cheaper than any they could buy. The point about home-produced food of this sort is that it is of an infinitely higher quality than any available in the shops.

Killing any animal is unpleasant and it is made even more so when you are, in effect, killing an old friend. However, it is something that you must harden yourself to, unless you want a garden full of geriatric animals!

It is a good idea to keep records of your animals – to write down how much honey the bees produced and when it was collected; the amount of milk your goats give night and morning through the year; the number of eggs you get each day, and so on. By doing so you can spot irregularities and changes when they occur.

Do not try to become a poultry-keeper, bee-keeper, goat-keeper, pig-keeper and rabbit-keeper all in one week. Do it slowly, getting used to the habits, ties and commitments of one type of animal at a time, making sure you can fit them easily into your daily routine. If you try to do everything at once, you will have disaster on your hands, and everything will go wrong. Finally, never keep animals of any type unless you are prepared to get your hands dirty!

Before keeping any of the animals discussed on the following pages, you should check with the local authorities to ensure you are not contravening any by-laws.

Keeping Pigs

IT IS COMMONLY SAID of keeping pigs that they are either 'muck or money'. This chiefly refers to the price of pork, which fluctuates almost more than any other foodstuff. Thus, if you keep pigs to sell (and if you breed you are likely to do so, for a sow will have eight or ten piglets each time she farrows and it would be nigh on impossible for one family to eat all of these!) this is a point that must be carefully considered. If kept in the right conditions, pigs are fairly easy animals to keep and rear, but are really hard work. The mucking-out of the house, which is at least a daily chore, is very heavy work and the pigs are extremely strong animals. I know of one lady, who, when she found herself looking after the household's pigs, devised a system of getting them into the yard – without going into it herself – by unhooking the door from outside the fence, and when the pigs were all safely in the yard eating, she would nip into the house and shut herself in to clean it. She never, therefore, came into direct contact with the pigs, which was purely, as she said, because they are quite strong enough to bowl you over in their enthusiasm to get to their food or their freedom.

Living requirements

There are three main ways in which you can keep pigs: the first is in a concrete sty, the second is in a permanent yard and the third is free-range. The first of these should not be considered, because it is unspeakably cruel. Pigs live by the snout – that is, their whole life consists of rootling through the ground; to deny them this by keeping them on concrete is unforgivable. The second is probably the method most people will have to adopt as few will have enough land to keep them free-range. The free-range system is in many ways the best, and for anybody who has a large amount of land – say 2.4 hectares (6 acres) or more – it is ideal, because pigs are the best cultivators of all; better by far than any mechanical equipment which is subject to breakdown. They will hunt out all the roots – weeds and all – turning the ground over and fertilizing it at the same time. In addition, when you come to kill and eat them, you will have the most delicious-tasting pork imaginable. The only way to obtain free-range pork is to keep pigs this way yourself. Such meat is never sold in butchers' shops.

In the free-range system, about ten pigs can be kept in an area of approximately 0.2 hectares (0.5 acres). When they have done their work of cultivating it, or the sow has a new litter, they should be moved on again. They should not be returned to that piece of land for at least three years, for the parasites that attack them will remain in the soil for this amount of time. These parasites, incidentally, are no threat to other types of livestock.

If there is no alternative but to keep pigs in a yard, it is a good idea to throw dried bracken, straw, etc, onto the ground every now and then, for the pigs to rootle through and turn over. Mud will not bother them – they love it. Obviously the size of the yard will determine the number of pigs you keep, as they should not be crowded. Your common sense and powers of observation should tell you whether they have enough room.

Whichever of these two systems you are adopting, the fencing and housing requirements are the same. Fencing is probably the most important aspect of keeping pigs, because they are great escapers. If the yard is bricked around to a height of 1 metre (3 ft 6 in), it is probably fairly secure. Failing this, it should be fenced with strong pig wire secured to posts (or corrugated iron bolted to them) that are driven very firmly into the ground. Pigs will lean against the fence and rub against it, soon dislodging the stakes and weakening the whole structure, unless it is really strong and firm. At the bottom there should be at least one strand of barbed wire to stop them nosing their way through underneath. The fence should be about 1.2 metres (4 ft) high; pigs can jump, and will do so, particularly if they are frightened!

Should your pigs escape (and you will be an exceptional pig-keeper if they never do), they are the easiest animals in the world to retrieve. Providing they know you and you have a bucket of their favourite food, they will follow you to the ends of the earth.

Housing for pigs can be as simple or as sophisticated

One of the simplest and best shelters is called the Roadnight Shelter **(left)**. It consists of one blocked wall – in this case, wooden – and one open with a curved roof of corrugated iron. A very effective method of preventing pigs from straying is to fence them in with pig wire **(above)**. If it is very firmly staked to wooden posts, the pigs will find it impenetrable.

BREEDS OF PIG

Large white
Long legged, large boned pig which is a fast grower and an efficient converter of food into meat. Makes good, lean bacon.

Gloucester Old Spot
White pig with black spots. Good at grazing and will eat grass and vegetables. Although hardy, it produces small litters.

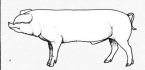

Landrace
Long and lean white breed with floppy ears and short legs. Very docile and make excellent mothers. Good for lean bacon.

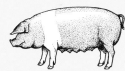

Saddleback
Black pig with a band of white across the shoulders. Very hardy all-purpose pig. Sows give milk plentifully.

Welsh
A very old lop-eared breed of Western England, which makes a good mother. Being small, it eats less than the Large White.

Large black
Black pig with deep sides. Hardy and economical to feed. Copes well in hot weather.

as you care to make it. As ever, the chief criteria are that it should be dry and draught-proof. The simplest form of housing, used to great effect by many, is a shelter constructed of bales of straw and topped with corrugated iron. If you have a shed, so much the better, particularly if the roof is covered with asbestos roofing material rather than corrugated iron, which tends to get rather hot in the summer, because pigs hate heat. Earth floors are fine. By and large, pigs do not soil their living quarters, preferring to do this outside, so the house should not get too evil (there are always exceptions!). Another alternative is a concrete floor, covered with wood – concrete on its own is somewhat cold. In either event, a layer of straw as bedding will be appreciated. Ideally you should be able to shut the pigs in, but if one side of the shed is open, make sure it is not in the direction of the prevailing wind or driving rain.

Although pigs prefer not to soil their sleeping quarters, this area should still be cleaned out daily, because if they are shut in at night they will muck somewhere. It will make your job of cleaning out easier if the accommodation is tall enough for you to stand up inside it.

Acquiring pigs

As with all livestock, it is best to acquire your pigs from a local farmer or dealer. Thus, the breed you buy will depend on what he has. Bear in mind that some of the new breeds, developed specifically to give the best (ie most) meat production, could be rather more highly-strung and susceptible to disease than some of the more old-fashioned types, owing to the intensive selective breeding to which they have been subjected. The Large White is a good and popular breed, as is the Landrace. Crosses between these two are also good pigs to keep, and all these breeds are renowned for being good-tempered.

There are two possible systems for small-time pig-keepers to adopt. One is to buy eight-week-old weaners, keep them for ten to twelve weeks (or longer if you prefer), and then slaughter them, and the other is to keep

Right: you can build a sty for your pigs if you wish to improve their living conditions. This can easily be constructed from building blocks, with a corrugated iron roof. If supplying windows, place them near the roof of the sty, opening outwards from the bottom, so the pigs have ventilation without a draught. The yard is easy to clean out and gives the pigs some exercise.

a sow and breed from her. The first method is undoubtedly the most economic and also the least trouble. It also means you can keep just a couple of pigs to eat yourself, and you can sell the rest.

Feeding

Most people will be unable to grow sufficient quantities of the root vegetables and potatoes on which pigs live, and will have to feed them supplementary grain. If you are aiming to fatten pigs for slaughter, then in any event you must give them some supplementary feeding. The best form of concentrates are the commercially-prepared pig nuts, but these are not cheap. (A point to bear in mind when assessing the economics of keeping pigs.) Eight-week-old weaners will need about 900 g (2 lb) of these per day, given in a morning and evening feed. This amount should gradually be increased to 1.8–2 kg (4–4$\frac{1}{2}$lb) by the time they are about four months old. A sow wanted for breeding will want more and then still more while she is pregnant and feeding her piglets. In addition she will want milk (preferably from goats if you keep them).

Besides their concentrates, pigs will appreciate a variety of other foodstuffs. Root vegetables are very important – Jerusalem artichokes, swedes (rutabagas), turnips, parsnips and so on – and these can be grown in their yard or patch of land so they can dig them out themselves. They like potatoes (although these are more digestible if boiled), and they appreciate some greenstuff. You can provide this by giving them cuttings from hawthorn or beech trees for example, or nettles. Other things they like are apples (windfalls), comfrey, grass, clover, any of the brassica greens and scraps of cooked meat or fish. It is sometimes possible to obtain factory throw-outs to feed to pigs. I have heard of one person who fed his pigs almost entirely on reject crumpets, and another who fattened his on turkish delight! (Make sure, if you adopt this system, that you do give the pigs their daily rations of nutritious food as well.) If the pigs are free-range and still clearing the ground, they will really only need the supplementary corn – the rest they should be able to forage for themselves.

Pigs drink lots of water, but unlike other animals such as goats, this does not have to be sparkling clean and clear. A very good, and most valuable, source of nutrition is the washing-up water from dirty plates, providing, that is, that no washing-up liquid or detergent was used. Give the water in troughs and make sure there is always enough in them.

Farrowing rails: these are essential at breeding times to prevent the sow from lying on her piglets **(right)**. A more sophisticated system can be made at home **(below)** from wood.

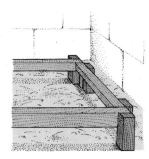

Drinking troughs: pigs must be given a lot of water which they can drink out of sturdy troughs. Check there is always enough water in them.

FEEDING PIGS			
System	**Housing**	**Feeding**	**Other Requirements**
Grazing out of doors	Hut made from straw bales or Roadnight corrugated shelter. Land can be reclaimed with this system.	If grass plentiful, feed once a day with meal or concentrated food, depending on pigs. Fresh water.	Sheltered, deep bedding. Electric or pig wire fences.
Limited grazing	Ark or movable house with yard or pigsty. Bring in at night.	Supplement food obtained from grazing. Swill is acceptable.	Deep bedding in the sty. Excellent fencing required.
Tethering	Movable house with tether accessible.	Supplement grass, feeding accordingly.	Deep bedding in hut. Harness, tether, chain, swivel, and stake.
Cottage sty and yard	Wood, brick or blocks 2.4 m × 2.4 m × 1.5 m (8 ft × 8 ft × 5 ft) to eaves with concrete yard sloping to drain.	Swill, garden waste, potatoes and comfrey. Give turf for minerals.	Troughs for food and water. Deep bedding in huts. Barrow and shovel for mucking out.

Management and breeding

Your pigs should give you remarkably little trouble and need very little attention. In hot weather, however, throw a bucket of water over them and another onto the ground. They dig holes in the ground to sleep in and they like these to be damp.

If you do want to breed from a sow, let her have one season first (this will be at about six months old), and then breed from her when she is about a year old. It is possible to artificially inseminate pigs, although the timing is critical, and you must be sure of what you are doing, too. The alternative is to take her to a local pig-breeder, providing he is willing to take her (some will not, because of the risk of infection). He will generally let her run with his boar for a few days until he reckons she has been served.

Gestation is 14 to 16 weeks, and a pig will usually have between 8 and 10 piglets, which she can rear easily. Shut her in the shed or house to have her litter. It is always a good idea to construct a farrowing rail in the shed where the sow is to farrow, to stop her lying on her piglets and crushing them. This is an arrangement of very strong bars, which should be raised about 22 cm (9 in) from the ground and sited a similar distance away from the wall. It must be strong – old iron bed rails are ideal – and firmly bracketed to the wall, or the pig will merely get her snout underneath it and wrench it free. The farrowing rails should be sited along the two walls of the sow's favourite corner of the shed, which is where she is most likely to have her piglets. It is a good idea too, to stack straw bales with gaps between them (like houses of cards) against the other two walls. Then, if the sow does move over there at any time, the piglets can escape into the straw. Lying on the piglets is no wilful act on the part of the sow; it is merely that she is so big and they are so small that she crushes them all too easily. An infra-red lamp (with a red bulb) suspended over one corner of the shed, where the piglets can get to but the sow cannot, is an extremely good idea. The piglets are then only likely to bother the sow when they want feeding, not having to seek warmth from her too. This is another way to help prevent them getting crushed by her lying on top of them.

The sow must be fed well and the piglets should be weaned when they are four weeks old. Male piglets should also be castrated at this time, otherwise the pork will be tainted – a condition known as boar taint. Castration is a pretty unpleasant job and will probably be one for the vet, although many backyard pig-keepers save money by doing it themselves.

Pigs can either be sold when they are about 12 weeks old, as previously mentioned, when they generally weigh about 40 kg (90 lb) and are known as porkers, or kept until they are about 72 kg (160 lb), when they are known as baconers.

A point to bear in mind: those who keep pigs on the small scale we are considering here do say that breeding pigs and fattening them are two different skills. It may be that you are good at both of them, but more usually you will be better at one than the other.

Killing a pig

The best and most acceptable way of killing pigs is to take them to the local slaughterhouse, or you may be able to find a local butcher to kill them for you. You can then have the meat you want (butchered and ready to go in the deep freeze) and sell the rest.

Keeping Goats

GOATS ARE BETTER back-yard animals to keep for milk than cows. They are cheaper and easier to care for, being more adaptable to varying living conditions, requiring less space and, by and large, less work. They give adequate milk yields – those labelled high-yielders will give up to 8 litres (14 pints) in summer, down to 1.2–1.8 litres (2–3 pints) in the winter – and providing they are properly fed and cared for, and milked in hygienic conditions, their milk will not be smelly or highly flavoured, as it is often reputed to be. In fact, few people could tell it from cows' milk, yet it has the advantage that it does not carry the tuberculosis bacillus. Besides making excellent cheese and yoghurt, it is also proven in many instances to help sufferers from such complaints as eczema and asthma. The other claim by antagonists that goats smell is really only applicable to male goats (billies) and most people would be advised not to keep them anyway, because they can be very temperamental and are only used to serve female goats (nannies).

If there is a branch of the Goat Society nearby, it is a good idea to join. They will give good advice about breeds as well as the practical aspect of goat-keeping.

Living requirements

Goats need a dry, draught-proof shed, preferably with a divided stable-type door, the bottom half of which should be about 1.2 metres (4 ft) high. If there is a window, it should be positioned high up and preferably hinged at the bottom to give ventilation without draughts. The floor should be concrete, and slope slightly to the back of the shed to aid drainage (there should be a couple of drainage holes for this, too). The size of the shed will depend on what space you have to devote to it, how many goats you are keeping, and so on. The basic requirement is that goats can stand up, turn round and lie down, but as they hate cold, windy or wet weather and on such days are best shut in the shed, it is kinder to provide them with a little more space. A shed 3 × 4.5 metres (10 × 15 ft) gives ample space in which three grown-up goats can move around.

There should be a hay rack on the wall (hung quite high, as goats are browsers rather than grazers, and therefore naturally reach upwards for food) and the floor should be kept covered in straw. Keep adding to this as it gets dirty and then clean it out when the floor level has raised 30–45 cm (12–18 in). Stack the dirty straw neatly and let it rot – it makes excellent garden manure.

Goats should be shut in the shed at night, but during the day they can be kept in one of two ways: either in a well-fenced run, or tethered in places that provide suitable food. If using the former method, the area will have to be rested from time to time to give it a chance to recover, so you must have at least a couple of such areas to devote to the goats. Fencing must be very strong; either drive thick wooden posts 60 cm (2 ft) into the ground and secure strong wire netting (that used for fencing sheep, not chickens, or goats will merely trample their way through it) between them, so that the fence is a good 1.5 metres (5 ft) high, or erect solid, closely-spaced paling fencing.

If you have access to lots of hedgerow land, where goats can safely be tethered, or alternatively have a lot of spare, scrubby land you want grazed, you can tether them in a different spot each day. Make sure there are no poisonous plants in reach, such as rhododendrons, privet, laurel, yew, ragwort or laburnum. Surprisingly, ivy is safe for them to eat, and oak leaves are manna to

goats. They also like flowers, vegetables and fruit trees – of which they will make incredibly short work, so keep them well away from any of these that you value.

In the winter, it is often advisable to keep goats in a concrete yard (providing them with food and tethering them out when you can). Muddy conditions can lead to foot troubles.

Acquiring goats

Note the plural in the heading – it is not fair to keep a single goat. They are sociable, gregarious and friendly, and one on its own will be miserable. Over two, have as many as you want, according to the land and time you have available and the amount of milk you need. The breed you have is largely a matter of personal choice, although some are renowned for giving higher yields than others, such as Saanen and British Alpine. It is best to be guided in this by what is available locally and by the advice of knowledgeable goat owners in the district.

You can get them from any age – as young as four weeks – if you have lots of time to devote to looking after them and do not want milk for 18 months or so. If you want milk from a goat straightaway, you will have to get one which has kidded (after which she goes on producing milk for about two years). The advantage of getting a young goat, apart from the cheaper cost (but weigh that against the cost of keeping her until she comes into milk) is that she will get thoroughly used to you, particularly if you give her the loving care and attention she likes to receive.

Feeding

Another misconception about goats is that they will eat anything. It is when they are forced into a bad diet that they give smelly, bad-tasting milk. In fact, they are very fussy eaters and will not, for example, eat anything that has dropped on the floor of their shed. Basically, goats need a meal night and morning of some sort of con-

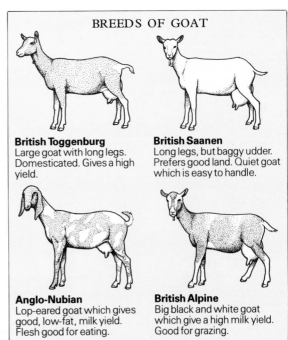

BREEDS OF GOAT

British Toggenburg
Large goat with long legs. Domesticated. Gives a high yield.

British Saanen
Long legs, but baggy udder. Prefers good land. Quiet goat which is easy to handle.

Anglo-Nubian
Lop-eared goat which gives good, low-fat, milk yield. Flesh good for eating.

British Alpine
Big black and white goat which give a high milk yield. Good for grazing.

KEEPING GOATS

System	Housing	Feeding	Other Requirements
Out of doors	Dry, draught-proof shed. Deep bedding to cut draughts. Should equal outside temperature to encourage growth of winter coat.	Roughage available from grazing. Provide hay at night. Feed concentrates when giving milk.	Salt licks. Access to water. Frequent inspection and handling to keep tame.
Strip grazing, rotational grazing.	Provide shelter although undercoat will protect from rain. Shut in at night.	Allows for fresh grass feeding. Strip grazed kale available in winter. Keep concentrates in dry bins and hay in airy shed.	Electric fencing with three wires 38 cm, 68 cm, and 100 cm (15 in, 27 in, 40 in) above ground. Salt licks.
Tethering with shed (not for young)	Roomy shed for when not tethered. Platform for play and exercise.	Move frequently to allow fresh grazing with bushes and branches available. Provide hay for shortage of feed.	Wide collar; tether-chain, swivel, harness and stake. Shade in sunny weather. Access to water and salt.
Yarding with shed	Both shed and yard as large as possible. Fence or wall for looking out but keeping them in.	Provide good variety; a garden for greens and grass from the roadside.	Take for walks for exercise and food. Salt licks and seaweed mineral supplements.
Indoors	Roomy pen with light and air. Sleeping platform.	Branches tied and suspended from ceiling. Scraps of bread and vegetables.	Walks for exercise.

Feeding: when goats are kept in a shed they must be given hay to replace their natural fodder. It should be placed in a rack above their heads **(above)**, because goats are naturally browsers and not grazers. In the wild, they will reach up to nibble branches **(below)**.

centrated food, which could be a formulated dairy food or one that your supplier mixes for you. It should contain broad bran, crushed oats and flaked maize, and possibly any of the following – peas, beans, molasses, barley, linseed cake and salt. This should be mixed with some root vegetables and greens; make friends with a local greengrocer and persuade him to let you have the offcuts from greens, rotting apples (dessert-types) and mouldy oranges – goats love them all! Midday snacks of sugar beet are also appreciated. Always feed goats in a metal bucket or bowl – they can become partial to plastic.

How much to give depends a lot on the age, size and temperament of the individual goat and what else she is eating during the day. Find out what her daily diet has been when you buy her, and gradually change or increase this as necessary. Concentrates are important for milk production, but if you feed too much they will be wasted, because they will not increase milk production over and above what is the normal average for that particular breed.

Clean drinking water must be readily available and the container will need frequent washing and cleaning. Goats will not drink from a slimy bucket.

Make sure hay is always provided in the hay rack in the shed, particularly if they are going out to eat on lush pastures during the day. Far from providing goodness, rich grass will just fill an empty belly with water and can cause bloat. In fact, it is unwise to let goats graze on really lush meadows for more than one hour a day. They also need a salt or mineral block to lick.

Feeding goats: if feeding goats concentrated food, always give it to them in a trough. This is much less wasteful than spreading it around on the floor.

CLIPPING HOOFS

Goats' feet must be trimmed every three weeks or so, or they will grow too long. The operation is best done by two people, with one to talk to and soothe the goat while the other does the cutting **(below)**. Proper shears **(right)** make the job easier (the horn is quite tough), although it can be done with a pruning knife. Always cut the hoof carefully.

Milk production and milking

Although it is not uncommon for a maiden goat to come into milk, goats will not normally do so until they have kidded. The first mating should generally be left until they are 15 to 18 months old (some people claim goats can be mated as young as 7 months and, providing they are properly fed, will suffer no ill-effects thereafter; others say this will stunt their growth). When they come into season – recognizable by much wagging of the tail, loud bleating, general nervousness and unease, and maybe a slight mucus discharge from the vulva – they should be taken to a billy as soon as possible. Make sure you choose a good one. The highest success rate in matings occur if the nanny is serviced early in her season. They come into season every 21 days, usually between September and February.

Gestation is about 5 months (155 days) and if you are milking the goat, stop two months before she is due to kid. Goats generally manage the birth quite happily if left alone, and usually produce two kids. If one (or both) is a billy, decide whether to get rid of him, or rear and fatten him for the table. He should be killed at about four months old and will taste a bit like lamb. Kids are usually taken away from their mothers soon after birth and hand-reared.

Milking must be done night and morning, every day of the year, and the loud bleatings will tell you when it is time! You should have a milking shed, separate from the goats' living quarters, which is kept immaculately clean.

A good procedure for milking is to brush the goat to remove all dust, wisps of hay, etc from her coat which might otherwise fall into the milk, and then take her to the milking shed. You will find it easier if you have a raised platform on which she stands for milking (goats are very low to the ground, which can make milking

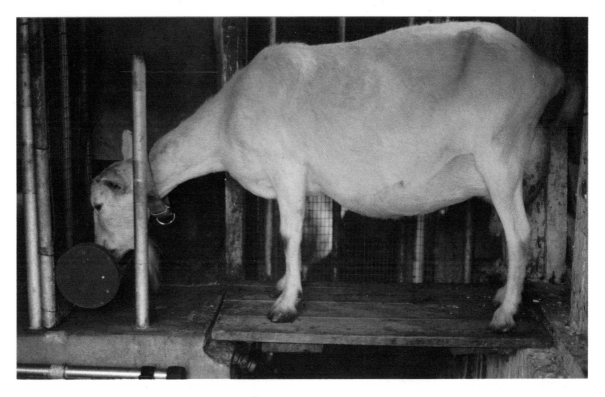

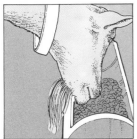

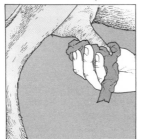

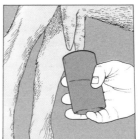

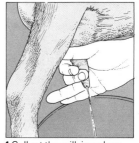

Milking goats: 1 Before the goat is milked, brush her coat and then take her to the milking shed. Give her some food to distract her attention.

2 Wash the udders with a clean, sterilized cloth before milking. Run your hands around the udders so that they are warm, and she is used to you.

3 Collect the first milk in a small bowl. It cleans and clears the flow. Throw it away, or it could turn the rest of the milk sour very quickly.

4 Collect the milk in a clean stainless steel bowl. Squeeze the teats unless they are small, when they should be pulled up and down.

tricky!). Lead her on to this and give her a feed to keep her occupied and still. Wash her udders with a clean, sterilized cloth and put a stainless steel bowl (buckets are considerably more expensive and often too tall to fit under a goat) beneath her. Run your hands round her udders to warm them and get her used to you, then give a couple of squeezes on each teat. This first milk should be wasted, because it cleans and clears the flow, so do not let it fall into the bowl. Also, as this milk has been in closest contact with the outside air, it could be rather warm, particularly in summer.

The milking technique is to gently squeeze and release the teats – a bit like squeezing a sponge – rather than to pull them up and down. If your hands are big and the goat's teats are small, however, you will find you have to pull the teats up and down; squeezing them will

be ineffective. As you get near the end of the supply, massage the udder and squeeze the teats hard to bring down the final drop. You will not hurt the goat, however hard you squeeze her teats.

The milk should be covered immediately with a clean tea towel, and then the goat taken to her day- or night-time quarters before she gets a chance to kick over the bowl. Strain the milk straightaway through a sterilized milk filter (available from goat suppliers) and cool it by placing it in its container in a large bowl of very cold water (or in the fridge), and then put it into a churn or jugs. It will keep fresh for two or three days, but it must always be kept covered as it picks up other flavours very easily. Alternatively you can freeze it as soon as it is cold – it will not separate and will keep for up to six months, or you can make cheese (see page 209).

Keeping Chickens

CHICKENS ARE POSSIBLY the easiest of all animals to keep and must be about the most productive. Not only do they provide you with lovely fresh eggs, but once they have outlived their egg-laying usefulness, they make excellent eating themselves. They need not take up much room or much of your time and if you have access to a lot of household scraps (scrounge them from your neighbours too), they can be quite economical to feed. However, be prepared for a fairly high initial outlay when you begin your hen-keeping venture. Proper hen houses are extremely expensive to buy (although they must be among the easiest of all animal accommodation to make yourself), chicken wire for fencing is very costly, and the hens themselves are by no means cheap to acquire.

One of the great advantages of keeping chickens is that it is usually very easy to get someone to look after them if you want to go away – a point that must be borne in mind when keeping livestock of any type. Whilst people might be reluctant to come and milk the goats or feed the pigs, they are almost always willing to shut the hens in at night, let them out in the morning and feed them, in exchange for the eggs the hens lay while you are away. Be prepared to come back to a messy hen house though – few neighbours will regard cleaning it as part of the bargain!

A less pleasant aspect is that chickens do fall unwell with various diseases and ailments, and by observing your flock, you will notice when things are wrong. You must, therefore, have someone in the house who can wring their necks when it is necessary – do not be like one person I know who took a chicken to the vet and asked him to put it down! In addition, it is not uncommon to go to the hen house in the morning and find that a hen has died in the night for no apparent reason. Just remove it, but do not eat it as it will not have been bled (ie the blood will not have drained from its veins as it does when you wring its neck and hang it – see page 150).

Living requirements

As always, you must have everything ready for your chickens before they arrive, and this means deciding how you are going to keep them. There are many different ways of keeping chickens, and they all have their pros and cons. The best thing to do is to decide which is the most convenient for you and be prepared for the people who tell you you are doing the wrong thing! Chickens can be kept free-range – that is, they have a house in which they are shut at night, but during the day they are allowed to wander and scratch at will. This is undoubtedly the best way from the hens' point of view – all poultry will be happiest and healthiest if allowed to wander at will. It also cuts down your feeding bills and provides you with the best eggs of all, but it is seldom practical for most backyard or garden hen-keepers. The area over which they roam will soon resemble a meadow – there will be no recognizable vegetable plot and little else of value to you.

A good alternative is to keep hens in movable arks – that is, a hen house complete with a fairly small covered run – the whole construction being moved every few days to a new spot. This is probably only practical if you have a fairly large area, such as an orchard, that you can use in this way, but it is undoubtedly very satisfactory as the hens continually have new ground at which to peck.

Finally, they can also be kept indoors all the time (the

shed will need to be larger than hen houses used in the other systems) on a sort of deep-litter system, or they can be kept permanently in a well-fenced run which also contains their house.

The last system is the one likely to be favoured by most people. If possible, it is better to have two areas that can be used as a run (perhaps side by side, with the hen house in the middle – providing it has access on both sides) so that the grass in one area will have a chance to revive while the other is in use. If this is not possible, because the area you have to spare is too small, you can keep hens in the same run permanently, although this is not ideal. It will not be the best-looking corner of your garden, but properly kept, it need not be an eyesore. Digging it out to a depth of 15 cm (6 in) and covering it with cinders and clinker, or gravel, can help.

The run should be fenced with galvanized wire erected to a height of 1.5–1.8 metres (5–6 ft). Bury it 30 cm (1 ft) or so into the ground to stop the hens scratching their way out and foxes burrowing their way in. Make sure the posts to which the wire is attached are firm in the ground. Obviously there must be a gate for you to go in and out, and if it is wide enough to take a wheelbarrow, cleaning out the hen house will be made that much easier.

Designs of hen houses are infinite, ranging from the very sophisticated (and expensive) to the home-made, constructed from bits of old timber, spare roofing felt, wire netting, etc. These are cheap, but perfectly adequate. Old sheds can easily be converted into magnif-

Hen houses: these can vary
from being ramshackle but
serviceable to quite
sophisticated, whether
movable or permanent.
Floor: raised off the ground
for ventilation and shelter for
the birds in bad weather.
Opening: preferably two —
one for you and one for the
chickens, but must be shut
up at night. **Windows:** for
light and ventilation. Could be
small holes in wall. **Roosting
perch;** for hens to roost at
night. If two perches, stagger
them or put at same height.
Laying boxes: one per three
or four birds.

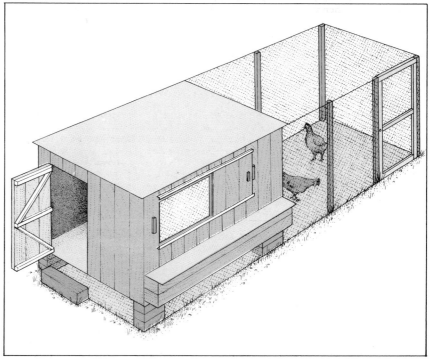

BREEDS OF CHICKEN

Rhode Island Reds
Fairly large birds able to
stand tough winters.
Prolific layers.

Marans
Pretty, plump birds,
good for eating. Lay
dark brown eggs.

Buff Rocks
Fairly large, with yellow
feathers. Lay tinted
eggs.

White Leghorn
Small white birds
which give white eggs.
Not very popular.

Light Sussex
Quite large pale brown
birds. Give brown
eggs.

icent hen houses. If your flock of hens numbers no more than about a dozen or so, there is no need for you to be able to stand up in the house, as long as you can reach in all parts of it to clean it, although this operation is undoubtedly easier if you can stand up.

Clean out the hen house and the droppings underneath as necessary. In dry summer weather, this will probably be about every six weeks. In wet weather and the winter, it will need doing more frequently if it is not to be smelly and unpleasant.

Opinions differ about the treatment of the run; some people are quite happy to leave it as it is (dusty and uneven in the summer, muddy and boggy in the winter), while others prefer to cover the ground with such things as dry bracken, dead leaves, general garden weeds and rubbish, in which the hens can scratch. Periodically this is raked up and composted. If you do not cover the run in this way, it will need digging over in the winter and covering with limestone granules, which you can buy. This will help to keep the run broken up and not too muddy. The hens will love it when you are digging, following closely behind you to grab the juicy worms.

Acquiring hens

There are various ways of acquiring hens; you can buy them as day-old chicks, point-of-lay pullets or older battery hens that have passed their peak of laying but will still continue to lay eggs for some time.

Day-old chicks: these are the cheapest to buy, but of course they have to be fed for up to six months before they start laying. The mortality rate is often quite high (out of seven, a friend has two left; five died in the first few weeks), and you do not know how disease-prone they are likely to be. They also need lots of care and attention. Some people say they must be kept in some sort of incubator, although this is not necessary if you are prepared to keep them in a warm box in the kitchen, out of the way of cats and children.

Point-of-lay pullets: these are chickens that are about six months old and have just come into lay. They will lay for you as soon as they have settled down, which can be up to two or three weeks, but is usually only a matter of days. By and large, they are the best bet, particularly for novice chicken-keepers. They are likely to be healthy and, providing you keep them properly, should remain that way. They are the most expensive to buy, but you do get an instant return, in the form of eggs.

Battery hens: this is a cheap way of getting hens. Battery farms sell them off when they are about 18 months old, and a sorry sight they are too, likely to be bald in places, with long claws from a lifetime of no scratching, and ugly clipped beaks lest they peck each other. They are unable at first to scratch, take a dust bath, perch, or anything. These instincts will soon return, and in a few weeks they will have changed completely. It is not a method of acquiring chickens which is wholly recommended though, because they could be diseased and many quite often die.

Whichever hens you buy, get them all at once. It is not generally a good idea to introduce new hens from an outside source into the flock, although many people will exclaim immediately that they have done so with no ill effects. If you buy them at different times and from different places, you could well bring in disease, infecting others that were healthy.

Deciding which breed or breeds to have will largely be a matter of whether you want brown or white eggs. It is better to go for hens that are known to do well in your area. Buy locally, if you can, from someone who has a reputation to protect.

The whole subject of breeds in chickens is one that has seen enormous changes in recent times, with the advent of intensive battery chicken production. Some people say the pure breeds of chicken are really only kept alive today by the poultry shows, while the breeds most commonly seen are hybrids produced by intensive selective breeding. The aim has been to produce birds which will lay the maximum number of eggs and this has been done at the expense of broodiness. Many of today's commercial breeds simply will not go broody; if you do want to breed from your chickens, it is perhaps safer to try to find one of the old-fashioned pure breeds.

Unless you want a lot of surplus eggs, you can estimate how many chickens you need on the basis of two hens per egg-eating person in the family. Be prepared for your egg consumption to go up if you keep chickens – it usually does!

The only real reason for keeping a cockerel with hens is if you want to produce chicks, although it is a good idea with free-range hens, as a cock will keep his hens in order. Controversy rages fiercely over whether hens are happier with a cockerel or not! By and large he appears to make their lives a misery, bossing them around and pecking them at random. A cockerel has a far more voracious appetite than his hens, so is much more expensive to keep, and if the hens will go broody, it is just possible he will turn the whole pack so at one time! In addition, his early-morning crowing can quite often upset neighbours.

Broody hens are instantly recognizable – they refuse

148

to move from the nesting boxes, sitting tight and clucking gently, they go off their food and they lay no eggs. Warm weather from April onwards is the time to watch for this. If you do not want a hen to be broody, put her in a cold box on her own, with no straw so she can not make a nest, and placed where she can see the others. Let her out at feeding time and check a little later whether she has gone back to the laying box. If she has, put her back in the isolated box.

Feeding and daily routine

What you feed your hens rather depends on how you are keeping them and what they are able to forage for themselves. Those kept in a run will need some concentrated grain night and morning. This is easiest (and most expensively) supplied in the form of specially prepared layers' mash or pellets. Of the two, pellets are the most economical. Mash, even when dampened, tends to blow away in a strong breeze. If you do not want to feed them this you can feed them about 125 g (4 oz) of grain (mixed corn or wheat) divided between the night and morning, and supplement this with a good supply of household scraps.

Chickens appreciate household scraps anyway – particularly greens. In addition they like potato and apple peelings, bacon rinds, cut-up banana skins, bread, fish scraps, etc, but avoid any plate-scrapings which are very salty. In the winter you can make this into a particularly delicious hot mash by mixing and mulching all the scraps together with hot water. The hens will love it! Avoid feeding them too many fatty scraps – if the hens get too fat, they will stop laying.

Concentrated feed can be scattered on the ground for the hens to scratch, or it can be fed in a container. Sophisticated feeders can be bought, in which you can

CLIPPING WINGS

Chickens should have the flight feathers on one wing clipped when they are six months old, or they will fly over fences. **Below;** spread out one wing. You can clearly feel the meaty part of the wing and will be able to see the long flight feathers. **Right:** clip these off at the base, using very strong scissors, as the feathers are very tough. It will not draw blood or hurt the bird.

Chicken feeders and drinkers: you can buy sophisticated food and water containers, or improvise with plastic bowls.

KEEPING CHICKENS			
System	**Housing**	**Feeding**	**Other Requirements**
Deep litter	Permanent hen house with no run. Add litter from time to time. Suitable for loft or garage. Perches and nests.	Scatter grain. Meal or mash in hopper. 100 g (4 oz) feed per bird per day. 75 g (3 oz) grain and 25 g (1 oz) protein. Hang up bunches of green food.	Clean, fresh water. Grit for gizzard. Calcium.
Straw yard	Permanent hen house with attached open yard, fenced. Littered with straw. Wooden house for roosting and laying. Perches and nests.	Mown grass provides green shoots. Also waste vegetables and scraps.	Keep food hopper in house. Shut hens in at night. Provide box filled with fine earth or sand.
Folding	Movable ark or house on wheels with movable run. Trundle on fresh grass daily. House for nesting and perching. Can be placed in orchard, or on grassland lying fallow.	Fresh green food, depending on time of year.	Level ground and predator-proof. Do not return to same patch too often. Good treatment for grassland.
Free-range	Fixed house with nests and perches. Access to field or runs. Carotene content of greens will give eggs deep orange colour.	Green food and insects supplied and grit in most soils.	Clean water. Shelter should be available when needed.

put more than one feed at a time. They have small holes, from which the hens pick out the grain.

Clean water is essential and hens drink an enormous amount. Again, you can buy special water containers, which are designed to help keep the water clean. A cheaper alternative can be made from a plastic bowl with an upturned flowerpot placed in it. With any luck, this will stop the hens from getting right into the bowl. They are prone to putting their feet in the water (and this is the nicest thing they do in it!), so the container needs frequent cleaning.

In addition, chickens need grit, which helps them to break up their food, and calcium or limestone to help them form egg shells. Those kept on chalky ground will probably not need extra calcium; in other cases either give them crushed oyster shells (available from your local corn merchant) or recycle the egg shells by drying them off in a slow oven and crushing them before giving them back to the hens. Each bird should have approximately 14 g ($\frac{1}{2}$ oz) of grit and limestone (or oyster shells) per week in the ratio of one to four grit to limestone.

If the hens have a run, the daily routine is to open up the hen house and let the hens out as early as possible – dawn is best. If left too long, the birds may start to peck each other. Feed them and give them clean water. Collect the eggs in the morning (most are laid between nine and noon and should be collected as soon after laying as possible to avoid breakages). Unless you are cleaning out the hen house or digging over the run, they need no further attention until their next feed at three or

four o'clock. Shut them into the hen house at about six o'clock.

Breeding

If you have a broody hen and a cockerel, you might like to try to hatch some eggs. It is fun to do, lovely to watch and you may be able to add to your flock.

When a hen goes broody, put her in a special box of her own, away from the others, with some straw so she can make a nest. She should not be able to get out of this, and ideally it should have a wire mesh bottom to allow damp and warmth to come up from the earth. Sit her on eight newly-laid eggs (some people will say ten or twelve, but you run a greater risk of breakages) and leave her. Take her off the nest to feed and perhaps have a dust bath, but the eggs should not be left for more than about 15 minutes or they will get too cold. Providing all goes well, the chicks will hatch exactly 21 days after the hen began sitting on them. There is nothing for you to do but wait until the tiny yellow chicks emerge.

The chicks need water but no feed for 24 hours. Put the water in a tiny container, otherwise they will fall in and drown. Thereafter they can be fed on chick pellets three times a day, or you can feed the mother grower's mash and watch her feed tiny crumbs to her babies.

You will be able to tell when the chicks are ready to leave the hen and become independent, because she will let you know she is clearly fed up with them! In an ideal world, it is better to integrate them into the flock slowly, as they are likely to get pecked and victimized at first. If it is not practical to keep them apart, they generally do not suffer too much if you put them in with the others. A few pecks maybe, but they are usually able to look after themselves before too long. Cock birds can be fattened for the table.

Incidentally, hens are not always good mothers. If you get a good one, the advice from old country folk is to keep her for as long as possible to rear chickens for you. It is best, though, to change the cock each year. If you keep the same one, he will mate with his daughters and your flock will begin to be inbred.

Killing birds

The most economical way of keeping chickens in terms of getting the maximum egg production is to keep them for two laying seasons (ie until they are about 18 months old) and then kill them and start the flock again. They will go on laying for some years to come, but although the eggs get larger, they become fewer.

How to wring a chicken's neck is shown in the photographs. However, do not expect your chickens to make good roasting birds. They have spent their lifetime pecking and scratching, which is likely to have made them strong and somewhat tough, but they will make lovely pot-boilers – perfect for casseroles and curries.

Eggs

Hens lay most eggs in the summer when the days are longer and lighter. In their prime, you can generally expect to get eggs for five or six days a week from one chicken. This amount will drop off in the winter, although from a flock of about ten birds, it is usual to get one or two fresh eggs each week, even in mid-winter. Hens can be encouraged to lay in the winter if you light the hen house well, so they have, in effect, about 12 hours of daylight each day.

Wringing a chicken's neck: 1 After stunning the bird, hold the legs with your left hand, letting the body hang down. Hold the neck close to the head with your right hand.
2 Pull neck down and twist firmly so head is bent backwards towards the back. If you pull too hard you will pull the head off. You will feel the neck break.
3 Hang the bird with its head down, so the blood drains out of its veins.

Keeping Other Poultry

IF ANYTHING, ducks are even easier to keep than hens, although it is by no means as usual to see them. Some people say that ducks do not need a pond and will be happy just as long as they have a container of water deep enough to immerse their heads and necks. I cannot see that they will be really at home in such circumstances, nor do I think it humane, and consider a pond (or, better still, a stream, so the water does not become stagnant) is really essential if you want to keep ducks.

Living requirements

Their living requirements are far more primitive and straightforward than hens. All that is necessary is a dry house containing some straw, in which they can be shut up at night to protect them from foxes. It needs no nesting box or roosting perch and, in fact, a packing case can be turned into an excellent duck house. A couple of large holes punched in the back will give adequate ventilation.

Eggs

Duck eggs are often considered to contain impurities, which is possibly one of the reasons why ducks are less frequently kept. In fact, the shells are porous, so if laid, for example, in the mud around a stagnant pond, dirty water could get into the egg. If the eggs are laid in clean surroundings they are perfectly good, clean and quite safe to eat. The best way to ensure this is to keep the ducks shut in their house until about ten o'clock in the morning. They lay their eggs before this time and therefore will do so in the house. The eggs are larger and

Other poultry: part of the duck's essential living requirements **(left)** is a pond or, ideally, a stream. It is cruel to keep them without one of these supplies of fresh water. Geese **(below)** only need a hut or a well-wired run.

rather richer than hens' eggs, but will not keep as long; they should be used within a week.

If keeping birds for the table, buy them when they are very young and keep them for ten weeks. Fatten them with barley meal and kill them when they are exactly ten weeks old, at which point they are at their best. They are also easiest to pluck at this stage; thereafter, they begin to moult and the new feathers which are coming through are much more difficult to pull out.

If keeping them for eggs you can get ducks as day-old-chicks or point-of-lay pullets, like chickens.

Feeding

Ducks are voracious eaters, but will thrive on grass and will keep down slugs and snails. They will also keep down the vegetable patch, so make sure they cannot get to it. They will need some grain in the night and morning. Feed it in a container rather than scattering it and if there is any left after an hour, feed them less next time. They will also appreciate their share of household scraps, in particular greens. They need as much clean drinking water, grit and limestone for their shells as chickens.

Breeding

You can, of course, breed from your ducks but they are lousy mothers. It is much better to give a clutch of eggs to a broody chicken and let her hatch them. She will do so in 28 days, but dampen the eggs each day in the final week, as ducks do. Do not let the chicks into the water until they are four weeks old – before this their feathers will not repel the water. If they are an egg-laying breed and you have extra drakes, kill them at ten weeks old and eat them. Ducks have their necks wrung in the same way as hens.

GEESE

Goose eggs are larger and richer still, and you can expect to get about a hundred a year from each bird. If you have a large orchard or patch of grass where they can graze, or have access to unlimited greens, geese are probably the cheapest of all poultry to keep. Although they have fallen from the favour they once enjoyed, they still make excellent eating and many people prefer them to turkeys at Christmas. One point about them, which may be considered either an advantage or a disadvantage, is that they are extremely aggressive and will chase after people they do not know. They are also very noisy, but much acclaimed as watchdogs and can easily intimidate anyone unused to them.

If you keep geese, there is no doubt that you must get the ascendancy over them and establish who is boss, particularly with the gander. The power of the human eye works well here; look your gander fairly and squarely in the face and let him know you will brook no nonsense. The way to deal with a goose if it does attack you is to grab it by its neck (which is easy enough to do if you are bold, as it advances with its neck forward). It is unable to do anything then.

Living requirements

Like ducks, they have very simple housing requirements and only need somewhere with four walls, a roof and a floor, in which they can be shut up at night to keep them safe from foxes. Alternatively they can be shut in a well-wired run (wire the top as well as the sides, for extra protection).

Feeding

Their staple diet, as mentioned above, is grass, but they cannot cope if it is really long; it needs to be of medium length, which they will crop as neatly as a lawn. If you want to fatten them, give them some grain too, and if you put this in their night-time accommodation, it will help to lure them inside. In addition, like all poultry, they need grit and limestone, and access to clean water. They drink great quantities of water, in fact, and as they immerse their entire heads as they drink, it should be given in a fairly deep container. Clean it as soon as it gets dirty.

Geese make dreadful mothers, and so if you want to breed some goslings, put the eggs under a large broody hen, who will be able to hatch between four and six at a time. They take upwards of four weeks to hatch, and if being hatched by a hen, must be turned each day in order to stop the contents settling. Sprinkle them with water, making particularly sure they are kept wet in the final week before hatching. Feed goslings on bread and milk to begin with and then on chick feed.

Breeding

Later of course, you can breed from your geese if you want to. They sometimes take a fair while to select a mate, but once done, they have paired for life. You can expect them to produce between ten to twenty eggs, but the eggs will seldom all hatch in a single clutch, so do not be too optimistic. Beware of the male, particularly at breeding time; he gets very protective and aggressive and it is best to stay well away from the nest.

Killing geese

Geese cannot be killed in the same way as chickens and ducks, because they are too big and strong. There are two ways of killing them, but for both, you must stun the bird first by giving it a hefty blow to the head with a heavy instrument. Then, either cut its throat at the bottom of the neck to sever the jugular vein, or hold the bird by the feet, with its chin resting on the ground. Get a helper to lay a wooden pole or metal bar across its neck and tread on either end of this to keep it in place. Then pull the legs up towards you to break the neck.

TURKEYS

These are the birds least frequently kept on a small scale, mostly because they have a reputation for being delicate and hard to rear. In addition, they are usually bred solely for their meat, although their eggs are actually very similar in taste to those of chickens. One turkey egg is approximately the equivalent in size to two hen's eggs.

A principal worry and objection to keeping turkeys is that they are likely to get a disease called blackhead if they come into contact with chickens. This contact can be as remote as you dealing with the turkeys after having been in the hen house. However, this is really no longer a problem, for modern turkey feeds contain the antibiotic which combats this disease. Providing you feed proper turkey pellets, you should encounter no problem.

Turkey eggs can be difficult to hatch; turkeys are not good mothers in that they are relatively large for the size of eggs they lay and, in their enthusiasm, they are apt to break them. It is better to use a broody hen if possible, and she can hatch from six to eight eggs. She will then rear the chicks, teaching them to eat and caring for them.

An alternative is to hatch turkey eggs in an incubator, kept at a temperature of about 38° C (101° F).

Keep the incubator in a place where the temperature is constant – in other words, inside the house is better than outside in a shed where the temperature will fluctuate. The trouble with hatching turkeys in this way is that young chicks are very difficult to rear as they are reluctant to begin eating. The trick to overcome this is to chop up onion tops and put them on top of their food.

A turkey house is similar to a hen house in design. The birds like to have perches, but make sure these are strong and solid. If you are able to keep the turkeys free-range, so much the better – they will wander around all day constantly pecking and eating.

Besides there being a market for turkey eggs, the chicks can easily be sold as one-day-old birds, or you can keep them and sell them at Christmas.

BREEDS OF DUCK AND GEESE

Embden
Large pure white bird which is the most popular goose breed.

Khaki Campbells
Prime layers, which give over 300 eggs a year. Go off lay early in year.

Chinese
White bird which is considerably smaller than Embden.

Aylesbury
Very popular duck which is kept for eating. White feathers.

Toulouse
Slightly smaller than Embden, with mostly grey feathers.

White Pekin
Long-necked bird which is also kept for the table. White feathers.

Keeping Rabbits

RABBITS ARE ONE of the most valuable of all animals to keep, because although there are no by-products, such as milk or eggs, just three breeding rabbits are quite capable of providing you with meat for the table at least once a week throughout the year. Not only is this meat said to be nutritionally better than chicken, pork or beef, but the animals can be kept at a very low cost, in a very small place, with extremely little labour.

Living requirements
Rabbits can be kept in hutches of various designs which are very easy to construct. The most important points are that they should be dry and draught-proof. Adult rabbits are generally best kept in individual hutches – let your common-sense dictate the size, but obviously the rabbit must be able to lie down and turn around without being cramped. The most usual material for construction is wood. If it is treated with creosote it will discourage the rabbits from gnawing, but make sure the creosote is thoroughly dry before putting the rabbits in the hutch or it will poison them.

Numbers of hutches can be housed in an old shed or garage (preferably one that lets in some light), in which event they do not need to be quite so strong or weatherproof. They must, however, be raised off the ground again as protection against rats and mice.

Cover the floor of the hutch with a thick layer of newspaper or woodshavings. This helps to prevent the wood from getting urine-soaked. On top of this provide straw bedding.

Rabbit hutches must be cleaned out at least three times a week, but by observing which corner of the cage

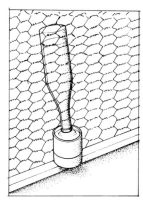

Rabbit hutches: like hen houses, these can easily be made at home. **Roof:** must be waterproof, so cover the top with roofing felt. Should slope towards the back and overhang for ventilation. **Door:** should be covered with metal grille. **Sleeping:** at one end of the cage, with a door to the outside for cleaning. **Siting:** should not face north, a prevailing wind, or against a stone wall. You can buy drinkers **(left)** or make them. **Right:** as the rabbit drinks, the water in the bottle replaces that in the can.

KEEPING RABBITS

System	Housing	Feeding	Other Requirements
Colony	Fenced and sheltered on grasslands. Fencing should be chain-link buried 15 cm (6 in) underground.	Grass and weeds available in summer. Concentrate or bran may be used for fattening. Hay should be available.	Water. Nest boxes for breeding.
Morant hutch folded on grass	Wooden ark with run moved to fresh grass daily. Covered sleeping portion.	Mash or grain as grass supplement. Hay in wet weather.	Water. Nest boxes. Wire mesh floor to prevent digging. Litter in sleeping portion.
Outdoor hutch	Weather-proof hutch made of tongue-and-groove board covered in felt. Good eaves with overhang.	Garden and wild greens. Hay. Bran mash from scraps. Roots in winter. Feed to appetite and remove unwanted food.	Food trough. Water drinkers. Nest box. Litter – straw, shavings, sawdust. Clip claws every six weeks if rabbits hutched.
Indoor hutch	Wood or wire cages in shed. Light and airy with room for circulating air.	Less food required than other types. Do not let rabbits get too fat. Provide variety.	Good lighting and ventilation. Artificial light in winter. Clip claws.

the animal soils (and it is likely always to be in the same place) you can make this chore easier for yourself. Wooden floors must be scrubbed and disinfected once a week. Rot down the hutch cleanings and use as manure (do not use straight on the ground – they are too rich in nitrogen and potash).

If you have space, rabbits will appreciate a run out in the open and you can keep them in a movable hutch which has a run attached to it. However, they must be shut into the hutch at night to protect them from foxes. Day-time runs (in which the rabbit is confined as time permits during the day) should be covered over the top and sides with strong wire mesh and should have a sheltered place at one end where the walls are solid. Allowing rabbits out in this way gives them some exercise as well as giving their hutches some ventilation.

Acquiring rabbits
As always, rabbits are best acquired locally, from a reputable source where you can see the rabbits are clean, healthy and well-cared for. Never buy young rabbits if the parents look dull, tired or in any way unhealthy. Which breed to have might depend a little on availability, but the New Zealand White is among the most popular. This is a medium-sized rabbit that gives a greater proportion of meat than some of the larger breeds – the Flemish Giant for example: It also has a beautiful pelt. The Californian is another popular breed and is sometimes also available crossed with a New Zealand. The Dutch is another possibility.

Feeding
Rabbits are vegetarians and traditionally associated with salad foods. However, if you want them to grow big they will not do so on a handful of greenstuff a day. Ideally, they should have some sort of grain supplement, probably best given in one of the commercially prepared rabbit foods. If you feel this will make keeping them less economic than it should be, devise a diet based on a wide variety of greenstuffs – both wild and cultivated, with household scraps – particularly bread and boiled potato skins, root vegetables and so on. They must have hay to nibble, given preferably a small rack attached to the side of the hutch, which means it is less likely to get absorbed into the bedding. In addition, give them such things as apple prunings or other branches to gnaw at. It will help to keep their teeth in good condition and might save the sides of the hutches.

Give them the greenstuff you have readily available and that you know they like. They will love any non-

BREEDS OF RABBIT
Three of the most popular breeds of rabbit are New Zealand White (**below**), Flemish Giant (**right**) and Californian (**below right**).

poisonous wild plants which you can collect from the hedgerows, such as chickweed, groundsel, plantain, coltsfoot, dandelion and all its relatives, meadowsweet, hogweed, dock, dead-nettle and so on, or trimmings from any of the vegetables of the brassica family. If you are feeding a handful of grain night and morning, give greenstuff in the middle of the day. The chief rules are to vary it as much as possible and to give only as much as the rabbit will clear up in about twenty minutes. Try to collect wild greenstuff from open, sunny positions rather than those that are heavily shaded, and preferably not from those places which are the favourite visiting spots of dogs.

Give food such as grain or scraps in clean bowls – heavy porcelain or stainless steel are the best but are also the most expensive. Old saucers will do, but be prepared for some of the food to be spilt.

Rabbits must have a good supply of fresh clean water, of which they drink a surprising amount. This can be given in a heavy porcelain bowl which is not too likely to be knocked over, or you can provide them with one of the automatic, drip-type drinkers which are commercially available.

Breeding
Does should be at least nine months old before they are mated for the first time and they must be in good, healthy condition. They should not be too fat, or they will be quite likely not to conceive. One buck is needed for every ten does, but if you do not want to keep a buck, share one with another rabbit-keeper or go to a breeder for mating.

Take the doe to the buck at any time (do not bring the

Picking up a rabbit: 1 Take hold of it by the ears and support it under its stomach. **2** Lift it, keeping your hand under its stomach, and steadying it by the ears. **3** Support it in the crook of your arm, talking to it to soothe it.

buck to her cage – fighting is more likely this way round). If she is not ready for mating, it will simply not take place. The chances are, however, that she will be. If she does not accept the mating, put her alone in a cage where a buck has been, without cleaning it out first, and leave her for a couple of days. Then try again.

Return her to a larger hutch and do not handle her too much after mating. Give her a nesting-box in the hutch – this being merely a box which should have an opening on one side or at the top. Some people say the doe is less likely to step on her babies if she hops into the box. Fill it with hay – straw is too hard and prickly at this time.

Gestation is 30 to 32 days, during which time the doe should be fed well on high-protein food, but not over-fed. She will appreciate carrots and should have the pick of the greenstuff. Give her lots of water and possibly some milk. A lactating doe can drink up to 4.5 litres (8 pints) of water a day.

When the babies are born, check them as soon as you can, taking care to disturb the doe as little as possible. It will help if you rub your hands in the bedding of the hutch, so she cannot smell you too much on the babies. Remove any that are dead or look particularly weak. Ideally she should not be expected to rear more than eight babies, so destroy any over this number.

The babies can leave the doe when they are six to eight weeks old (the longer time is better in winter). In fact, they are often slaughtered for the table at eight weeks old. If you prefer to let them get a little larger, feed them from this time in the usual fashion, beginning by giving them three feeds a day, but slaughter them by the time they are five months old. The doe can return to the buck as soon as she looks fit and healthy. It is better not to

leave it too long; if she is left unmated for long periods, she may become sterile.

Sexing rabbits

Young rabbits can be kept together in large hutches of separate buck and doe colonies. To find out which is which, put each rabbit on its back, holding it still with one hand. Gently press down on the sexual organ. In the male, it will be cylindrical-shaped and usually protrudes very slightly. The female organ is a slightly oval orifice.

Examining rabbits

Obviously you should check and examine your rabbits frequently to ensure they are healthy, and also to see that their claws are not growing too long. Rabbits kept in captivity will need their claws cut from time to time as they will not be worn down naturally. Although the ears are useful as an initial way to hold and steady the rabbits, never lift them without supporting them under their rear end as well. Once in your arms, it is better to hold a rabbit by the back of its neck rather than by its ears.

Killing rabbits

There are various ways of killing a rabbit. If you have an air gun, shoot it in the back of the head between the ears, pointing the gun slightly downwards. If you are very sure of yourself, you can kill it with a sharp, strong blow to the head. Use a stout piece of wood and strike the rabbit (as if you mean it) just in front of the ears. Or, break its neck by twisting the head and pulling it backwards with one hand, whilst forcing the neck downwards with the other hand (pushing firmly on the back of the neck).

Keeping Bees

UNLIKE THE OTHER ANIMALS discussed in this book, bees have never been domesticated, although man has been keeping them, or at least collecting the fruits of their labours, for centuries. Providing you are able to keep bees, it is well worthwhile doing so, for even one hive is likely to provide you with all the honey you can eat, in return for remarkably little work or worry. Honey can almost always be used in the place of sugar – from sweetening drinks of all types to making cakes, puddings and all manner of other cooked dishes, and it is far better for you.

As always, there is more than one way to keep bees and all bee-keepers will have their own ideas about the best way to do so. Described here, in brief and simple terms, is a method of keeping bees to enable you to farm your own honey, but perhaps more than with any other animal, it is important to get help and advice from bee-keepers in your area if you are a complete newcomer to the subject. And do not be surprised if they advocate different ways to those described here to deal with various situations!

Can you keep bees?
Before deciding definitely to keep bees, it is very important to discover how you react to being stung. Some people react very badly indeed and in such cases, keeping bees could be a positive danger. Accompany a local bee-keeper on an inspection of a number of hives; you will probably get stung and you can then judge your reaction. In addition, join your local branch of the Bee-keepers' Association and try to attend one of the courses they run for newcomers to bee-keeping.

About stings
If you keep bees, you will get stung, and probably sooner rather than later. When this happens, it is advisable to remove the sting. Scratch it out from your flesh using a hive tool or, failing that, a fingernail. The bee leaves a poison sac with the sting, plus the mechanism that continues to pump the poison from the sac into you, and so, if you squeeze the sting, it will merely send the poison shooting into you, causing more irritation and swelling. Generally, the pain stops in a few minutes and the swelling subsides in a few hours. If it is really painful, bathe the sting with witch hazel or soak with diluted Epsom salts.

Equipment
Certain equipment is essential if you mean to keep bees, and the fact that it can be expensive to acquire is another good reason for making certain you want to keep them. For yourself you will need a bee-veil (worn over the face and very essential – stings to the face or throat can be extremely unpleasant, not to mention dangerous, to anyone); gloves (later you may dispense with these, finding them rather cumbersome, but wearing them to begin with helps to give confidence to a novice bee-keeper); and wellington boots (into which you tuck your trousers – themselves tucked into long socks, so the bees cannot get inside your trouser legs). You might also want a bee-suit, which offers complete protection, but is expensive unless improvised out of a pair of overalls. In any event, always remember that bees climb upwards, and so will climb up sleeves but not down trousers, and protect yourself accordingly.

For the bees, you need a hive with all its relative component parts, a hive tool to lever out the frames and a

Bee-keeping equipment: it is very important that you should be dressed in the correct protective clothing before inspecting any bee hives **(above)**. As well as the distinctive bee-veil, you should wear gloves, wellington boots, and perhaps a bee-suit. If you do not have one, tuck your clothes in, as bees climb upwards. **Left:** making bees drowsy with a smoker before working in the hive.

smoker. This is used whenever you want to open up the hive; in it you burn anything which smoulders, such as dried grass, fir cones or insulation board. The smoke subdues the bees, as their reaction to it is to gorge themselves with honey, making them somewhat dozy and therefore less likely to sting. This is the condition you want them to be in if you have to work in the hive.

The hive

This is the most expensive item of equipment, but may often be acquired second-hand, which will help cut the cost. Scrub and disinfect it, and check whether it is in need of the odd nail or piece of angle-iron to make it thoroughly sound.

The two most common types of hive used in the United Kingdom are the WBC and the modified National. The WBC is the traditional, rather pretty beehive that is shaped slightly like a pyramid. The National is more usually recommended for beginners, and there is always a ready market in second-hand National hives if you find bee-keeping does not suit you after all. Both are made of wood, but the WBC hive is double-walled, improving insulation, and therefore more expensive. The commercially-available hives are made from western red cedar, but the do-it-yourself enthusiast could use almost any wood to construct a hive.

National hives basically consist of boxes, filled with frames, piled on top of one another.

The frames are constructed so that the distance between them when they are fitted into the box corresponds with the spacing from the centre of one honeycomb to the centre of the next, based on the measurements taken from wild bees' nests. This means that there is just enough room between frames for the workers to make honeycomb, for the queen to lay her eggs, for the cells to be capped and for the nurse bees to tend them.

In the first year after acquiring a colony of bees, a hive is likely to consist of three boxes – two for the queen and the developing colony and one empty one above the crown board where the feeder may be placed (see below). In a good year this might be fitted with frames for the bees to make honey. In the next year, when the colony has greatly enlarged, the number of boxes is likely to be increased to five or six. At the end of the honey-making season, when many of the bees will have died (through their hard work of the last six weeks or so) the hive can be reduced down to one or two boxes for the winter.

Siting

Do not site any beehives near a public footpath, road or railway track, where people could be bothered by the flight of the bees, nor under heavy trees where the spot is likely to be damp, nor in a frost pocket. Ideally, they should be in a place that is shaded from the rest of the garden by a fairly tall screen (which is not right up against the hives). When planning where to site your bees, get advice from a local expert, who can advise of the possible problems.

Acquiring bees

It is always best to acquire bees from a local bee-keeper, for two major reasons: the first that bees are adapted to a particular region and its climatic conditions; bees from another district are unlikely to do as well. The other reason is that it is easier and more convenient to go back to the source, should anything go wrong with the bees.

Probably the easiest way to start a new colony is to acquire a nucleus from an experienced bee-keeper. This, in effect, is a mini-colony, consisting of about five frames of drawn comb with a laying queen. It probably numbers about 5000 to 8000 bees (whereas a full colony numbers on average 40,000 to 60,000 bees). A bee-keeper should not let you have this nucleus until it is certain that the queen is laying, and this means that early June is the most likely time for acquisition.

The nucleus is put into the centre of the lowest box, which is then filled on either side with frames of foundation. Another box of foundation is placed above this.

The initial aim is to build up the colony, but the queen will lay according to the food coming in. As there will not be many spare bees to go out to collect nectar, it is necessary to give supplementary feed. This is done in the form of sugar syrup made to the formula of 900 g (2 lb) of sugar dissolved in 550 ml (1 pint) of hot water, cooled to room temperature. Feeders can be bought, but it is just as easy to make them. Pierce the lid of a 650 g (1½ lb) tin with very small holes, put the syrup in the tin and press the lid firmly into place. Then invert the tin over the hole in the crown board and put another box on top. Put the roof on the hive. The bees will extract the syrup gradually through the holes.

The amount of feeding will depend a little on the weather, but aim to feed them up to about 18 kg (40 lb) of sugar in the first year.

It is unlikely that you will get any honey in the first year, but if the weather is ideal in July (ideal really meaning hot, sunny, sultry days with rain at night to encourage maximum plant growth) you can replace the feeder with a super full of foundation frames, from which, at the end of the season, you could get between 4.5–9 kg (10–20 lb) of honey.

As the colony builds up over the first few weeks, it will help if you move the frames around. The bees are likely to build up comb on the centre frames, this being the most congenial place to work. Every fortnight or so, open up the hive, remove the frames of foundation at the outer sides of the lower box and replace these with the frames of drawn comb from the centre of the top box. Put the frames of foundation back in the top box, but be careful not to split the brood. By the winter you will have two full boxes of drawn comb which is ideal for wintering. The bees will cluster on them and survive happily.

Removing honey

Honey may be taken from the hive from the end of July until the end of August, depending on the nectar flow in the area. Put a board with a one-way bee-valve under the supers and, when the bees have gone down to the lower boxes (after about 48 hours), remove the top frames. To extract the honey, you must first remove the wax cappings on the cells and this can be done with a large uncapping knife which is drawn across the frame, or a special uncapping fork (keep the wax for making candles or polish!). Some bee-keepers even use an electric carving knife; it will do the job but soon gets clogged-up with wax. The frames are then put into a special contrifuge or honey extractor (an expensive item of equipment that can usually be hired from your local bee-keeping association, but if you have more than two

A WBC HIVE

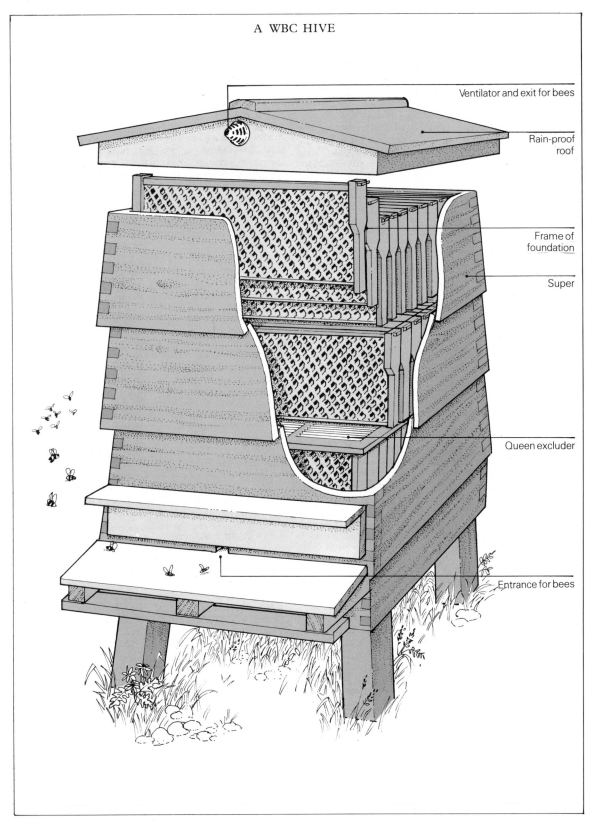

Ventilator and exit for bees

Rain-proof roof

Frame of foundation

Super

Queen excluder

Entrance for bees

Extracting honey: the frames full of honey are placed in a honey extractor, and the honey collects in the bottom tray. This is done somewhere free of dust and bees.

hives, it is probably worth investing in one). This spins the frames round at speed so the honey falls into the bottom of the drum. From there it is filtered into the honey tank, which is a special compartment, from whence it can be drawn off into jars. The maximum amount of honey you could expect from a single frame is 2.2 kg (5 lb); the maximum in a super (box of eleven frames) is 22.5 kg (50 lb).

It is usual to extract honey from all the boxes above the queen excluder. This means you will be leaving 9–13.5 kg (20–30 lb) of honey in the lower boxes, which will not be enough to feed the bees through the winter. They must therefore be fed as described above and you will need to give them syrup made with about 13.5–16 kg (30–35 lb) of sugar. Start feeding around the beginning of September, The colony will have dropped down to about 30,000 bees by this time and this figure could drop even further to about 10,000 by the end of the winter.

Subsequent management
In the following years, you will find it is necessary to replace frames of old, drawn comb in the lower boxes with new foundations. Basically it is unwise to keep frames much more than three years, because the cells begin to get congested with the skin shed by the larvae and the cocoon shed by the pupa and other foetal matter. Each larva sheds five skins, and the queen probably lays an egg in the cells every 25 days or so. If the frames are left longer than three years, they begin to turn black and can harbour minor diseases.

The hive should be inspected every fortnight from May to July to make sure the queen is laying and to see if there are any queen cells. These are much larger than ordinary cells and will protrude out from the comb. If no action is taken the colony will swarm.

You can either remove the frame and destroy the queen cells, or you can make an artificial swarm. The idea is to split the colony and to do so you find the old queen in the hive, and put her and the frame of eggs she

is on in another box with some frames of drawn comb. Leave these on the current site (with the supers of honey) and put all the brood frames, including the queen cells together with the drones, on an adjacent site. When the foraging bees return, they will automatically go into the old hive on the site they know. This hive then will house the queen and all the foraging bees, and is known as an artificial swarm.

Meanwhile, in the adjacent site, which contains the nurse bees and the queen cells, panic will set in as there is no food coming into the colony. The bees will, therefore, tear down all the queen cells except for one. The new queen will emerge, leaving the hive, get mated and come back to start laying, thereby beginning a new colony. If you only want one colony, go into the original hive, find the queen and either destroy her or give her away. Then unite the two colonies by putting the queen into the hive. The bees will follow her.

Bee-keepers should renew the queen in a colony every two years, because it is in this time that she is at her most efficient as an egg-laying machine. The colony, of course, can go on indefinitely as the worker bees are constantly being replaced.

Swarming
If you inspect your bees regularly and follow the procedure outlined above, experienced bee-keepers would claim that there is no reason for bees swarming. They will only swarm if conditions in the hive become overcrowded, or if a new queen hatches. Queen cells are produced when the queen gets older and produces less of something known as queen substance, which the bees groom from her. Providing there is enough of this to go round, the workers are happy and the rearing of queen cells is inhibited. The older queens produce less queen substance, making the colony more likely to swarm.

If the bees do swarm, about half of them will leave the hive, with the queen. They will cluster on a nearby bush or tree (or even a fence or building), and unless they are collected by a bee-keeper, they will probably move off to their chosen new home a day or two later.

Collecting a swarm
If the swarm has settled onto the branch of a tree, place a white sheet, measuring about 1.2 × 1.2 metres (4 × 4 ft), on the ground beneath it. Hold a strong cardboard box or straw basket directly under the largest part of the swarm and give the branch a sharp shake. This will cause most of the bees to fall into the box. Invert the box over the sheet and carefully prop up one side with a small stone. After an hour or so, all the bees left on the tree and those flying around nearby will have joined the swarm in the box.

Return to the box at dusk, remove the stone and cover the box with the sheet, so the bees are safely trapped inside. Then take the swarm to the site where it is to be hived. The hive should consist of a floor, a single brood chamber filled with frames of foundation, a crown board and a roof. Place a board about 45 cm (18 in) square in front of the hive and support it so that it slopes up to the entrance. Spread the white sheet out evenly over the board and shake the bees out of the box in front of the entrance. Bees naturally run uphill when they are frightened, so they will run up the sheet into the hive. If the weather is cold and windy, feed the swarm about 2 litres (4 pints) of sugar syrup.

Food from the Countryside

THE COUNTRYSIDE, inland rivers and lakes, and the shoreline with its coastal waters, all harbour rich crops of edible plants, animals and fish, and yet few of these areas are exploited to anything remotely approaching their full potential. Admittedly, all wild produce from these areas should be treated with respect and a fair measure of caution, but this does not mean they need to be neglected in the way they are at the moment.

The countryside is home to all manner of fungi, fruit, nuts, herbs, plants and flowers, many of which can do much to enliven our daily food and which will cost nothing more than the time needed to find and pick them. Fungi are probably the most neglected of all free food, as literally millions of edible fungi go uncollected each year. Such a fact, whilst unfortunate, is wholly understandable, for undoubtedly some species are deadly poisonous and unless you are able to identify them for certain, there is no foolproof test that will tell you whether a particular fungus is safe to eat or not. Having said that, however, the number of extremely poisonous fungi is remarkably small, and there are many more that are delicious and safe to eat. It is worthwhile learning to identify the poisonous ones, so that you can gather and eat the others with impunity.

There are countless edible wild plants and herbs that grow in great abundance, but again go largely uncollected. Be adventurous, and on the look-out, as you explore your surrounding countryside, and always ask people who have lived in the district a long time if they know of anything that grows in the nearby woodlands or moorlands that is good to eat.

The practice of consuming wild produce is as old as time itself, and many of the plants that abound along the grass verges of our modern roads today were attributed with great healing powers by country folk not so long ago. Although I have not examined the possibilities in this book, many can be used to make soothing lotions and balms or infused with hot water to make teas.

When picking plants from the wild, there are a few simple rules that everyone should observe in order to ensure their own survival, as well as that of the countryside. Make sure that you know that what you are picking to eat is edible and not poisonous; if you cannot find someone who is definitely able to confirm this for you, leave the plant alone. Most produce – fruit, flowers and fungi in particular – is best gathered on a sunny, rather than a rainy day, as the wetness is likely to encourage quicker decomposition. Place your gatherings into an open shallow basket, rather than a polythene bag (in which they will be crushed), and pick only the quantities you know you can deal with at any one time. Try to gather only from places that are relatively unpolluted. Most plants are best if gathered young.

Proper respect for the countryside and wild life is of paramount importance. It is illegal to pull up wild plants by the roots in many places and, in any event, it is unnecessary for your purposes. In the same vein, do not strip plants of their leaves and flowers – this could easily kill them. Nor should you take all the flowers or seeds from annual plants, or they have no hope of being able to re-seed and grow again.

The countryside is home, too, for a number of wild animals and birds which can add great variety and interest to our dinner tables. There are extensive and complicated rules and regulations surrounding their capture and killing, however, and it is as well to acquaint yourself with these.

Rivers and inland lakes or reservoirs can be fished to provide food, but there are increasing restrictions surrounding this age-old practice too, and it is now regarded as a desirable and rather exclusive sport. The equipment used is sophisticated, expensive and infinitely variable, and has progressed far from the stick-and-bent-pin image of one-time stream-side fishing. Likewise, the techniques are something of an art-form, and successful fishermen are highly skilled craftsmen. All this need not put you off, for simpler techniques are as successful now as they ever were and are still widely practised.

The seashore and its immediate coastal waters is another rich store-cupboard of edible goods. The seashore supports a number of plants, as well as various edible seaweeds and the many sea creatures that bury themselves in the sand or live among the shoreline rocks.

Herbs and Plants

THE LIST given below of edible roots, leaves and flowers is by no means complete, for to include all the wild plants that can be eaten, wholly or in part, would easily fill a book this size. This is a classic instance for asking like-minded people in your area what they have managed to harvest from the countryside, more particularly as so many plants belong to specific regions. In addition to those mentioned, look out for wild vegetables, because nearly all those cultivated have their wild counterparts. Cabbage, carrots, celery, parsnip, radish, salsify, turnip and watercress are all there for the taking, although it is unlikely, of course, that they will all grow in the same area.

Beech: pick leaves when they are very young and tender. They make a lovely addition to salads (if you do not eat them all on the way home).

Broom: grows abundantly on heathland and dry moors. Pick the flowers when still in bud and pickle them in vinegar or salt. Alternatively, sprinkle them over salads as a decorative and tasty garnish.

Burdock: grows in abundance in hedgerows, roadsides and along the edges of woods. Eat the young leaves as a salad vegetable; chop the leaf stems raw into salads, or simmer them gently and serve with butter as a vegetable. Scrape and boil the root to eat like salsify.

Chickweed: grows as a weed in most gardens as well as on wasteland everywhere. Strip off the tiny leaves by running a fork down the stems and cook them like spinach or use raw as a sandwich filling.

Chicory: grows particularly where the soil is chalky. The leaves can be used raw in salads and the root can be ground to make a drink that is often used as a substitute for coffee. To do this, clean the roots thoroughly and cook them in a moderate oven until they are dry and crisp, then grind them in a coffee grinder. Let them steep for some minutes in boiling water before straining and drinking the liquid.

Comfrey: a much-neglected and under-used plant that grows commonly in ditches or damp ground near river banks. Used for centuries as a healing medium (setting bones and helping tissue knit together were its prime uses by the herbalists), it makes a pleasant alternative to spinach and is cooked in the same way.

Cowslip: widespread along hedgerows and roadsides,

and particularly noticeable in spring with its umbrella-like clusters of tiny white flowers. These can be infused to make a refreshing drink, or the liquid can be used as a delicate flavouring for puddings. The young leaves can be used as a salad vegetable and the adventurous might like to use the root to give a different aroma to their homemade beer.

Dandelion: one of the commonest, yet most useful of all wild plants. Found growing abundantly in all wasteland and open grassy spaces, it was not so long ago that the plant was cultivated in many vegetable gardens, and it still is in parts of the world. The leaves make a tasty and nutritious salad vegetable, but should be picked young – in springtime before the well-known yellow flowers appear – when they are at their least bitter and most tender. They can also be cooked like spinach, and many people recommend mixing them with the leaves of spinach or sorrel (see below), both raw and cooked, in order to reduce the rather bitter taste. The roots can be dried in the sun, then roasted and ground for a superb coffee substitute. They can also be cooked as a root vegetable or used to make wine.

Dead nettles: pick young leaves and cook like spinach. The flowers can be used to make a pleasant drink.

Dog rose: the value of the hips of the dog rose is discussed more fully on page 166. The flowers have a pleasant, if not very substantial, culinary use. They can be used to flavour jams, jellies or honey. Painted with egg white and sprinkled with caster sugar, the resulting crystallized petals make a pretty decoration for light puddings. Try them as an unusual sandwich filling or as a delicate garnish to a light salad.

Fat hen: one of the commonest of all garden weeds, it will also be found growing on wasteland. It is rich in iron and is another substitute for spinach.

Hawthorn: one of the most useful and versatile of all wild hedgerow crops – the young leaves are lovely eaten raw as a salad vegetable; the flowers can be made into a fresh-tasting, wicked liquor by packing them into bottles with brandy and caster sugar (pick the flowers before noon on a sunny day and use only the petals); and the berries can be made into jelly. It is even said that the hawthorn's magic powers will sweeten the mood of a bad-tempered man!

WILD PLANTS

1	Dog rose	12	Poppy
2	Beech	13	Jack by the hedge
3	Broom	14	Primrose
4	Chicory	15	Plantain
5	Burdock	16	Sorrel
6	Chickweed	17	Marsh samphire
7	Comfrey	18	Salad burnet
8	Dandelion	19	Stinging nettle
9	Cowslip	20	Horseradish
10	Dead nettle	21	Lime
11	Fat hen	22	Hawthorne

Horseradish: grows in abundance on wasteground. Peel the roots and grate them to make horseradish sauce or cream.

Jack by the hedge: grows in abundance on the outskirts of woods and in hedgerows. The leaves can be chopped over salads (they have a slightly garlicky flavour), or they can be made into a sauce to accompany meat.

Lime: the healing properties of this tree were such that many years ago they were planted by royal command along roadsides. They are still found in such locations today, and the leaves make a good salad vegetable or sandwich filling. The flowers, picked and dried, make a refreshing tea that is renowned for being extremely soothing.

Marsh samphire: found on salt marshes. The young leaves can be cooked like any leafy green vegetable.

Plantain: widely found growing on wasteland, the young leaves can be used raw in salads or cooked like spinach.

Poppy: another plant whose contribution to the family larder cannot be claimed as a great money-saver. However, the seeds contained in the brown seed heads that follow the red, papery flowers, can be used to flavour cakes, biscuits and bread, or sprinkled over salads.

Primrose: the flowers of this spring plant can be used to make a refreshing drink or they may be crystallized in the same way as rose petals. Gather them sparingly though: there are all too few of them left after the heavy picking they have suffered in the past.

Salad burnet: commonly found in grassland, particularly on chalky soil. Crush the leaves slightly and use them in salads, or add them to cool long summer drinks.

Sorrel: throughout the spring, wood sorrel may be found in woodland and shady places; common sorrel is found on grassland and heaths. Both are widely neglected in the wild and yet can make a tremendous contribution to the family food. Use sorrel raw in salads, or cooked in soups, soufflés, omelettes, stuffings and sauces for meat and fish, or as a vegetable accompaniment. It does contain a lot of oxalic acid, so do not eat it every day of the week, or cook it in an aluminium saucepan.

Stinging nettle: another much-neglected plant that is widespread and grows in great abundance. Pick it when very young – ideally no more than 15–20 cm (6–8 in) high – and cook them like spinach (the stinging formic acid is destroyed in cooking), use them as a flavouring for soufflés and omelettes, or make them into soup.

Herbs

Only the herbs most easily found have been listed below, but again search for the wild relatives of the cultivated herbs in your garden. If you are lucky you will find balm, borage, parsley, fenugreek, basil and lovage, and quite possibly others too. If you find borage in quantity you can use it as a salad vegetable, cook it like spinach or use it as a base for soups. If you have a large enough quantity of herbs, you can preserve them (see page 195).

Angelica: may be found in damp places around the outskirts of woods, near streams etc. Although classified as a herb, its main culinary use is as a decoration for puddings or as a flavouring for cakes. For this, the stems are candied by simmering and steeping them in heavy syrup over a period of a few days.

Fennel: needs seeking out but may be found on waste and damp ground and often likes coastal locations. The leaves may be used fresh or dried – chopped, to impart the characteristic aniseed taste to a variety of dishes, and the seeds which are gathered in the late autumn can be dried and ground like peppercorns.

Marjoram: grows in grassy wastelands, and particularly on dry, chalky soil. Use the leaves fresh or dried in the same way you would cultivated marjoram.

Meadowsweet: grows abundantly in most locations, but particularly in damp, shady ground and near marshes. Both leaves and flowers may be dried and used for flavouring, or to make a refreshing, soothing drink.

Mint: various types of mint grow wild, the commonest probably being corn mint, which appears on heaths and woodland clearings, and water mint, which likes damp locations. Use whatever you can find in all the ways you use the mint you grow in your garden. Make a good supply of mint sauce to last you through the winter. Mint makes the loveliest, most refreshing, ice cream, too.

Thyme: one of the most widespread of all wild herbs, it grows in grassland and heath. It can be used just like cultivated thyme, although some say the flavour is milder. It is attributed with many healing properties, and can even be taken like snuff to clear the nasal passages!

Woodruff: found in woodland and hedgerows. The leaves may be picked and dried, whereupon they are said to smell like 'vanilla, new-mown hay and honey'. Besides its many medicinal uses, woodruff can be used to flavour sausages and hamburgers. It also gives a pleasant flavour to wine or long, cool, summer drinks.

WILD HERBS

1 Angelica
2 Fennel
3 Meadowsweet
4 Marjoram
5 Thyme
6 Mint
7 Woodruff

Fruit and Nuts

THE WILD FRUITS of the hedgerow can be used in a variety of ways – eaten raw as a dessert in some cases or as the principal ingredient for a pudding, to make jams and jellies, in chutneys or pickles, as garnishes to a meat course, and for wine or soft drinks.

Nuts have just as many culinary uses and, as an important source of protein, they can often be used as the principal ingredient of a meal. They also make superb additions to stuffings and sauces and are invaluable as a garnish.

Soft fruit

Barberry: once common, disease has rendered this shrub a rarity now, but it may still be found in different locations. The bright red berries appear in July. Beware of the thorns when picking; they are vicious. Use berries for jelly or as a sauce to go with meat.

Bilberry: (also known as the blueberry and whortleberry.) Generally found on heath and moorland, these bushes may be found nestling among the heather. They often grow singly some distance apart from one another, so you will need time and patience to gather more than a handful of berries. These are small, round and blue-black in colour, and they appear from July to September/October. They make excellent jelly and wine or can be used in all types of fruit pudding.

Blackberry: the commonest of all wild fruits, and widespread in hedgerows, wasteland, woodland outskirts and so on. The familiar black fruits appear from August onwards, but folklore has it that they should not be picked after the end of September when 'the Devil spits on the berries'. In fact, this is sensible advice: those picked in October are soft, mushy and seldom worth the trouble. Blackberries may be used in jams, jellies, chutneys and for all manner of puddings and sauces, or in wine-making.

Cloudberry: found on northern moors where the ground and atmosphere is damp. The fruits are similar to blackberries in shape but a pale, pinky colour and they grow on very low shrubs. If you can gather enough and they are ripe, they can be eaten raw as a dessert. Otherwise, use them in any way you would blackberries.

Cranberry: another fairly rare shrub, found in marshy and boggy land. The principal, or traditional, use for the hard, dark red, shiny berries is as a sauce to accompany roast turkey. They also make a good stuffing for all sorts of meat, or can be used in puddings.

Elder: both the flowers, which appear from June to July, and the berries, which follow them from August to October, are valuable crops. The elder tree is widespread, growing freely in woodland and wasteland. The clusters of white flowers can be made into a drink by pouring boiling water on them (let it cool and chill it before drinking) or into wine. They impart the most wonderful and subtle flavour to gooseberry puddings, jams or jellies, and they can also be dipped in batter and

Nature's harvest: some of the many foods which can be picked in the countryside.

165

fried in deep fat to make the most delectable of all fritters. The berries are ready for picking when they are black and hanging heavily from the branches. They can be mixed with other fruit in jams, jellies or puddings; made into sauces and chutneys; used to flavour spiced vinegar; or made into superb wine. Dried, they can be substituted for currants in cakes and biscuits.

Gooseberry: careful searching of woodland and hedgerows will yield numbers of wild gooseberry plants in widespread locations. The familiar green bomb-shaped fruits appear from July onwards. Use them in any of the ways you would use their cultivated cousins, such as in tarts, fools, jams and wines.

Raspberry: wild raspberries and mulberries grow, if not in profusion, at least in fair abundance in hedgerows and on heathlands and need only careful seeking. The berries are ripe from July to September. They can be used in all the ways suitable for cultivated fruit, but if you only find a few, use them to flavour vinegar for a salad dressing, or mix them with other fruit.

Redcurrant: this grows naturally as a wild plant, and also in wild locations, having been seeded by birds from cultivated specimens. Look for it particularly along hedgerows or at the edge of a wood, near a stream. The round, red fruits appear in July and may be used in the same way as cultivated ones.

Rose hips: the orangey-red berries appear on the wild rose or dog rose in late August/early September until about November. They can be made into a syrup which is very rich in vitamin C and, besides making a wonderful drink has endless application in flavouring puddings, ice creams, milk shakes etc. Cut the hips in

half, or put them through a mincer, and then boil them for about thirty minutes. Let the contents of the pan drip through muslin or a jelly bag overnight. To each 600 ml (1 pt) of liquid, add 450 g (1 lb) of sugar and boil again.

Rowan: this tree may be found anywhere, particularly in cool woods. The heavy clusters of orange berries appear from August to November and can be used with crab apples to make a jelly that is a wonderful accompaniment to meat. They can also be made into wine.

Strawberry: these grow in open woodland and on heaths and also need careful seeking. The tiny fruits, similar to those of the alpine strawberry, ripen from late June to August and have an infinitely sweeter flavour than any cultivated variety. They are also rich in vitamin C. Ideally, eat them raw, with ice cream to make them go further or, better still, with champagne over them.

HARD FRUITS

Bullace: the typical, small plum-shaped fruits of the tree may be red, purple, yellow or green, and the tree is actually the ancestor of all cultivated plums. It is found in hedgerows and often in a neglected corner of a cottage garden. The fruits are similar to the sloe (see below) in that they are very tart, but this will diminish if they are left until after the first frost. They can then be used in fruit pies, or perhaps more wisely in chutneys or wines.

Crab apple: this is the ancestor of all cultivated apples and will still be found growing singly in hedgerows and occasionally in woods and on heaths. The crab apple has been widely crossed with cultivated varieties of apples, and many of these have found their way back into the wild hedgerows, so the crab apples you find might well

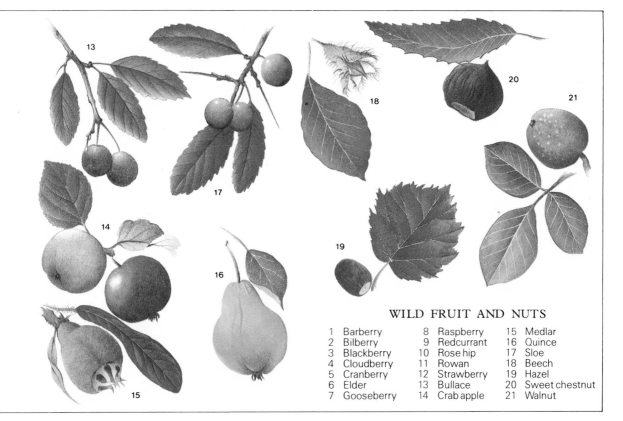

WILD FRUIT AND NUTS

1	Barberry	8	Raspberry	15	Medlar
2	Bilberry	9	Redcurrant	16	Quince
3	Blackberry	10	Rose hip	17	Sloe
4	Cloudberry	11	Rowan	18	Beech
5	Cranberry	12	Strawberry	19	Hazel
6	Elder	13	Bullace	20	Sweet chestnut
7	Gooseberry	14	Crab apple	21	Walnut

be variable in colour, size and taste (true wild crab apples are incredibly sour). Pick them as you find them from July to November and use them to make jellies, sauces, puddings, chutneys or pickles, according to their sweetness.

Medlar: although a native of the Mediterranean, it is not uncommon to find a wild medlar tree. The brown fruits are somewhat pear-shaped with a five-leaved calyx at the top end. They are not ready for picking until at least November, or when they look as if they are turning rotten. They make a delicious alternative to apple sauce to eat with pork, or may be roasted in the oven and eaten as an accompaniment to meat, or as a pudding (with honey and cream). They also make a delicious jelly.

Quince: like the medlar, the branches of these trees grow large and contorted and will occasionally be found in hedgerows. The hard, yellow, pear-shaped fruits are ready for picking in October. They cannot be eaten raw and are most frequently used in jelly.

Sloe: the small, bluish-black berries are the fruit of the thorny blackthorn which still makes up many of the densest hedgerows. The berries eaten raw are extremely sour, although they can be mixed with apples to make a jelly, or even a fruit pie. If you are going to do this, pick them after the first frost which takes away a little of the tartness and makes the skins a little softer. The more usual (and luxurious) use of sloes is to make sloe gin: prick the skins with a skewer, mix with an equal quantity of sugar – less if you do not want the gin too syrupy – and pack into bottles. Top up with gin and leave for two or three months. Strain off the liquor and either eat the berries or add them to an apple pie.

NUTS

Beech: trees are widely spread and the nuts appear in September and October, although only once every three or four years. Four nuts are usually contained in the brown husk. They can be eaten but it is generally considered better (or at least less fiddly) to make them into oil. Grind them in a coffee grinder, put them into a muslin bag and press it with a heavy weight, letting the oil fall into a bowl.

Hazel: known also as cobnuts, these trees are widespread in woodlands and hedgerows and yield their tasty harvest mainly in September and October. Pick them and leave them in their shells until you want to use them.

Sweet chestnut: the prickly green cases, each containing up to three nuts, begin to fall off these tall trees in October. Like beech nuts, they must be peeled once they have been extracted from the outer husk, and they also have an inner skin which makes them very bitter unless it is removed (which is not easy!). It is more usual to cook them before eating them, either by roasting in the embers of the fire, or to make soups, stuffings or as additions to casseroles. Puréed, they can be used in a number of puddings, and the patient can make marrons glacés, which cost a king's ransom to buy. This is done by repeatedly boiling the peeled nuts with sugar and glucose, letting them steep in the syrup between boilings.

Walnut: only a very few of these trees exist in the wild, but they are worth looking for. The nuts ripen at the end of October, although you can pick them earlier for pickling. The uses of the walnut are myriad and they can enhance a number of meals, both sweet and savoury.

Fungi

AS ALREADY MENTIONED, it is imperative to be able to identify fungi if you intend to gather them for eating, and the best way to learn to do this is undoubtedly to spend time collecting with someone already experienced in the art. To this end, some local natural history groups (or the British Mycological Society) run Fungus Forays, and these are well worth attending.

Most fungi are found in their greatest numbers in woodlands – particularly those of beech and oak – where the ground is rich in leaf mould and, therefore, humus. In general, they like warm and damp, but not water-logged, conditions. Although some of the edible species appear in the spring, most are found in the autumn and will be growing in profusion if the summer was good and the autumn is wet, but not cold.

The most important exceptions to the woodland habitat are the field mushroom and the horse mushroom, and these are probably the most coveted and sought-after of all wild, edible fungi. They have infinitely more taste than their cultivated cousins. Both occur in meadows and pastures (the horse mushroom, as its name suggests, likes those frequented by horses, and also, cattle – look for it near cowsheds or horses' shelters in fields and along gallops used by racehorses out on exercise). In a good year they will start springing up towards the end of the summer and continue through until November. They often appear year after year in the same spot (although equally they may not) so remember it and keep it to yourself.

There are some simple, but essential, points that should be observed when collecting fungi, and adhering to them will help further to ensure safety.

Picking fungi: though fungi might be tempting and attractive, there are some vital points to remember when picking them in the countryside. The most important of all is to be absolutely sure of what you are picking. If you cannot identify a fungus, do not pick it, as it could be poisonous. Collect mature, perfect fungi which you know to be edible, and be certain that they have not been polluted by dogs, or any other animals.

Harvest fungi by twisting them by the stalk so they break free at the base. Pulling them out of the ground is selfish as it destroys the whole plant; cutting the tops off with a knife will hamper certain identification as the base of the stem is often a guiding feature in this. Collect them on a fine day, not when it is raining, as this will lead to very quick deterioration of the fungi. Put them into an open receptacle – ideally a shallow basket, not into a polythene bag, which provides the perfect conditions for very quick decomposition.

The fungi you collect should be mature, but not so old that they are beginning to decay. Do not pick young mushrooms, the tops of which are still bunched or buttoned. Their identification characteristics will not have developed and a poisonous species could easily be mistaken for an edible one.

Pick only perfect specimens (or as near perfect as possible); not those that are ragged, torn or slimy. Go through them again when you get home, and discard any that you feel are suspect. All wild fungi must be cooked before eating – never eat them raw. Also, they should be cooked or dried (see page 188) as soon as possible after collecting – and they should be washed very thoroughly first.

It is important to stress again that you should never eat any fungus, unless you are absolutely certain it is an edible species. Testing by tasting is crazy; a remarkably small amount of a deadly species could kill you. Similarly, even though you know a species to be edible, if you are trying it for the first time, eat only a little; it might disagree with you even though the rest of your family can eat plateful after plateful!

EDIBLE FUNGI

1	Field mushroom		sponge-cap
2	Horse mushroom	14	*Boletus erythropus*
3	Brown wood mushroom	15	Shaggy ink cap
4	Wood mushroom	16	Giant puffball
5	Parasol mushroom	17	Common puffball
6	Shaggy parasol	18	Cauliflower fungus
7	St George's mushroom	19	Hedgehog fungus
8	Oyster mushroom		or wood hedgehog
9	Chanterelle	20	Blewit
10	Horn of plenty	21	Wood blewit
11	Morel	22	Yellow swamp russula
12	Cep	23	Bare-toothed russula
13	Bay boletus or bay	24	Blackish-purple russula

Edible fungi

Field mushroom (*Agaricus campestris*): found in damp grassland from August to November, often growing in a ring.

Horse mushroom (*Agaricus arvensis*): found in pastures grazed by horses, cattle and sheep, near cattlesheds, hayricks, etc, from June/July to November.

Wood mushroom (*Agaricus silvicola*): found in damp woodland from August to November.

Brown wood mushroom (*Agaricus silvaticus*): found in woodland in August and September. Pick when flesh is white or pinkish, not when it has turned brown.

Parasol mushroom (*Lepiota procera*): found at the edges of woods and in grassy clearings in woods or by roadsides from July to November. Pick as cap is beginning to open, and discard the stem.

Shaggy parasol (*Lepiota rhacodes*): found in shadier places in woodland and favours rich soil. Occurs at the same time of year as the parasol mushroom.

St George's mushroom (*Tricholoma gambosum*): found in hedgerows, sand dunes and chalky grassland from the end of April to June. Use in soups or stews.

Oyster mushroom (*Pleurotus ostreatus*): found growing on dead tree trunks, branches or stumps, particularly beech. Found throughout the year, but is commonest in autumn and winter. Pick when young and stew slowly, or dry.

Chanterelle (*Cantharellus cibarius*): found in woodland – particularly that of beech and oak, from July to Novem-ber (June to December in very good years). Stew in milk; needs slow cooking.

Horn of plenty (*Craterellus cornucopoides*): found growing among dead leaves in woodland in August or September to November. Search hard; it is not always easy to see in the leaves. The thin flesh makes it good for drying.

Morel (*Morchella esculenta*): found in hedgerows, wood-land clearings, grassy banks. Also likes rich, bare soil. Appears in April and May.

Cep (*Boletus edulis*): found in woodland, beech in particular, from August to November. Good for drying.

Bay boletus or bay sponge-cap (*Boletus badius*): found in woodland, particularly of conifers or where the soil is poor or chalky, in August and September (to November in a good year).

Boletus erythropus: found in woodland, particularly conifers, or on poor soil from September to November. Do not worry about the blue colour to the flesh when cut or broken.

Shaggy ink cap (*Coprinus comatus*): found on roadside verges, rubbish tips and other places where organic rubbish is buried, from May to November. Gather while gills are still white, discard stems and scrape scales from caps.

Giant puffball (*Lycoperdon giganteum*): found in wood-land and grassland from July to October. Eat when young and the flesh is white, not yellow.

Common puffball (*Lycoperdon perlatum*): found in

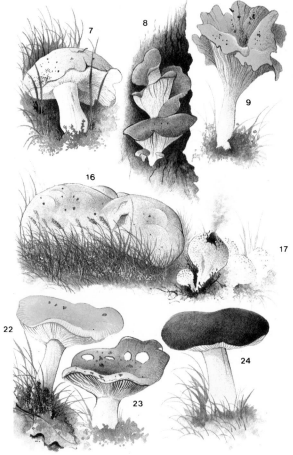

POISONOUS FUNGI

1	Death cap	8	*Clitocybe dealbata*
2	Destroying angel	9	*Clitocybe cerrussata*
3	Fly agaric	10	*Paxillus involutus*
4	Panther cap	11	Livid entoloma
5	Fool's mushroom	12	Sulphur tuft
6	*Inocybe fastigiata*	13	Devil's boletus
7	Red-staining inocybe	14	Yellow-staining mushroom

woodland and grassland from June to November. Pick when flesh is white.

Cauliflower fungus (*Sparassis crispa*): found near pine trees, sometimes growing on the stumps, from September to November. Eat when young, or dry.

Hedgehog fungus or wood hedgehog (*Hydnum repandum*): found in woodland from August to November. Needs boiling for twenty minutes or so or else it tastes bitter.

Blewit (*Tricholoma saevum*): found in pastures and other grassland, often in gardens, as well as in woodland and hedgerows, from October to December.

Wood blewit (*Tricholoma nudum*): as for blewit. Pick when underneath and stems are tinged violet.

Yellow swamp russula (*Russula claroflava*): in wet ground under birch trees in September and October.

Bare-toothed russula (*Russula vesca*): found in woodland, particularly of beech and oak, from June to October.

Blackish-purple russula (*Russula atropurpurea*): found in woodland, particularly under oak, from July to November.

Poisonous fungi

Death cap (*Amanita phalloides*): found in woodland, particularly oak and beech, from July to October. It is deadly.

Destroying angel (*Amanita virosa*): found in woodland from August to October, but is rarer than above.

Fly agaric (*Amanita muscaria*): found in woodland or near coniferous and birch trees from August to December.

Panther cap (*Amanita pantherina*): found in woodland, particularly beech, as well as on heathland and grassland. Occurs from July to October.

Fool's mushroom (*Amanita verna*): found in woodland, usually beech, from July to October.

Inocybe fastigiata: found in woodland, particularly beech, from July to October.

Red-staining inocybe (*Inocybe patouillardii*): found in woodland, particularly of beech, and grows near paths or near the outskirts of the wood. Occurs from May to November.

Clitocybe dealbata and *Clitocybe cerrussata*: found in coniferous woods.

Paxillus involutus: brown roll-rim found in woodland of all types from June to December.

Livid entoloma (*Entoloma sinuatum*): found woodland, parkland and some gardens, favouring clay soils. Occurs from August to November.

Sulphur tuft (*Hypholoma fasciculare*): found in large groups round the base of trees. Can be found at any time, but usually from July to November.

Devil's boletus (*Boletus satanas*): found under beech trees in particular, but look under all trees that grow on calcareous soils. Usually occurs from June to August.

Yellow-staining mushroom (*Agaricus xanthodermus*): found in pastureland from August to October.

Fishing

SEA FISHING IS BIG BUSINESS and the increased commercialization of the fishing industry over recent years has undoubtedly affected the catches of those fishermen who like just to row gently out from the shore, cast off a line and see how lucky they can be. However, the oceans are bountiful and there certainly is food to be caught for those with the patience.

From the beach: the diligent can catch much without even leaving the shore and barely getting their feet wet. On a rocky beach try searching the rock pools at low tide, turning over the rocks one by one. If you are lucky you can get bucketfuls of prawns (shrimps) this way.

Another way of catching prawns (which mainly frequent rocky coastlines) is by suspending a net from the rocks into water that is about 1.2–1.5 metres (4–5 ft) deep. You can make the net by fixing it to the rim of an old bicycle wheel (remove some of the spokes first). Tie a rope to the hub, lower it into the water so the net is just covered and leave it for five to ten minutes. Pull it up and the chances are you will have a decent catch.

Long line: this is a line laid down the beach at low tide, the ends secured through a wooden board which is buried into the sand to anchor it. All the way along the line are short traces – 15–22 cm (6–9 in) long – which have baited hooks on the ends of them. As the tide comes in, it will bring a number of fish in with it and they, hopefully, will take the bait. When you go back at the next low tide, there should be a line full of fish. If you live in an area where crabs (which unfortunately are unlikely to be the edible kind) abound, and are apt to take your bait, put little corks on the traces. This will lift them as the water flows over them, taking them out of reach of the crabs.

Trot line: this operates on the same principle as a long line, but this time the line is set up parallel to the shoreline and is anchored securely at either end. It may be 9–12 metres (30–40 ft) long and is held off the beach by posts. Traces with baited hooks hang from it and these may be buried in the sand when the line is set up at low tide. Go back at the following low tide and see if you have had any luck.

Rod and line: those with plenty of time can try fishing with a rod and line from the beach, casting into the water at high tide. The length of line needed will depend on the sea bed and whether it drops away quickly, but on a normal beach you will need a line of at least 64 metres (70 yd), so you will need to be something of an expert angler (and a fanatic – it is not the quickest way to catch a meal). You could bait the line with up to about thirty hooks on small traces – this being the most you could probably hope to haul in without a mechanical winch.

For those prepared to get wet, there are two further possibilities of catching fish without using a boat.

Lobster-pots: these basket-type pots are specially

designed so that lobsters and crabs can swim into them, but cannot swim out. Although they are often put in 10 metres (30 ft) of water or so from a boat, they can be put closer to shore around wrecks, rocks or estuaries where lobsters and crabs are known to be. They should be weighted to keep them on the bottom and their position marked with buoys. Visit them periodically.

Seine net: you need a few helpers for this. A long net about 1.5 metres (5 ft) deep and 15–23 metres (50–75 ft) long is anchored, at low tide, at one end to the beach, and two people take the other end and wade out as far as they can go. They then walk back onto the beach in a wide arc, making a sweeping movement with the net. As the net comes up onto the beach, it should bring an ample catch with it.

If you have a small boat, other possibilities will open up to you, but remember that it is unwise to go more than about 1.6 kilometres (1 mile) offshore, and that far only when weather conditions are good. If you cannot swim, it is unwise to go out of your depth.

The sensible plan of operation when considering offshore fishing is to try to determine where the fish are

Left; lobsters can be caught in pots strategically placed around rocks, close to the shore. If you have a boat, you can leave them further out.

Below: it is not necessary to take to the sea to fish. If you are patient you can collect a big catch from waters around the shoreline.

going to be, so that you keep the chances of a fruitless mission to a minimum. You can ask more experienced fishermen who may be willing to share their knowledge with you, or you can learn by observing the sea bed at low tide. If there are gulleys or outcrops of rocks for example, these are the places where the fish will gather when they come in, so position your boat above them.

There are various techniques for fishing from a boat, and what you do will depend on the equipment you have and whether you are going for bottom-living fish such as plaice, sole, dab or flounder, or those that mainly frequent the mid-water, such as bass, mackerel, pollack, etc.

Rod and line: if you are fishing with a rod and line, you can do so with bait or flies. Using flies (small feathers tied onto the hook meant to simulate flies on the water or tiny fish swimming through it) is the sporting way; using bait gives you more of a chance, as the fish are more likely to go after a tasty meal. If looking for bottom-living fish, you do so with the boat at anchor and the line is weighted so the bait remains on the bottom. If going for the mid-water fish, let the boat drift; generally it stays sideways to the tide, gently moving down the tide, and you should play the line through the water. This means gently pulling it so the fish are attracted by the lures. In either case, the line can have several traces with hooks running off it, so that you can hope to catch more than one fish at a time. As soon as you feel a bite, haul the line in; if you have gone through a shoal of mackerel, for example, you may have a fish on each hook and if you are quick and have a small outboard motor, you may have

Bait: there are many different types of bait available, but one of the most traditional forms is the lugworm **(above)** which can be dug up from the beach in the early morning. Equally, the size of the spinner **(right)** can vary according to the type of fishing you plan to do and the size of fish you wish to catch.

time to wheel the boat round and go through the shoal again.

Fishermen fishing the bottom often help the size of their catch by attaching what is known as a 'rubby-dubby' bag to the anchor. This gory item is a bag crammed full of fish guts, which exudes a highly alluring juice into the water, thereby attracting the fish to it.

Long line: you can let a long line out from the boat; it operates on the same principle as the one described for use from the shore. Tie one end of the line to an anchor, row out and drop this, then let the line unravel as you move down the tide line and attach the other end to an anchor with a marker buoy. You can leave the line until the next day, then come back and haul it in.

Seine net: this can be done on the same principle as that already explained for shore-line fishing, except a boat can be used instead of two people wading out. The other end should still be anchored to the shore.

Trawl net: if your boat has a motor you could try dragging a trawl net behind it, and you can use one designed to go along the bottom or one for mid-water. The net is wide open at the front and tapers towards the end, a bit like the toe of a sock. All types of fish can be caught in this way.

What will you catch?

This depends on where you are fishing and the time of year, as well as the day-to-day weather conditions, the temperature of the water, and so on. You can catch whiting all the year round, although they are most plentiful in the winter. Robin huss, dab, flounder and sole are also year-round catches, but sole are always difficult to catch as they mainly feed at night. Spurdog (a superior type of huss) may be caught from December to June and plaice from June to December. Fishermen generally believe April and May to be quiet months, but this may be when considered in the light of the summer months when mackerel, bass, gurnard (flying gurnard), tope and garfish (gar) swim into reach. In the late summer you can hook the evil-looking conger eel. You may be lucky and get some fish apparently out of season. It is not unknown, for example, to catch thornback ray (skate) in early summer when it comes inshore to lay its eggs. Normally it lives at greater depths than those considered here.

Not all the fish mentioned above may be to your liking, but they are worth tasting, at least once. The rather unpleasant meat of the tope, for example, takes on quite a different character if soaked overnight in vinegar and water (it turns quite white), and the flesh of the conger eel is delicious if cut into bite-sized pieces, coated in batter and deep-fried.

Bait

All sorts of fish can be used for bait; an oily piece of mackerel, for example, offers infinite temptation. The traditional bait is the lugworm, for which you need to get up early and go and dig at low tide. Their presence is detectable by the worm-like casts they throw up in the sand; people will tell you not to dig directly into these, but look for the blow-hole a little way off and dig under that. Better still is to find a patch of beach that is riddled with casts and just dig! There are two types of lugworm – the blow lug and the black lug. The latter is better – bigger and more favoured by fish; inevitably it is harder to find. If you find a patch, dig like crazy and grab hold of them as they disappear from you.

Coastal plants and seaweeds

A few edible plants that are found living close to the sea are mentioned here, together with some edible seaweeds. Seaweeds are rich sources of iron and minerals and yet, once again, are sadly neglected by most people. They tend to be treated with the same disdain and suspicion given to fungi, but, like them, they can provide a tasty, and free, meal. Always wash seaweeds very thoroughly in cold running water before cooking them; they are likely to be salty and full of grit etc.

Coastal plants/Rock samphire: grows on cliff faces and, more accessibly, among the shingle and rocky outcrops of many coastlines. Pick the leaves and cook like other greens.

Sea beet: known also as sea spinach, it grows widely on sea shores, even on shingle. The leaves can be picked and treated just like cultivated spinach.

Sea holly: grows on sandy or shingle shores, but is less common now owing to the heavy picking it has suffered in the past. The roots were traditionally peeled and boiled before being crystallized in a heavy syrup.

Sea kale: another plant that grows on sandy or shingle shores. Pick off the big leaves, strip them to leave the stems, boil these and serve with melted butter.

Sea purslane: this plant likes the salty marshes found near the coast. The leaves may be used in salads.

Seaweeds/Carragheen or Irish Moss: the reddish-purple fronds (which may turn green in very strong sunlight) of this seaweed can be found in shallow pools, clinging to rocks and stones. Gather it when young, wash it well and simmer it slowly in the ratio of one part seaweed to three parts milk or water, adding sugar to taste. The seaweed will dissolve, at which point it can be strained and flavoured to make a blancmange or jelly, for the mixture will set firm when cold. You can dry it by washing it and putting it in the sun. Use as gelatine.

Dulse: the fan-like fronds of dulse may be found in shallow waters or hanging onto rocks on lower shores. Discard the older parts, once gathered, as these tend to be tough; the younger parts are more tender and can be used raw in salads or cooked like a green vegetable..

Kelp: found round the low-tide mark on seashores, particularly those that are rocky. Kelp may be treated in the same way as carragheen to provide vegetable gelatine. It may also be used raw in salad.

Laver: this is one of the most commonly-used seaweeds and its purply-green fronds, which turn black when dry, grows on all manner of stones and rocks found on the seashore. It particularly likes those that become covered with sand. It is probably most often used to make laverbread, which in fact is a sort of purée, which the Welsh once widely considered to be a breakfast delicacy when rolled in oatmeal and fried with bacon. To make the purée, wash the seaweed thoroughly, then simmer it, changing the water as it begins to stick, until it is thoroughly mushy. It is also traditionally used as a sauce to go with lamb or, more accurately, mutton.

Sea lettuce: the translucent green fronds of this seaweed will be found on all parts of the shoreline, sometimes floating in shallow water, sometimes in rock pools and sometimes hanging onto stones or rocks. It can be washed and cooked like a green vegetable.

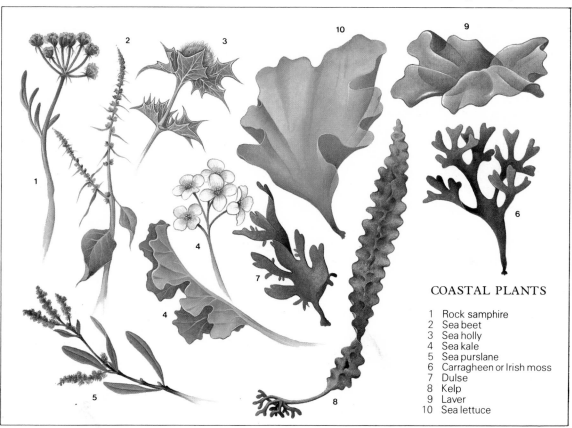

COASTAL PLANTS

1 Rock samphire
2 Sea beet
3 Sea holly
4 Sea kale
5 Sea purslane
6 Carragheen or Irish moss
7 Dulse
8 Kelp
9 Laver
10 Sea lettuce

Food From the Seashore and Coastal Waters

NUMBERS OF EDIBLE FISH can be gathered from the seashore without the use of a fishing line or net, nor is it necessary to take to the waters in a boat. These fish are the shellfish, in particular the molluscs, that mainly live on the rocks or in the sand or rock pools that line the water's edge.

Molluscs: shellfish, and molluscs in particular, certainly should be treated with caution but, by and large, they do not deserve the reputation they have for causing frequent and dire food-poisoning. They feed by pumping water through their shells, filtering out the food particles as they do so, and any bacteria contained in the water tends to be retained with the food particles. Therefore, molluscs found near sewage outlets should be left well alone, and it is wise to do the same with those living on piers, jetties or other possible sources of pollution. Instead, collect them only from a clean, unpolluted stretch of water.

Some people advise against collecting molluscs during the warmer summer months. Although no harm need come to anyone eating them at this time, it is sound advice for two reasons: the first is that this is their breeding season, so they will necessarily not be in prime condition, and the second is that the warmer temperatures of the water provide slightly more conducive conditions for bacteria to work.

The other important point about shellfish of all kinds is that they decompose very quickly after death. Never collect any that are already dead (if the shell is open, or if they do not hold fast to their rocky stronghold, this is a sure sign). They should be alive at the moment of cooking, which should be done as quickly as possible after collection, having first been washed very well in clean water.

Cockles: these small molluscs are also found in tidal mud or sand, and frequently inhabit the mouths of rivers. They generally live just under the surface and are visible either by the narrow veins of mud showing up against the sand or from the fact that the area looks a little darker or muddier than the rest. You can usually find a fair number of cockles in one spot. Scoop them out with your hands or dig them out with a blunt-pointed rake and put them carefully into a bucket or bag. Soak the cockles for several hours in a bowl of clean, salted water, having first washed off any clinging mud and sand. They will filter the water through their shells, getting rid of sand and waste matter. Then put them into a large pan with a small amount of water over a gentle heat. Shake the pan until the shells open. Pick the fleshy meat out of

the shells and use as cocktail snacks, or add to fish salads, soups, stews, sauces, pies, etc.

Clams: a great favourite in the United States of America, clams are most frequently found in the, often muddy, sands exposed between tides. They are among the largest of the molluscs, and usually live quite deep beneath the surface of the sand or mud, so you will have to dig for them. They can be eaten raw, but they are often difficult to prize open. Do so by inserting a sharp knife (preferably a special oyster one) between the shells at the hinge and twisting it. Cut off and discard the fleshy siphon. Alternatively, they can be persuaded to open by shaking the shells in a saucepan over a medium heat for a few minutes.

To cook them, boil for five to ten minutes, then remove from the shell. You can eat them like this, fry them, or add them to soups, stews or sauces.

Limpets: these single-shelled molluscs cling to rocks, jetties, piers and the like, but should be gathered only from clean rocks which are washed daily by the incoming tides. Prize them free with a knife (you can kick or knock them off if you take them by surprise) and treat them like cockles, soaking before cooking. They are much tougher than either clams or cockles and will need long, gentle simmering if they are not to be chewy.

Mussels: these bi-valves are found on rocks close to estuaries and the shoreline. Because they are so susceptible to pollution, be particularly sure that you only gather them from clean places. To be absolutely certain, take them only from the low rocks that are washed by each tide, gathering them, therefore, at low tide. Discard any with broken shells, or those that do not close immediately the shell is tapped.

Scrub the shells and soak them for five or six hours in cold water, preferably with a handful of oatmeal added. The mussels will feed on this, excreting the dirt in their shells. Discard any that open or float to the surface in this time. Cook by steaming over a gentle heat, like cockles, or by baking them.

Oysters: these are increasingly difficult to find wild, and most are reared in commercial beds. If you do find them, it is a treat indeed, but do not let your enthusiasm mar your judgement – if you find them in polluted waters, leave them alone.

Oysters live in shallow waters, often near or attached to rocks or stones. The greatest delicacy is to eat them raw; prize the shell open by inserting a sharp, strong knife at the hinge, twist it, then use it to free the oyster from the outer shell. Add a squeeze of lemon juice and just let it slide down your throat. Oysters can also be used in recipes suitable for other shellfish.

Razor fish: these long-shelled bi-valves are very hard to find, as they generally live in the sandy shores that are only exposed at the lowest tides. They are worth searching for, however, as the flesh has a superb flavour. They will burrow furiously into the sand as you get near them. Either dig them out with a deep-pronged fork, or try sprinkling salt over their holes. This will bring them to the surface, so be ready to grab them. Wash the shells, discarding any that are broken or open, then soak them in cold water in the usual way. Steam like cockles or mussels.

Winkles: may be gathered from among the seaweed found on the rocks on the middle or lower shores. Rinse them and then leave them to soak in cold water. Cook for about ten minutes in boiling water. Let them cool, and then get to work with the pin.

Shellfish: there is a wide variety of shellfish which can be caught on the beach or in rock pools, without having to venture far into the sea. However, never let your enthusiasm get the better of your judgement, by eating shellfish which may have died before you caught them. The penalty of food poisoning is not worth the pleasure of eating a few extra fish. Some of the shellfish to be found around coastal waters are as follows: **1** oysters; **2** winkles; **3** whelks; **4** cockles; **5** limpets; **6** mussels.

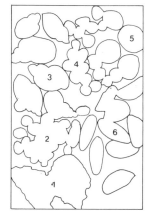

Freshwater Fish

HOW OFTEN freshwater fish will supplement your diet depends on where you live and how law-abiding you are! The great majority of freshwater situations in the United Kingdom – rivers, lakes and reservoirs – cannot be fished officially unless you obtain a rod licence and a licence to fish. In most instances these are issued by the local water authority, except in the case of privately-owned lakes, reservoirs and stretches of river, in which case, permission has to be sought from the owner. In addition, there is a closed season for coarse fishing.

Fishing licences are expensive, so as the prospective fisherman you have to estimate whether you consider it worthwhile to buy one. Fishing with a rod and line is the sporting way to catch fish and it is a highly-developed skill in which there are numbers of permutations. Those who are well versed in the art can undoubtedly make their licence pay for itself in terms of fish caught, although many such skilled fishermen are mainly interested in the sporting element.

There are countless different species of freshwater fish, many of which are edible. The chief ones – and those most coveted by the sporting anglers – are salmon, sea trout and the other types of trout. In addition there are bream, carp, perch, pike, roach, char, barbel, chub, gudgeon, tench, greyling (grayling) and eel – all of which may be eaten, although some may be an acquired taste!

Besides rod and line fishing, some less sporting people use trot lines in fresh water. A trot line is a single line which has several traces, each of which carries a hook. The line may be secured to a post driven into the bank and it is not an uncommon practice to peg out several trot lines at a time. Left overnight, they will often yield a profitable catch when checked the next day.

Experienced people will tickle trout, and can pull fish after fish out of the water. The technique is to put your hand gently into the water (in a known trout river obviously!) and wiggle your fingers. As the trout drifts over your hand you continue the wiggling movement, tickling the belly, until, with one quick movement, you get your hand round it and flick it out onto the riverbank.

Trot lines: secure baited traces to one long fishing line, which should be weighted. Tie each end to a post driven into the riverbank and leave overnight.

Nets: secure one end of a fishing net to the riverbank and hold the other, with the net resting on the river bed. As the fish swim into the net, wade into the river and pull them out. This is best done after rain, when the river is rising, and is easier with a helper.

Eel baskets: these resemble lobster pots, but are smaller. They are baited with fresh meat or fish, weighted, and left in the river. Check them regularly.

Seine nets: with the aid of a helper, secure one end of a long net to the riverbank, or hold it. The helper holds the other end of the net and wades through the river in a wide arc, sweeping the net through the water to catch the fish.

It is not unusual to use nets strung across a river to catch fish, in particular to catch salmon as they come upstream. The best time to do this is after rain, when the river is rising. The net is anchored to one side of the river, with the bottom of the net resting on the river bed. You hold the other side and as you feel the fish swim into it, you can wade into the river and pull it out. On very wide rivers it is possible to practise a version of seine netting (see page 173).

Eels can be caught in special eeling baskets, placed in the stretch of river that these fish are known to frequent. Those people with strong stomachs can also land a reasonable catch, by sharpening and straightening the prongs of an old kitchen fork, lashing it to a strong stick and using it to jab eels in shallow stretches of water. Find them by turning over the stones.

You can increase your chances of catching fish by learning to recognize where they are. Bream, for example, tend to swim in shoals, and can be spotted by areas of muddied water in an otherwise clear stretch of river, while pike are lazy fish that often lie quietly in wait for their prey in the deepish water of a reed bed. The somewhat muddy taste of pike, incidentally, can be greatly reduced by soaking it in vinegar and water.

Fish will be attracted to all sorts of bait – worms, maggots, garden slugs, and even bits of cheese, bread and potatoes. If you are being lawful in your fishing activities, however, you should check with the authorities or water-owners; some do not allow the use of live bait at all and you have to fish with artificial flies or lures. If you are fishing with rod and line, it pays to have a net, too, to help you land big fish. Another method is to use a gaff – a long pole to which is attached a sharp, strong, metal hook. A gaff is traditionally used to pull pike out of the water after they have been caught on the line; some unsporting people use them to pull out fish which they have not first caught on a line.

Freshwater fishing: this is considered to be more of a sport than a means of finding food.

Animals and Birds

THERE ARE NUMBERS of animals and birds found living wild which make very good eating, but the laws surrounding the killing of them are as complicated as they are manifold. Anybody considering farming the countryside in this way would be well advised to acquaint his or herself with the basic outline of such laws, in the hope of being able to ward off trouble, if it occurs!

At its very simplest, it is illegal to shoot or kill any wild animal or bird anywhere except within the boundaries of your own property, unless you have permission from the owner of the land. Even then, you can only kill the animal within the permitted open season and only if you hold a game licence. This actually also applies to the wild game which stray on to your property, in search of your tastiest vegetables: you can kill them, providing the previous owner did not reserve the rights to shoot, providing they are in season, and providing you have paid sporting rights to the local rural district council. Also, of course, if you intend to shoot wild animals or birds, you must hold the relevant firearms licence. In addition, there are extremely strict and complicated laws relating to the sale of wild game.

The animals that live wild in the United Kingdom and are generally considered good eating are rabbits, hares and deer. Others can be eaten, such as squirrels and even mice, but they probably have a rather limited appeal! Rabbits and hares are known as ground game and may be taken throughout the year (although hares must not be sold between March and July); there is a season for deer, but this varies a little depending on the type of deer and the locality.

The birds include pheasant, partridge, quail, woodcock, wild duck and geese, ptarmigan, snipe, grouse, blackgame, capercailye and pigeon. Some people consider other birds, such as rooks, worth shooting, too. All the birds mentioned have a close season, with the exception of pigeons and rooks, which may be taken all the year round. No reasonable person would ignore these seasons, incidentally, for they are imposed to protect the animals during their breeding seasons.

Rabbits: rabbits will be found in all wild habitats – woodland, scrubland, moorland, etc. A few years ago, the rabbit population diminished severely when it was hit by an epidemic known as myxomatosis. There are still incidences of this disease around, so if you catch a rabbit, check to see it is healthy before considering eating it. The eyes are the tell-tale feature: in a diseased rabbit, they will be swollen and runny. Rabbits should be paunched (de-gutted) as soon as possible after killing, or the meat will be tainted. Some people say they should not be hung like other game, but you may well find that the meat has a better flavour if you do hang it for a few days before cooking. Skin it after this (see pages 210 and 211 for instructions on paunching and skinning).

Hares: hares are found on open ground, but they exist in far less abundance today than at one time, owing largely to modern farming methods. You can consider yourself quite lucky if you catch a hare. The best way to do so is to try to find their homes (seats) and runs. Hares should be hung for at least a week (two if you can face it) and then paunched and skinned. This is a considerably more unpleasant job than it is with rabbits, as the animal is likely to be pretty high, but the cooked results should make it worth it, for jugged hare is a treat indeed.

Deer: some four hundred years ago, eighty percent of the deer population was found in parks, where it was sport for kings and aristocrats, and fair game for the

Game birds: these can only be shot within their recognized seasons, in order to protect them when they are breeding. Different laws apply in different countries, relating to poaching, seasons and licences for guns, but always make sure you are well acquainted with those which apply to you. Otherwise, you could find yourself having more to deal with than just a few birds!

brave poacher. Modern high costs of fencing parks and feeding deer have meant that many such parks have been abandoned and the deer allowed to take to the wild. Hence the wild population of deer is almost greater today than it has ever been. Shooting deer is a bigger job than shooting rabbits. They can be killed outright with a shotgun, but it is more advisable to use a rifle – and then only if you are a good shot. It is inexcusable not to kill any animal outright. If you do kill a deer, the best thing is to take it to your local butcher who will deal with it for you. Skinning and butchering it yourself is a pretty tough job.

Game birds: the open seasons for the best-known game birds are available, and these should always be observed. It is an interesting fact that nearly all the game birds (not the wild fowl, such as ducks and geese) that are seen in the fields and woodlands today have been

Setting a snare: these are one of the most common methods of catching ground game, but are certainly not one of the most humane. The snare is set up outside the burrow of the animal **(left)** and the height of the noose is adjusted according to the game **(above)**. A general rule is to measure four fingers for rabbits and the full width of the hand for hares. In theory, the snare works by trapping the animal's head within the noose, which tightens and strangles the prey **(below)**. However, it can ensnare other parts of the animal instead, leaving it in agony.

hand-reared by gamekeepers; there simply would not be the numbers in existence otherwise, as modern farming methods, in which chemical sprays are used to abolish many of these birds' favourite foods, have greatly reduced the various populations.

Game birds should be hung by the neck for about a week in a cool, well-ventilated place. In cold conditions they can be hung for longer. Although they are often hung with their feathers still on, they are best plucked as soon as possible after killing, as a warm bird is the easiest to pluck (see page 216 for instructions). The insides are left in during the hanging.

Killing other than shooting
Shooting wild animals and birds is the most common, and undoubtedly the most humane, way of killing them, but countryfolk have numbers of other ways. You must judge for yourself the relative efficacy and cruelty of such methods, for few can be relied upon to kill the animal outright.

Snares are probably the most common method used to catch rabbits and hares. Made from a variety of materials, such as horsehair, rawhide, cord, steel wire, etc, they operate on a noose principle – the snare being set up outside the rabbit's burrow, so that when it emerges, its head will go into the noose. It tightens and,

theoretically, strangles it instantly. However, it is just as likely to tighten around its stomach or leg, causing a long, agonizing death, or it may easily ensnare dogs and cats. If you do use snares, go and inspect them frequently to make sure no animal is suffering a slow, drawn-out death.

Another method is to use nets, especially when trapping rabbits. A long net is set up, supported on pegs and placed between the rabbits' feeding grounds and their burrows at night-time. A dog is then normally used to drive them back towards their burrows, and as they run into the net it closes about them. In fact, it is so designed that they catch their heads and ears in the mesh, and are unable to escape backwards. However, this method merely traps them and you still have to kill them. The other form of net commonly used is a smaller purse net. This is placed over the burrows and a ferret is put down into the hole to drive the rabbits up into the open and into the net. If you are considering using this method, you must also keep ferrets.

In the past (and probably still) all numbers of ways have been used to trap and catch game birds, but few can be recommended as being remotely humane. Traps of all kinds, which were once widely used in the poaching of wild animals, are highly illegal and using them will deservedly incur heavy fines.

Free Firewood

UNFORTUNATELY, very little firewood is free for the taking. All woodland, after all, belongs to somebody and, theoretically, you should ask the owner – whoever it might be – before you even pick up kindling. If you are able to gather kindling, remember that it really means small bits of dead twigs and branches that have fallen to the ground. It does not mean, as many people seem to think, branches that are up to 15 cm (6 in) in diameter and 2 metres (6 ft 6 in) long, that can be persuaded to part easily from the parent tree. It is because of this kind of abuse that many authorities and owners of woodland will no longer grant permission to collect kindling.

Small dead branches of wood, incidentally, will start a fire infinitely quicker and better than the firewood you chop up for kindling, and if the source is there, it is much quicker to go and gather an armful of twigs than to start chopping up old packing cases or splitting down large logs.

The only trees that you can chop down for firewood (or anything else) are those that are growing in your garden. Before attacking them, however, you should check with the local authority that they do not have a preservation order on them. These are imposed by the local planning office for all manner of reasons, quite possibly because your neighbour has complained at the sound of the chain saw starting!

If you own a patch of woodland, there is a legal limit imposed on the amount of timber you can cut down each quarter of the year. Also you must have a felling licence, although if you are felling fruit trees, or trees that are less than 7.5 cm (3 in) in diameter and 1.5 metres (5 ft) tall, for example, this is not necessary. There are a few other categories of tree that are also exempted from the licence regulation so check with the local authority or Forestry Commission before you begin.

Felling a tree

Felling a tree is simple if you know how and extremely dangerous if you do not. Seek the advice of experts, and watch them at work, before attempting it yourself, and even if you know what you are doing, it is sensible to seek advice if the tree is in anything but perfectly straightforward circumstances – ie if it is very large, leaning heavily, close to a deep ditch, telegraph poles, other trees, etc, or growing on very uneven ground.

Instructions for felling a tree that is standing perfectly erect, with nothing to obstruct it as it falls, are given below, but a word about power saws first. Nobody should use one of these without first having had proper training; they are extremely dangerous in inexperienced hands and can wreak appalling injury. Forestry commissions run courses for outside organizations (although not for individuals as such) and it would be well worthwhile trying to attend one of these if you have a lot of potential felling on your land. Failing that, stick to the axe and hand saw. They may take longer, but they are generally safer.

If you cut down trees, it seems only right that you should plant new ones. This way you are acting in a responsible manner conservationally, and doing your bit to ensure future generations do not inherit a landscape denuded of trees. Plant young trees – the younger they are, the better they are likely to take and establish themselves. If you are planting hardwood, it will be twenty years before you can chop it down for firewood. Ash is better: it should be ready for chopping again within about 12 years.

Felling a tree: 1 Chop a large wedge in the trees on the side that you want it to fall.

2 Chop similar-sized wedge slightly above first on other side of the tree.

3 Exert pressure on the same side of the tree to make it fall in the direction planned.

4 Once the tree is felled, trim off the branches and chop the trunk into logs.

Left: before felling a tree, it is vital that you plan which way it is to fall, and to ensure that you have an escape route if the tree falls in the opposite direction.

How do they burn?

Ash is generally regarded as being the best wood for burning. Beech and oak are good, but slower-burning, and they do not give out the same heat. Oak, in particular, needs to be mature to be at its best. Elm is not bad, but it must be thoroughly dry. Old fruit trees, such as apple, plum and pear make good burning. Most conifers should be treated with respect; they burn well, but are great spitters, so are best used in an enclosed wood-burning stove. All logs should be left to dry before burning (stacked inside a dry shed), otherwise they soot up the chimney with a black, gooey resin. This will soon close up the chimney altogether – hence the reason for the large, ingle-nook fireplaces of the past; they allowed access for somebody to climb up the inside of the chimney and scrape off these sooty deposits.

Burning peat

For those who live in very peaty areas, it is possible to utilize this for fire fuel. The peat should be cut out of the ground (usualy from valley bottoms) with a special peat-cutting tool or a spade. Then it must be stacked until it has dried irreversibly. Peat reaches a point where it cannot re-absorb moisture, when it becomes very cake-like and hard. It can then be chopped into convenient sizes and stacked ready for burning. It burns slowly and does not give out a fierce heat.

Splitting logs: 1 Drive a wedge into the end of a log, using a sledgehammer.

2 Drive the wedge in carefully so as not to splinter the wood.

3 Continue driving more wedges down log until it splits in half.

4 Once the log is split, it can be chopped into smaller pieces as required.

Preserving your Produce

WHILE THE AVERAGE consumer has to buy out-of-season produce from the supermarket, the gardener can enjoy his or her own produce, which has been preserved in some way. The satisfaction of growing and harvesting your own food can be enormous and you can enjoy the results of this work all the year round if you store your own produce. Eating June strawberries in the middle of a cold, grey February can bring back memories of the summer.

Of course, all foods taste best if they are harvested and eaten immediately, but there are few countries with a climate which is temperate enough to provide such extended growing seasons, so the food must be preserved in some way.

In all methods and types of preserving, it is of great importance that you know which produce may be safely preserved and which may not. Any reliable preserving recipe – especially the cooking temperatures and times – should be carefully followed. No one should risk food poisoning. If there is any question of the safety and reliability of a preserved food, do not tempt fate – throw it away.

It is a good idea to keep a record of each batch of produce preserved, recording what it was, how much it weighed, how long it took, the shelf life, and so on. You will soon become adept enough to develop a rhythm of planting, harvesting and preserving which will fit the flow of the seasons and the natural growing and maturing patterns of fruit, vegetables, meat and poultry.

Fruit and vegetables

The methods of storing and preserving depends on the individual fruit or vegetable. Most vegetables are best preserved by freezing, but root vegetables are the easiest of all, being stored in sheds, in the ground or in boxes of sand. One popular method of preserving vegetables is to keep them in vinegar to create pickles, chutneys, relishes, sauces and ketchups. Some delicious combinations can be created if you use your imagination.

Some fruit and vegetables can be dried . While the original texture will alter quite markedly, dried fruit and vegetables can be used in a variety of ways, either as they are, or after being soaked in water.

Fruit is well suited to freezing, although the method will again depend on the individual fruit. Soft fruit, such as raspberries, can be frozen, but will be rather mushy in texture when they are eaten. As well as being frozen in its original state, fruit is sometimes better preserved in syrups or purees.

Making wine, beer and cider at home has become a great success. Many wine-making kits are available but most are inadequate and, in trying to cut corners, eliminate the best qualities of home-made wine. The most important factor in wine-making is patience. Drinking the wine too soon is usually the cause of those shudders which can accompany the first sip of a glass of home-made wine. If it is made properly, however, it can be a real pleasure.

Goats' milk

Goats' milk is a good source of a range of dairy products, with yoghurt and soft cheeses being the most popular. Soft cheeses are easier to make than hard and require less time to mature.

Preserving fish

Most fish can be preserved by salting, pickling, drying or freezing but, whichever method you choose, do it as soon after catching the fish as possible. Herring, mackerel and cod can be salted, but this is an acquired taste. Pickling fish is done in much the same way as for fruit and vegetables, using vinegar as the preserving agent, but it will not keep as long.

Poultry

Killing poultry is easily done at home, although you may find it difficult at first. While it is fairly straightforward to skin a rabbit, plucking a chicken is a more arduous process but will become quite simple after a time. Poultry can be successfully frozen if you prepare the bird first, by removing the head and innards, and trussing or jointing it. Eggs may be preserved by a number of methods, while pickling is done in the same way as for fruit, vegetables and fish.

Preserving Vegetables

VEGETABLES CAN BE STORED and preserved in a number of different ways, some of which leave the vegetable in its natural state so that it can be used as if it had just been harvested, and others that change its nature somewhat, but still allow you to enjoy your home-grown produce all the year round.

Root vegetables store most successfully in their natural state, and they can also be frozen. Freezing is probably the most successful method of preserving most other types of vegetables in order to keep them as close as possible to their natural state. A few vegetables, such as the salad crops like lettuce and endive which have too high a water content for successful freezing, can really only be stored when they are turned into a cooked dish, such as soup, which is then frozen.

Leaving in the ground
All root vegetables, and some others such as leeks which have a very long harvesting season, can be left in the ground through the winter and dug up as you want them. However, there are three main objections to such a storage method: firstly, that you are unable to use the ground for anything else; secondly, that the ground may be so hard and frozen that you cannot get a fork into it; lastly, that it can be very cold work – picking brussels sprouts when they are frozen to the plant and the frost or snow is thick on the ground is few people's idea of fun!

Clamping
This is a somewhat old-fashioned way of storing potatoes and root vegetables, for which you need a spare patch of ground. Cover this with a layer of straw, then pile the root vegetables (take off all leafy tops first) on top in the shape of a pyramid. Cover with more straw, then dig a ditch around the heap, throwing the soil over the top. Ensure some straw protrudes through at the bottom to allow for ventilation, and pat the earth hard and flat with the back of the spade. The advantage of clamping is that vegetables keep freer of disease than they do when stored in a shed (see below); the disadvantage is that in a very cold area, or harsh winter, it does not give adequate protection against a heavy frost.

Storing in a shed
By and large, it is probably easier to store root vegetables in a dry, cool, frost-proof, gloomy shed, and there are various ways of keeping them therein. Remember not to wash them before storing, or they will rot. You can make a sort of mini-clamp by piling the vegetables in a corner of the shed, separating the layers with straw and protecting them with some sacking. Or you can layer them in containers, separated by sand or peat which prevents the vegetables from drying out or shrivelling. Use wooden boxes or dustbins and put a 5-cm (2-in) layer of sand or peat in the bottom. Put a single layer of the root vegetable (carrots, parsnips, beetroot, salsify, winter radish, etc) on top, arranged neatly and close together. Top with another layer of peat or sand, and then continue layering in this way. The containers must be kept in the dry, cool shed.

The very lazy might like to try piling up their swedes (rutabagas) in a corner of the shed and using them from here as required. Beware of storing vegetables in a garage, incidentally, particularly one in use, as they could easily take up the taste of petrol fumes.

In sacks: most root vegetables can be stored in heavy paper or hessian sacks, but not polythene, which holds in the moisture, so will make them rot. Storing in sacks is a good way of keeping potatoes; pile them into the sack, leave it open for a couple of days, then close it up and

Making a clamp: if potatoes and root vegetables are stored in a clamp, they will be freer of disease than if they were stored any other way. Place the vegetables which are to be stored on top of a layer of straw on the ground **(left)** and cover them with more straw. Dig a trench around the heap and throw the soil on top of the straw, patting it down with a spade. Leave some straw protruding from the bottom to ventilate the clamp **(above)**.

Stringing onions: before beginning, check that all the onions you want to use have been dried and have long stalks. Knot the stalks of four onions together, and plait a strong piece of string around them, so that they hang properly when you hold them up. As you add each onion, knot the stalks around the string, making sure that the bunch always hangs evenly. When you have strung enough onions, hang up the bunch in a cool, dry place.

store in a shed as above. Potatoes must be kept away from the light or they will turn green.

In boxes: onions and garlic can be stored in shallow slatted wooden fruit boxes, but make sure the vegetables are thoroughly ripe before laying them down. Then just put them into the boxes in single layers and stack the boxes one on top of another.

In strings: the other traditional way of storing onions is in strings or ropes and these should again be kept somewhere cool and frost-free. There are various methods of stringing.

In nets: onions can also be hung up in nets, but check them frequently to make sure none are rotting and infecting others. This is also a way of storing ripe marrows (zucchini) or pumpkins; they will keep for several weeks. Pumpkins can be stored by just putting them on the shelf in the shed, as can marrows, but they will not keep very long. Cauliflowers can be kept for a few weeks if hung upside down by their roots in a cool shed.

DRYING

A few vegetables can be dried, although this is more frequently done with herbs (see page 195). Runner, French and haricot beans, peas, mushrooms and onions can all be dried.

Runner and French beans: pick beans when young, and top, tail and string them if necessary. Wash the vegetables and slice the runners. Plunge into boiling water for about three minutes, rinse quickly in cold water, then spread them out on a clean tea towel or a

thick wad of kitchen paper. When they have dried a little, spread them out on oven trays and leave in the coolest possible oven until they are quite dry and crisp. This takes a few hours. Pack into jars with effective air-tight lids and keep in a cool, gloomy place. They should be soaked for several hours in cold water before being cooked in the usual way. However, they will lose all their valuable vitamins if stored this way, and so should ideally be frozen to preserve their nutritive value.

Haricot beans: leave the pods on the plants until autumn when they have turned quite white. Pick the whole plant and hang up in a dry, cool place which has good air circulation. When they feel quite dry, either shell the beans or put them in a sack and beat and shake it to separate the beans from the pods. Spread the beans on sheets of paper or trays until they are hard and dry. Store in jars and use as recipes dictate.

Peas: either pick them young, pod them and follow the method for runner and French beans, or leave them on the pod and follow that for haricot beans. The latter tends to be less successful, unless you grow a variety specifically for drying.

Mushrooms: you can dry those you collect from the countryside, but they must be absolutely fresh and the very best specimens. Peel them if they look dirty, otherwise wipe them clean with a damp cloth. Remove the stalks and either thread the caps onto a piece of string (making sure they do not touch each other), or put them in a single layer on a wire cooling tray. Hang strings in a warm place (such as above a boiler or in an airing cupboard) and put the trays in the coolest possible oven.

Drying vegetables: only a few vegetables can be dried **(above)**. Runner beans and peas are dried slowly in the oven and the plants of haricot beans, and some peas, are hung up to dry. Mushrooms **(below)** are dried on strings in the oven, and onion rings **(right)** are plunged into boiling water and oven-dried.

Leave until they are dry and crisp and can easily be crumbled, then store in an airtight jar. For frying or grilling, boil them in a little water for about 15 minutes, or soak for an hour or two. They can be added as they are to soups and stews to cook with the other ingredients.

Onions: peel and cut into 0.5 cm ($\frac{1}{4}$ in) slices. Separate into rings and plunge into boiling water for half a minute. Drain and rinse quickly under cold water. Drain on a tea towel and then follow the procedure for drying beans. Soak the onions for thirty minutes before using them.

SALTING

This is the old-fashioned way of preserving runner beans, and it is still favoured by some people, although it has been greatly superceded by deep freezing. Cucumbers, which will not freeze, can also be preserved in salt.

Runner beans: pick the beans when young, top and tail them, then string, wash and slice them. Put a 1 cm ($\frac{1}{2}$ in) layer of salt in a jar, which can be plastic, glass or earthenware (do not keep an earthenware jar on a stone or brick surface because they are both porous), then a layer of beans. Continue until you have used up all the beans, or filled the jar. Cover the jar and leave it for a few days. You will find that as the beans shrivel, they reduce in size, leaving some space in the top of the jar. Top this with more beans and salt. Finally, seal the top of the jar and store it until you want the beans. Take out as many as you require at a time, wash them well in cold water and then cook in the usual way.

Cucumbers: salt cucumbers as soon as they are picked,

188

SALTING VEGETABLES

Above: preserve runner beans by layering them in jars with salt. **Below left:** sprinkle thinly sliced cucumbers with salt, cover with a plate and leave overnight. Drain the slices and dry with paper. Place layers of cucumbers and salt in jar and seal.

specially produced for freezing. Only freeze vegetables which are in prime condition; discard any that are bruised, damaged or generally tatty.

Pack vegetables for the freezer in meal-size quantities, either to cater for the family or for the number of guests you usually entertain at one time. This is less important for those vegetables that you open-freeze first (lay them out individually on trays and freeze them before packing them into bags and containers); they remain separate when frozen and may be tipped individually from the bag. Open-freezing takes a little more time, but produce treated this way is easier to handle than solid blocks of vegetables. It is suitable for such vegetables as peas, beans (of all types), courgettes (zucchini), baby carrots, etc.

It is usual practice to blanch vegetables before freezing them, although you will find people who argue against this practice in some instances. Blanching stops the action of enzymes and thus helps to retain the colour, flavour and texture of the vegetable. It also preserves the vitamin content. A special blanching basket should be used and the prepared vegetables are then plunged into boiling water for the prescribed time (see chart). After this they are plunged into ice-cold water for the same length of time to prevent the cooking process continuing.

A large pan of water should be used when blanching, as it is essential that the water returns to the boil within one minute when the vegetables are immersed in it. The recommended amount is 2.8 litres of water to 450 g of vegetables (6 pints to 1 lb), and it is inadvisable to put more than this amount of vegetables into the blanching basket at one time. The same water can be used to blanch about six batches of vegetables, but only use the water to cool them once. For cooling, fill a bowl with cold water

while they are still fresh and crisp. Slice them fairly thinly and place in a shallow container. Sprinkle heavily with salt, press a plate on top and leave overnight. The next day, drain the cucumber and pat it dry with kitchen paper or a tea towel. Layer with salt in a jar in the same way as for runner beans, finishing with a layer of salt. Seal the jar and store it. When they are needed, wash the slices well under cold water and leave them to soak for an hour in cold water. Then use them in salads, as garnishes, etc.

Storing tomatoes
Tomatoes can be frozen once they are ripe, although they can only be used for sauces, soups or stews thereafter; frozen tomatoes are no good for salads because they are too mushy.

FREEZING
Overall, this is probably the most successful method of storing vegetables and nearly all vegetables can be frozen. Because it is so successful, however, there is often a temptation to freeze too much, so try not to fall into this trap. Freeze only as much as you need to last you until the next fresh harvest and bear in mind that frozen food does have a limited life; it does not last indefinitely.

Vegetables should be frozen as soon as possible after picking, so only pick at one time the amount you can reasonably process straightaway. If you intend to freeze a sizeable proportion of any one type of vegetable, it is sensible to grow one of the varieties that have been

Storing tomatoes: a crop of tomatoes, which was harvested in October when the fruits were still green, can be stored until Christmas. Wrap each tomato in newspaper, and place carefully in a spare drawer or box and keep them indoors.

FREEZING VEGETABLES

VEGETABLE	PREPARATION	BLANCHING TIME
Artichokes, globe	Cut off stems and coarse outer leaves. Remove the choke if you wish; wash thoroughly in cold water.	7 minutes, or until tender, in water with lemon juice added. Blanch five at a time and drain.
Asparagus	Cut off the woody, lower stems and wash spears well. Sort into various thicknesses.	2 minutes for thin stems. 4 minutes for thick stems.
Aubergine (Eggplant)	Wash and cut into 0.5 cm ($\frac{1}{4}$ in) slices. Drop these into water with lemon juice added to avoid discoloration. Can be open-frozen.	4 minutes.
Beans, broad	Choose young beans and shell them. Can be open-frozen.	2 minutes.
Beans, French	Wash and cut off the ends. Choose young ones and leave them whole.	2 minutes.
Beans, runner	Wash, trim off ends and slice or cut into 2.5 cm (1 in) lengths.	2 minutes.
Broccoli, purple sprouting and calabrese	Choose small, tender shoots. Cut off tough stalks and leaves, wash thoroughly in salted water and grade into thick and thin stems.	3 minutes for thin stems. 4 minutes for thick stems.
Brussels sprouts	Choose small, firm sprouts; remove outer leaves and wash in salted water. Grade into sizes if they vary. Can be open-frozen.	3 minutes (4 if they are big).
Cabbage, white	Choose a firm-headed variety which is young and crisp. Shred and wash thoroughly in salted water.	2 minutes.
Carrot	Young carrots are best. Wash them (you can rub off the skins after blanching) and cut off tops. Leave whole and open-freeze. Larger carrots should be washed, scraped and cut into slices.	4 minutes for whole carrots. 3 minutes for sliced carrots.
Cauliflower	Choose compact, white cauliflowers and cut into small florets. Wash well. Can be open-frozen.	3 minutes in water with lemon juice added.
Celeriac	(If wanted for cooking, not for eating raw.) Peel and cut into cubes.	4 minutes.
Celery	(If wanted for cooking, not for eating raw.) Choose crisp young stalks. Cut off roots and leaves, wash thoroughly and cut into even-sized lengths.	3 minutes in water with lemon juice added.
Courgette (Small zucchini)	Choose young, firm courgettes. Cut off ends, wash and either cut in half lengthwise or into even slices. Can be open-frozen.	1 minute.
Kale	Choose young shoots, trim off thick stalks and older leaves. Wash thoroughly.	3 minutes.
Kohl rabi	(If wanted for cooking, not for eating raw.) Choose young ones, peel and cut into even-sized slices or chunks.	3 minutes.
Leek	Cut off roots and green top leaves. Remove outer leaves. Wash very thoroughly; leave thin-stemmed ones whole, providing you are sure they are free from all dirt. Split thicker ones into even-sized lengths. Can be open-frozen.	4 minutes if left whole. 2 minutes if sliced.
Marrow (Large zucchini)	Choose young, firm ones. Peel, discard seeds and cut the flesh into even-sized, fairly large chunks.	2 minutes.
Parsnip	Choose young, unblemished parsnips. Cut off tops and tails, peel them and cut into slices or chunks.	2 minutes.
Peas	Choose young ones. Pod them and grade into sizes if they are very variable. Can be open-frozen.	1 minute.
Pepper	Make sure the flesh is unmarked. Wash, slice and remove seeds and white membrane. Can be open-frozen.	3 minutes, but blanching is not really necessary.
Potato (new)	Choose small, even-sized potatoes and scrape or scrub them.	About 6 minutes (so they are almost tender).
Potato (old)	Can be prepared in various ways (duchesse, croquettes, etc) but raw, they are only worth freezing for chips. Peel, cut into chips. An alternative method is to partly fry the chips, until just tender, but not turning brown. Cool quickly and freeze. Can be open-frozen.	3 minutes.
Salsify	Choose young roots, peel and cut into even-sized lengths.	2 minutes in water with lemon juice added.
Seakale beet	Choose those with tender midribs. Remove leaves (and use or freeze like spinach – see below) and cut ribs into even-sized lengths.	3 minutes.
Spinach (including spinach beet and New Zealand spinach)	Use young, unblemished leaves and process immediately after picking. Strip leaves from the stalks and wash thoroughly.	2 minutes. Drain well and press with a plate to remove excess water.
Sweetcorn	Choose young cobs. Remove the green husks and silky tassels and sort into sizes. If you like you can cut the kernels from the cobs and freeze them.	4 minutes for small cobs. 6–8 minutes for larger ones. 3 minutes for kernels only.
Tomato	(For use in stews, soups, etc.) Choose firm tomatoes and wash and dry them. Freeze whole.	No blanching.
Turnip	Choose young, small turnips. Cut off the ends, peel and cut into chunks. Small ones can be left whole.	3 minutes (4 if freezing whole).

METHOD OF FREEZING VEGETABLES

1 Clean and peel the vegetables to be frozen and chop them into small pieces or slices of equal size.

2 Place basket of vegetables in a large pan of boiling water. Time the blanching process when the water regains its boiling point.

3 Plunge vegetables into a large pan of cold water, filled with ice cubes. Drain, dry and freeze – either in bags or with open freezing.

and tip some ice cubes into it. Drain the vegetables well after cooling, patting them dry with some kitchen paper, before packing, labelling and freezing.

Follow the normal freezer rules of packing vegetables into rigid plastic containers or polythene bags, excluding as much air as possible in both cases. Label them with their name and the date on which they were frozen and then keep a freezer log so you can use produce in rotation.

Left is a chart giving instructions for preparing vegetables for freezing, and giving the length of time they should be blanched in boiling salted water, unless otherwise stated. Not all those vegetables included in the growing section of this book will be found on the chart; this is because some are really not worth freezing. It has already been mentioned that most salad vegetables have too high a water content to freeze successfully, and they do not retain their crispness when thawed. Some root vegetables, such as Jerusalem artichokes or swedes are best stored in the manner described on page 186, or they can be frozen as a purée or a soup. The exception to this is if you want to freeze a small selection of mixed vegetables – including a variety of roots – to add to stews or casseroles. In this case, prepare and blanch all the different vegetables individually and then freeze them together in a bag. Beetroot and red cabbage are two vegetables that can be frozen, but are more usually preserved by pickling (or, in the case of beetroot, in boxes of sand); the results are not really worthy of the freezer space they would occupy. A few other vegetables, such as chicory, which are absent from this list, can be made up into cooked dishes and frozen, but they are not really worth freezing *au naturel*.

PRESERVING IN VINEGAR

In addition to the methods of storage and keeping vegetables discussed so far, many vegetables can be preserved by making them into pickles, chutneys, relishes, sauces or ketchups. Although these vary in appearance, texture and taste, they share the common factor that the vegetable is preserved by the action of the vinegar added to it. In most instances, various spices are added to the mixture to give additional flavouring.

Pickles, chutneys, relishes, sauces and ketchups may all be used as flavour garnishes to a variety of cooked or raw dishes, or they may be added to dishes, such as soups, stews, casseroles, etc, during the cooking to give

additional flavour. Differences between them are as follows:

Pickles: a preserve in which the aim is to retain the shape, colour and texture of the vegetable, whilst preserving it in spiced vinegar.

Chutneys: a preserve in which the vegetable or vegetables are cooked slowly with vinegar, spices and sugar, and often with such ingredients as dates or sultanas, to a jam-like consistency.

Relishes: a preserve in which the vegetables are chopped coarsely and either cooked quickly or not at all, so that their crispness is retained.

Sauce: a preserve made from one, or more, vegetables which are cooked with vinegar, sieved and then re-cooked to achieve the consistency of thin cream.

Ketchup: similar to a sauce in consistency, but generally made from only one vegetable and designed to give a very concentrated flavour.

Basic techniques and preparation

The most important thing to remember in the preparation of all these preserves is that any cooking must be done in an aluminium, stainless steel or enamel-lined pan, as vinegar will react with copper or brass in such a way that the taste of the preserve will be tainted. For the same reason, use wooden spoons and stainless steel knives, rather than metal ones, and nylon or stainless steel sieves. Vinegar will corrode metal tops, although those that are specially treated to be vinegar-proof are available. Failing this, use jars with air-tight plastic screw-tops or with clip-on lids fitted with thick rubber bands. Jars for all these preserves must be air-tight or the vinegar will evaporate.

Pickles

Spiced vinegar is normally used for making pickles, and this is made quite simply by steeping various spices in vinegar, ideally for at least a month. If sweet pickles are wanted, sugar can be added to the vinegar as well. Whole spices should be added, because powdered ones will make it cloudy; those most frequently used are cinnamon, allspice, cloves, mace and peppercorns. If you want to produce a hotter flavour, you can also add bruised root ginger, mustard seed and crushed dried chillies. Add about 6 g ($\frac{1}{4}$ oz) of each spice to 1 litre (2 pints) of vinegar, or more if you want a spicier taste. The most commonly-used vinegar is a good malt type, which is brown, but

Preserving fruit: this is the equipment needed when following any of the instructions given on these pages. **1** wooden spoon; **2** stainless steel knife; **3** nylon or stainless steel sieve; **4** aluminium, stainless steel or enamel-lined preserving pan; **5** jars either with clip-on lids and rubber bands, or air-tight screw-tops.

use a white distilled vinegar if you want a light-coloured pickle.

Choose young, unblemished vegetables which are still crisp and fresh. Wash and prepare them according to the individual recipe you are using (ie chop them, shred them or leave them whole). They must then be steeped in salt for at least 24 hours to draw out the excess water they contain. This would otherwise dilute the vinegar, giving a poor, watery flavour and reducing the storage time. Either sprinkle the vegetables liberally with coarse salt (not table or iodized salt which can spoil both the flavour and the appearance of the pickle) or steep them in a brine solution, made from 450 g ($\frac{1}{2}$lb) of salt to 2 litres (4 pints) of water. Dry salting is best for very watery vegetables such as marrows and cucumbers; soaking in brine is generally recommended for all others, but make sure the vegetables are thoroughly submerged by placing a saucer or plate on top. After soaking for the prescribed time (according to the recipe you are using) the vegetables should be thoroughly washed and drained.

If the vegetables are to be pickled raw, they are then packed into clean jars to about 2.5 cm (1 in) of the top. Any water that collects at the bottom of the jar should then be drained off before the jar is filled to 1 cm ($\frac{1}{2}$ in) of the top with the (strained) spiced vinegar. The jars are then topped with air-tight lids.

In some recipes the vegetables are cooked (beetroot, carrot and mushrooms for example), in which case they should be packed into warm jars while they are still hot and covered with the spiced vinegar in the same way as before. Keep all pickles for at least one month before using.

Vegetables suitable for pickling: beans (runner or French), beetroot, cabbage (red or white), carrot, cauliflower, celery, courgette, cucumber, marrow, mushroom, onion, pepper and tomato (red or green). They may be pickled individually or in a variety of combi-

Pickling: 1 Wash and chop or slice the vegetables to be pickled.

2 Steep the vegetables in salt or brine, cover with a plate, and leave for 24 hours.

3 Wash the vegetables well, drain them and prepare the pickling vinegar.

4 Either pack in jars when raw, or cook the vegetables, add vinegar, and seal.

the top of the vegetables or round the edges of the pan. If you think the mixture has become too solid (and remember it will thicken still further as it cools), add a little more vinegar.

The hot chutney should be poured into warm, clean jars and covered immediately with screw-top or clip-on, air-tight lids. The flavour will mature and mellow during storage, and all chutneys should be kept for a few months before they are used.

Vegetables suitable for making chutney: beetroot, marrow, pepper (red and green), pumpkin, tomato (red and green). Fruits: apple, apricot, blackberry, damson, gooseberry, orange, pear, rhubarb.

Relishes

Vegetables should again be fresh, crisp and young and they are prepared by washing and then chopping them into small, coarse pieces. Cooking will depend on the individual recipe, but many relishes are similar to pickles in that the vegetables are left raw. The spiced vinegar and, usually, sugar is added to them. It is usual to mix vegetables in relishes.

Vegetables suitable for making relishes: tomato, pepper and celery; sweetcorn, pepper and onion; cucumber and onion; beetroot and cabbage, and so on. Most relishes should be kept for about two months before using.

Sauces and ketchups

These are prepared in the same way, the chief difference having already been explained. As with chutneys, it is not so important to use crisp, young vegetables, but you should use those that are well-flavoured, and discard any bruised or damaged parts. The vegetables should then be washed, and chopped finely or minced, before being

nations. In addition various fruits (see page 201), may be pickled as well as hard-boiled eggs (see page 217).

Chutneys

It is not so important to choose crisp, young vegetables, but make sure all blemished parts of those used are cut away and discarded. By and large, the vegetables are prepared by chopping them finely or mincing them to ensure the finished chutney has a smooth, even texture. The vegetables are then cooked slowly with the vinegar, spices, sugar and any other additions (such as fruit or sultanas) for a long time. Malt vinegar is most generally used, although white, distilled vinegar can also be used. It may be spiced as for pickles or the spices may be added during the cooking – ground spices can be added direct, whole spices should be tied in a muslin bag and suspended in the mixture throughout cooking, and then removed. Spices used are similar to those used to spice the vinegar in pickle making, and individual recipes will specify them. Most chutney recipes include sugar, and brown sugar generally gives the better colour.

If vegetables are particularly tough (onions for example) it is often advisable to soften them first by cooking them in a small amount of water or vinegar in a covered pan. Once they are soft, add the rest of the ingredients and the remaining vinegar and continue the cooking with the pan uncovered. This aids the evaporation of the liquid which is essential to achieve the thick, pulpy consistency.

Chutneys generally require a good one or two hours' cooking, by which time there should be no liquid left on

Chutney: 1 Dice or mince clean, unblemished vegetables and fruit.

Relish: 1 Wash and coarsely chop the different vegetables to be used.

2 Cook slowly with vinegar, sugar and spices. Granulated sugar gives a light chutney.

2 Add spiced vinegar to the vegetables and either cook or leave raw, and bottle.

cooked together with the vinegar and spices as stipulated in the individual recipe. When the vegetables are soft and pulpy, they should be pushed through a sieve, after which they are returned to a clean pan and simmered again until the mixture is the consistency of thin cream. If sugar is to be used in the recipe, it is generally added after the vegetables have been sieved, and additional vinegar may be added at this time too. When the required consistency is reached, the sauce should be poured into clean bottles and topped with sterilized air-tight tops or corks. If using corks, let them steep in boiling water for about 15 minutes first. This sterilizes and also softens them, so it is easier to push them into the bottles.

Sauces and ketchups made from vegetables which have a low acid content – tomatoes and mushrooms in particular – may ferment during storage, so they have to be sterilized. In such instances either screw the caps loosely, or tie down the corks, otherwise they will blow out during the sterilization process. Put a false bottom on a pan which is deep enough to take the bottles, so that water can be added to come up to the bottom of the screw tops or corks. The false bottom can be made from thickly folded newspaper or by using a piece of slatted wood. Put the bottles on top of this, but make sure they do not touch each other or the sides of the pan. Pour in sufficient warm water to come up to the bottom of the corks or bottle caps and heat this to a temperature of $77°C$ ($170°F$). Keep it at this heat for thirty minutes, then remove the bottles and screw them up tightly. These sauces and ketchups should be used quickly once they have been opened. Those that do not require sterilizing will keep for several months once opened, as will pickles, chutneys and relishes.

Sauces and ketchups: 1 Wash, peel and chop vegetables. Cook with vinegar and spices until thick.

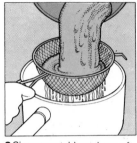

2 Sieve vegetables when soft and pulpy into a clean pan. Bring mixture back to the boil, then leave to simmer.

3 When the consistency of thin cream, pour carefully through plastic funnel into clean bottles, top with air-tight corks and label.

4 Vegetables with low acid content must be sterilized in a pan of hot water, and the tops secured. Separate bottles with pads of newspaper to prevent them cracking.

STORING AND PRESERVING VEGETABLES

The most successful and usual methods of preserving or storing vegetables are given in the chart below.

Vegetable	Method of storing or preserving	Vegetable	Method of storing or preserving
Artichoke, globe	Freeze	Cucumber	Salt or freeze as a soup.
Artichoke, Jerusalem	Leave in the ground or freeze as a soup or purée.	Garlic	In slatted wooden boxes or tied in strings.
Asparagus	Freeze.	Kale	Freeze.
Aubergine (eggplant)	Will keep for a fortnight in a cool place, or freeze immediately.	Kohl rabi	In boxes of sand.
Beans, broad	Freeze.	Leek	Leave in the ground or freeze.
Beans, French	Dry or freeze.	Marrow (large zucchini)	Hang in nets in a cool, airy place or freeze.
Beans, haricot	Dry.	Okra	Freeze.
Beans, runner	Dry, freeze or salt.	Onion	Hang in strings, or in slatted wooden boxes.
Beetroot	In boxes of sand or peat, or pickled.	Parsnip	In boxes of sand or clamps.
Broccoli	Freeze.	Peas	Freeze or dry.
Brussels sprouts	Freeze.	Pepper	Freeze.
Cabbage, white	Freeze. (Savoys can remain in the ground until wanted.)	Potato	Clamps, or in hessian or paper sacks.
		Pumpkin	On shelves or hang in nets in frost-free shed.
Cabbage, red	Pickle.	Radish (winter only)	Boxes of sand.
Calabrese	Freeze.	Salsify	Freeze.
Carrot	In boxes of sand, clamps or freeze.	Scorzonera	In boxes of sand.
Cauliflower	Will keep for three weeks if hung upside down in a cool shed, or freeze.	Seakale beet	Freeze.
		Shallot	Hang in strings or nets, or pickle.
Celeriac	In boxes of damp sand.	Spinach (all sorts)	Freeze.
Celery	Freeze.	Swede (rutabaga)	Stacked in a cool, frost-free shed.
Chicory	Freeze in made-up, cooked dishes.	Sweetcorn	Freeze.
Courgette (small zucchini)	Freeze.	Tomato	If green, in dark drawers until ripe, or freeze.
		Turnip	In boxes of sand.

Preserving Herbs

THE FEW HERBS that are evergreen – such as thyme and bay – can be picked and used the whole year round, but in order to enjoy the benefit of the subtle flavours of most other herbs throughout the year, it is necessary to preserve them in some way. The traditional method of doing this is to dry them, and this may be done in a number of ways (see below). Some herbs can also be frozen and this is usually a more successful way of treating such herbs as chervil, parsley and chives – chives, in particular, do not dry well.

A simple way to freeze herbs is to chop them and put them into ice-cube trays. Top up with a little water and put into the freezer or ice box. When they are frozen they can be removed from the trays and packed in polythene bags or boxes. The little frozen blocks can be used to flavour soups, sauces and stews and need only to be stirred into the mixture as it is cooking. Another way to freeze herbs (suitable also for basil, tarragon and mint) is merely to wash and drain them dry before popping the sprigs into polythene bags. They will become limp as they thaw so are not really much use for garnishes. Instead, crumble them into the dish they are to flavour while they are still frozen. Herbs frozen in this way will keep only for about three months in the freezer before becoming discolored.

If you are planning instead to dry herbs, be careful about when you pick them. All are best picked on a warm, sunny day in the morning after the dew has left them. Pick them just before the flowering season; after this the leaves – which contain the flavour – toughen. Choose only perfect specimens, with undamaged, unblemished leaves. Discard any that are withered or dead. Tying herbs in small bunches and dipping them for a few seconds in boiling water and then refreshing them quickly under the cold tap helps to clean them and to retain their colour, but it is not an essential part of the operation. If you do this, shake off excess water and dab them on kitchen paper to get them as dry as possible.

Treatment of dried herbs

When the herbs are quite crisp and brittle to the touch, they are dry. Either crumble them with your fingers or crush them with a rolling pin, discarding any tough stalks. If you want a finer powder, pass them through a sieve. Store the crumbled herbs in air-tight jars and keep them in a cool, dark place.

Use them as required, but remember their flavour is more concentrated than that of fresh herbs as the water content has been evaporated, just leaving their essential oils. When substituting dried herbs for fresh in a recipe, it is only necessary to use a third, or half as much.

Preserving herbs: 1 Rinse sprays in cold water.

2 Carefully pat dry with kitchen paper.

Drying herbs: 1 Strip the leaves from the stems and spread them out on muslin on trays. Place in a cool oven, and leave them for an hour, turning them over once. Turn off heat but leave them in the oven to cool. Crumble or crush herbs and store in labelled air-tight jars.

2 Spread the herbs out on racks and place in an airing cupboard, or on top of radiators, turning them occasionally. They will have dried after a couple of days, when they should be crumbled up and stored in labelled, air-tight jars.

3 Tie the different herbs in separate bunches and suspend them in either a muslin or a paper bag in a dry, warm place with a good circulation of warm air, such as an airing cupboard or over a solid fuel stove. When dry, crumble them up and store labelled, in air-tight jars.

Freezing herbs: one of the simplest ways of preserving herbs is to freeze them. Chop them up, place in ice-cube trays, top with water, and freeze. Stir them into sauces and soups as needed. Alternatively, wash and dry sprigs of herbs such as basil and oregano, place in plastic bags and freeze. To use them, crumble them up into dishes while still frozen. However, the flavour of preserved herbs diminishes after a few months, so only dry or freeze a few at a time.

Preserving Fruit

FEW TYPES OF FRUIT lend themselves to being stored in their natural state, in the way that root vegetables do (see page 186), and in fact the only fruits which can be kept raw in this way for longer than a month are the later varieties of apple. These can be wrapped individually in special oiled paper and stored in boxes, or placed carefully in the kind of thick cardboard trays seen in greengrocers, or put in polythene bags which have perforated holes in the sides. In all cases, the apples should be placed somewhere such as an attic or cellar where the temperature is constant and cool.

The most common ways to preserve fruit are freezing and bottling. Bottling was once the only way, but in recent years freezing has taken over in popularity, being both quicker to do and, in many instances, keeping the fruit closer to its natural raw state. Pickling, jam, and jelly making are other methods that are still widely practised as ways of preserving or using a glut of fruit. A few fruits may also be dried.

DRYING

This method is particularly suitable for apricots, peaches and plums, but apples, pears and grapes may be dried too. The principle of drying fruits is much the same as that for drying vegetables (see page 188), although it is particularly important not to let the temperature of the oven rise above 50°C (120°F) or Gas Mark 0–¼ for at least the first hour, otherwise the skins will either harden or burst.

Apricots, peaches and plums: choose the largest varieties possible and select fruit that is unblemished, ripe, but firm. Wash the fruit if necessary, then halve the apricots and peaches. Plums can be left whole. Cover wire trays (which will fit in the oven) with muslin and lay the fruit out on these, in single layers, not touching each other, with the cut surfaces uppermost. Place in an oven heated to the temperature recommended above and leave until the skins start to shrivel. After this the temperature can be raised very slightly.

These fruits are dry when no moisture comes out of them and the skin does not break when you squeeze them gently. Apricots and peaches will take about 24 hours; plums – not being cut in half – will take up to twice this time. Remove from the oven when dry, put on wire trays and leave for 12 hours before packing into boxes layered with greaseproof or waxed paper.

Drying fruit: a few fruits can be dried, in which state they will keep for several months. When they are needed for cooking, they are soaked in water, and sometimes sugar, until soft. Dried, soft fruit is also delicious eaten as it is.

Drying apricots, peaches and plums: place washed and halved fruit on muslin-covered trays and leave in oven until the skins shrivel.

Drying apples: peel, core and slice apples. Thread them on to thin wooden rods or canes and dry in an oven. Pack in layers or waxed paper in boxes.

Drying pears: peel, quarter and core fruit and drop in salted water to keep colour. Dry on muslin-covered trays in the oven.

Drying grapes: wash and dry grapes, then spread on muslin-covered trays and leave in oven. Allow to cool, then store in dry jars.

FREEZING FRUIT

Fruit	Method of freezing	Fruit	Method of freezing
Apple	Sugar-freeze; poached in light syrup, or as a purée. (NB If sugar-freezing or freezing in a light syrup, the apple slices can be prevented from discoloring by dropping them into a bowl of water and lemon juice as they are prepared, and by adding lemon juice to the syrup.)	Melon	Cut flesh into cubes or balls and cover in a light syrup.
		Loganberry	All methods are suitable; choose according to the use for which they are required.
		Mulberry	All methods are suitable; choose according to the use for which they are required.
Apricot	Sugar-freeze; poached in heavy syrup, or as a purée.	Peach and nectarine	Sugar-freeze, or poached in heavy syrup.
Blackberry	Open-freeze; sugar-freeze, or as a purée. They can also be frozen in a heavy syrup if wanted for pies, crumbles, etc.	Pear	In light syrup (treat as for apples to prevent discoloration).
		Plum and gage	Sugar-freeze; poached in heavy syrup, or as a purée.
Blueberry	Open-freeze; sugar-freeze, or in a light syrup.		
Blackcurrant	Open-freeze; sugar-freeze, or as a purée.	Raspberry	All methods are suitable; choose according to the use for which they are required.
Cherry	Open-freeze; sugar-freeze, or in a light syrup. Choose red varieties and pit them before freezing.	Rhubarb	Open-freeze (but the cut pieces should be blanched for one to two minutes first); in heavy syrup or as a purée.
Damson	Open-freeze; poached in a light syrup, or as a purée.	Strawberry	All methods are suitable; choose according to the use for which they are required.
Gooseberry	All methods are suitable; choose according to the use for which they are required.		

Open freezing: 1 Hull soft fruit. Place fruits on paper-lined trays, not touching each other, and freeze.

Sugar freezing: 1 Dip individual fruits in sugar, then pack into boxes, label and freeze.

Freezing in syrup: pour cold syrup over fruit in freezer boxes. Before freezing, cover with greaseproof paper.

2 When fruit is firm, pack it in freezer bags or boxes, label and return it to the freezer.

2 Another method is to place layers of fruits and sugar in freezer boxes, ending with a layer of sugar. Freeze.

Puréeing: sieve soft fruit into freezer boxes. Add sugar either before freezing, or when cooking.

Apples: the best way to dry these is in rings. Choose crisp, sweet apples; peel and core them, then slice them into 5 mm ($\frac{1}{4}$ in) rings. As you cut these, put them into some lightly salted water to help prevent discoloration. Pat the apple rings dry on sheets of kitchen paper, then thread them onto thin wooden rods or canes. Hang these in the oven heated to the temperature given above. They should dry in about six hours, by which time they will feel rather leathery and look dry and shrivelled on the outside. Spread them out on a wire tray and leave for a good 12 hours to dry.

Pears: choose ripe, but firm fruit and peel and quarter them. Cut out the cores and drop the quarters into lightly salted water to help prevent discoloration. Spread the quarters out on muslin-covered wire trays and put these in the oven heated to the temperature given above. They will take about the same amount of time as the apple rings to dry.

Grapes: the seedless variety are the best for drying and should be dried when they are just ripe. Wash them and pat them dry on sheets of kitchen paper. Spread out individually on muslin-covered wire trays and put in an oven heated to the temperature given above. The grapes are dried when the skins are shrivelled and do not burst when you squeeze them gently.

FREEZING

Nearly all fruit freezes well, although different methods suit different types of fruit. For all methods, choose ripe, but not over-ripe fruits, which are not bruised or blemished in any way. Fruit is best frozen within a couple of hours of being picked.

As mentioned, there are various methods of freezing fruit, each of which is suitable for particular types. In addition to the type of fruit though, the method of preservation will be determined by the use to which the fruit will be put. If it is to be eaten whole in its straight, unfrozen state, it is best to open-freeze it (see below), although this is the most time-consuming method. Fruit which is to be used in cooked pies or crumbles may be sugar-frozen, and if it is intended for mousses, etc, it is best to freeze it as a purée.

All frozen fruit must be thawed before using it in any way, although soft fruits which are to be used raw in a dessert can be thawed to a chilled state. The exception to this rule is if the frozen fruit is to be stewed; in this instance it can be heated gently from its frozen state.

Open-freezing: this is most suitable for soft fruits such as strawberries, raspberries, blackberries, etc. As with vegetables that are open-frozen, each fruit remains separate, so that as much as is wanted at any one time can be taken from the freezer bag. Wash the fruit only if absolutely necessary (the drier the fruit, the more satisfactory the frozen results), hull it, then place each fruit separately on a tray; they should not touch one another. Freeze until the fruit is firm, pack it in freezer bags, seal it and then label it before returning it to the freezer. When thawed, the fruits will be considerably softer than if fresh, but will still retain their shape.

Sugar-freezing: this method is also suitable for soft fruits, but the fruit will be very mushy when thawed and is thus best used in cooked puddings. Wash the fruit if necessary, hull it, then either roll each fruit in caster sugar, or put them in a dish, sprinkle with sugar (add as much as you like according to taste), and stir gently when the sugar has dissolved. Pack the fruit into rigid containers, seal, label and freeze. Another way of sugar-freezing is to layer fruit and sugar in rigid containers.

Freezing in syrup: this is suitable for stoned fruits and those which tend to be less juicy, such as apples and pears. They may either be frozen in a heavy or light syrup, according to your taste, what you want to use the fruit for and the type of fruit. Soft fruits are best frozen in a heavy syrup, while the more delicately flavoured fruit, such as pears or melons, are better in a light syrup. For heavy syrups, dissolve 450 g (1 lb) of sugar in each 575 ml (1 pint) of water; for a lighter syrup, halve the amount of sugar. When the syrup has completely cooled, pour it over the prepared fruit, packed into a rigid container. Make sure the fruit is submerged in the liquid before putting on the lid, by placing a piece of crumpled greaseproof paper on top of it.

It is advisable to poach most stoned fruits – apricots, peaches and plums – before freezing, or else the skins are likely to become tough during the freezing process. They need only a few minutes simmering and it is best to use a heavy syrup. When they have cooled completely in the syrup, they can be frozen in the normal way.

Freezing in a purée: puréed fruit is useful for all sorts of cold mousses, soufflés, ice creams, sauces and so on. It is also a good way to freeze fruit which is slightly over-ripe or imperfect (although all bruised or damaged parts should be discarded as they could affect the taste). Soft fruits, such as raspberries, strawberries and blackberries, can be sieved and frozen immediately. Sugar can be added before freezing, or on thawing before use. Other fruits – gooseberries, blackcurrants, apples, apricots etc

BOTTLING FRUIT

1 Wash, peel, stone or core fruit, according to its type. Carefully cut it into evenly-sized pieces.

2 Pack the larger fruits into clean bottles. This is easier if the insides of the bottles are wet.

3 Pack a little soft fruit into jars, and cover with syrup. Add more fruit and syrup in stages.

4 Fill jars of larger fruit with syrup. Ease out any air bubbles carefully with the blade of a knife.

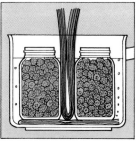

5 Seal lids of jars and place in a deep pan of water with a false bottom, for the hot water bath, quick method.

6 Secure lids but do not seal and place jars on newspaper in the oven for the oven method, wet pack.

PROCESSING TIMES

Hot water bath method
two minutes: Apple slices, blackberries, blackcurrants, gooseberries, loganberries, mulberries, raspberries, rhubarb, strawberries (unsoaked)
ten minutes: Apricots, cherries, damsons, whole plums
twenty minutes: Peaches, halved plums, strawberries (soaked)
forty minutes: Pears

Oven method
thirty to forty minutes: Apple slices, blackberries, blackcurrants, gooseberries, rhubarb
forty to fifty minutes: Apricots (whole), cherries, damsons, loganberries, mulberries, raspberries, strawberries (unsoaked)
fifty to sixty minutes: Apricots (halved), plums (whole), strawberries (soaked)
sixty to seventy minutes: Peaches, pears, plums (halved)

– should be lightly cooked and then liquidized or sieved. The purée must be quite cold before freezing.

BOTTLING

Just about all types of fruit can be bottled, and a good supply of bottled fruit can be an invaluable standby for winter puddings. The bottles or jars should be made of thick glass with either a screw top or a clip-on lid. In both cases they should also have a thick rubber ring that fits round the top of the jar and ensures a truly air-tight seal. If air is allowed into the inside of the jar, the fruit will quickly ferment.

When planning to bottle fruit, check the bottles carefully first to ensure none have chips around the ring. If they do, they are useless, for again the seal will not be air-tight. Make sure the lids are in good working order too – that the glass disc (on metal-topped jars) is not chipped or cracked, that the metal top is not bent or rusty, and that the spring clips are strong. Test to ensure the seal is air-tight by filling the jars with water, putting on the rubber ring and the lid and then standing the bottles upside-down on a table. If there is any sign of leaking after five minutes or so, the bottles should not be used. Wash those you do intend to use in hot water just before filling them with the fruit but do not dry the inside, or you will spread germs, even with the cleanest teat towel. Instead leave them to drain turned upside-down.

Choose only perfect, unblemished fruit and grade it according to size so that fruit of similar size is bottled together. Prepare it according to its type; apples and pears should be peeled, cored and sliced or quartered (put them into cold, lightly salted water as you prepare them to prevent discoloration); apricots and peaches should be halved and stoned, and the peaches should also be skinned; cherries, plums and damsons can be bottled whole, or plums may be halved and stoned if you prefer – wash them all first; rhubarb should be cut into small chunks, and will pack better into the jars if it is steeped in hot sugar syrup overnight; all soft fruit such as blackcurrants, raspberries, loganberries, strawberries, etc, is bottled whole and should have the minimum of handling. Some people say that the flavour of bottled strawberries is better if they are also soaked overnight in syrup and their colour can be improved by adding a few drops of edible red colouring to the syrup.

Fruit is usually bottled in a sugar syrup, and although there is no reason why it cannot be bottled in plain water, the flavour is not as good. Make a syrup with about 225 g (8 oz) of granulated sugar to 575 ml (1 pint) of water – vary the strength according to the fruit and your taste.

Pack the fruit evenly into the bottles, using the handle of a wooden spoon to push down and position the firmer fruits, such as apricots, etc. Fill the jars with the firm fruits and then pour in the syrup, jerk the bottles sharply to release any air bubbles and top up with more syrup. When bottling soft fruits, it is better to tip syrup into the jars up to the level of the fruit when they are a quarter filled, then a half and then three-quarters. This gives a better distribution of fruit and syrup. Tighten the lids, and if they are screw tops, undo them a quarter turn – this prevents the bottles bursting during the sterilization process which follows (spring clips are designed to avoid any danger of this happening).

Bottled fruit must be sterilized to prevent the growth of organisms and bacteria which would otherwise spoil it, and there are various ways of doing this. Two of them are described below – the hot water bath, quick method and the oven method, wet pack. In addition there is a hot water bath, slow method (which is similar in principle but cold water is used, the water takes longer to come to the required temperature and a thermometer is essential), oven method, dry pack (in which the jars are not filled with syrup until after the processing – a method which is not recommended for all types of fruit) or a pressure-cooker method.

Hot water bath, quick method

Pack the fruit into 1 kg (2 lb) jars and fill them with hot syrup, before securing the tops as described above. Put them into a deep pan or any other large pan (a fish kettle is ideal if you do not have a specially designed sterilizing pan) in which there is a false bottom; if the pan does not have one you can improvise by using a wire grill or placing thickly folded newspaper, cardboard or a towel in the bottom. The bottles must not touch one another – separate them with pads of folded newspaper to be on the safe side. Pour warm water (just above blood heat) into the pan to cover the bottles and put the lid on the

Testing for pectin: the amount of pectin contained in the fruit can be determined by taking a teaspoon of the cooked fruit pulp and, having let it cool, shaking it together in a jar with some methylated spirits. If there is a lot of pectin present, it will form a large clot **(right)**. If it has a medium pectin content, it will form several smaller clots **(below left)**. If it is poor in pectin, the fruit breaks up and does not really form clots at all **(above left)**. Pectin can be added to fruit whose content is poor either by mixing it with fruit which is rich in it, or adding a tablespoon of lemon juice to every 900g (2 lb) of fruit. Commercial pectin can also be used.

pan. Bring it up to simmering point – 88°C (190°F) – in about 30 minutes and simmer. Remove the bottles using bottling tongs (or tip some water out of the pan and hold the jars with an oven cloth) and tighten the metal screw tops. Leave the bottles overnight to cool before testing the seal.

Oven method, wet pack
Pack the fruit into 1 kg (2 lb) jars as previously described, and top up with boiling syrup to about 1 cm (½ in) from the tops. Dip the glass lids and the rubber bands in boiling water and put them on the jars, but do not screw on the metal tops or do up the clips. Stand the jars on a sheet of asbestos, a piece of cardboard or some thickly folded newspaper in the centre of an oven heated to 150°C (300°F) or Gas Mark 2. Make sure there is a good 5 cm (2 in) between the bottles at all points, then leave them for the times given on page 198. Remove them one by one, preferably onto a wooden surface and either fasten the clips or screw on the metal tops. Test for seal the next day.

Testing the seal
Between 12 and 24 hours after processing the fruit, you can test it to see that the seal is correct. Unscrew the metal top, or release the clip, and pick up the bottle by the glass top only. (Put your hand underneath the bottle to catch it, just in case.) If the top remains in place, the seal is perfect. If the lid comes off, check the jar to see if there is a crack round the top and check the rubber band to make sure it has not perished. The fruit can be reprocessed, but it is better used immediately. Label the bottles and store them in a cool, fairly dark place.

MAKING JAM
This is another way of preserving fruit, although it tends to change the nature of the fruit even more than bottling does. Jam does not have the same extensive application for making puddings and desserts as bottled fruit, but nevertheless, it is still a popular way of using a crop.

Jam is a thick jelly-like preserve, made by boiling fruit and water together with sugar to reach a setting point. The set comes from pectin – a substance contained in fruit cells, which once released, reacts with the sugar. Some fruits are rich in pectin, such as apples, black- and redcurrants, damsons and gooseberries; others are poor, such as cherries, rhubarb, pears and strawberries. In between these are a number of fruits – apricots, blackberries, plums, loganberries and raspberries – which have a medium pectin content. This means that unless additional pectin is added to the fruit, the jam will be rather less firm than that made with those which are rich in pectin.

Even though fruit for jam-making is to be cooked to a pulp, only good-quality, unblemished, fresh, just-ripe fruit should be used. Over-ripe fruit tends to lose its pectin and damaged or bruised fruit could affect the taste of the jam. Hull, wash and drain soft fruit such as raspberries and strawberries; peel, core and slice apples and pears; strip berries from the stem and halve apricots and plums, remove the stones and cut the flesh into quarters.

The fruit should then be cooked in a large pan over a gentle heat, adding water if necessary (most soft fruits such as raspberries and strawberries do not need water, but the individual recipes will state this). The pan is not covered during the cooking. Sugar is usually added after the fruit has formed into a pulp and the simmering has caused the volume to reduce considerably. Use granulated or preserving sugar, which dissolves quickly, and use the exact amount stated in the recipe. This will vary according to the pectin present in the fruit, so be sure to follow the recipe exactly, rather than add more or less to suit your taste. If you add too much or too little sugar, the jam will not set properly and the flavour will also be impaired. It is a good idea to warm the sugar in a gentle oven before adding it to the fruit, and make sure it is thoroughly dissolved before bringing the jam back to the boil.

The jam should then be kept boiling until it reaches

Making jam: 1 Peel, stone or core the fruit, according to its type, and then wash and drain it well.

2 Cook in a large pan with water if necessary. Add the sugar when the fruit has turned into pulp.

3 To test for the setting point, tip up a spoonful of jam. Setting point has been reached when the jam flakes.

4 Alternatively, allow some jam to cool on a cold saucer. If the jam forms a skin, setting point has been reached.

5 Remove scum from jam with a slotted metal spoon. Add a knob of butter to remove any final traces.

6 Fill jars with jam, cover tops with waxed paper and secure wet cellophane covers over rims with bands.

setting point. This can be determined by temperature – setting point is 104°C (220°F) – using a special jam or sugar thermometer, or by using one of the following tests:

Saucer test: put a little of the jam onto a cold saucer and let it cool. If the surface of the jam forms a skin which wrinkles as you touch it gently with your fingers, the setting point has been reached.

Flake test: take out a spoonful of jam, using a wooden spoon. Hold it for a minute to cool it, then tip the wooden spoon sideways; if the jam drops off the edge of the spoon in large flakes, setting point has been reached.

When it reaches setting point, the jam should be allowed to stand for a few minutes and then the scum must be taken off the surface, using a slotted metal spoon. A knob of butter stirred into the jam will remove all final traces of scum, and the jam can then be poured into warm, clean jars which have been left to dry. Fill the jars to the rim and place a waxed circle of paper on top (these are sold specially for jam-making). Wet a cellophane cover (also sold for jam-making), stretch it over the top of the jar and secure it with a rubber band round the top of the jar. Providing the jam is still hot and the cellophane was wetted first, it will give an air-tight seal. Label the jars with the contents and the date of making and store in a dry, cool place until wanted.

Jelly and pickling
Fruit jellies are similar to jams, except that they should be absolutely clear with no pieces of fruit in them. To achieve this, the fruit is placed into a jelly bag after it has been cooked, and allowed to drip slowly into a bowl or basin. The liquid is then boiled with a specific amount of sugar until setting point is reached. As only the liquid from the fruit is used, similar quantities of fruit make considerably less jelly than jam.

Many fruits can also be pickled in a similar way to vegetables (see page 191), although they do not need salting or soaking in brine first. Instead, the usual practice is to simmer the prepared fruit with the spiced vinegar, which is also sweetened, and when it is soft it is transferred to jars. The vinegar is boiled further to reduce it and make it more syrupy and it is then poured into the jars, too. Fruits which make good pickles are damsons, blackberries, gooseberries, apricots, peaches, pears, plums and crab apples.

STORING AND PRESERVING FRUIT
The most successful and usual method of preserving or storing fruit is given in the chart below.

Fruit	Method of storing or preserving	Fruit	Method of storing or preserving
Apple	Store later varieties wrapped in oiled paper or in boxes; otherwise freeze or dry.	Gooseberry	Freeze, bottle or make jam.
		Grape	Dry or make jelly or wine (see page 206).
Apricot	Can be kept for up to a month in wooden trays in a cool, airy place, providing they were only just ripe when picked. Otherwise, freeze, bottle, pickle or make jam.	Loganberry	Freeze, bottle or make jam.
		Melon	Freeze
		Mulberry	Freeze, bottle or make jam.
Blackberry	Freeze, bottle, pickle or make jam.	Peach and nectarine	Freeze, bottle or make jam.
Blueberry	Freeze.		
Cherry	Freeze, bottle or make jam.	Pear	Freeze, bottle, dry or make jam.
Crab apple	Pickle, make jam or jelly.	Plum and gage	Freeze, bottle, dry or make jam.
Crab apple	Pickle, make jam or jelly.	Quince	Make jelly.
Blackcurrant	Freeze, bottle, make jam or jelly.	Raspberry	Freeze, bottle or make jam.
Red and white currant	Freeze, bottle or make jelly.	Rhubarb	Freeze or bottle.
		Strawberry	Freeze, bottle or make jam.
Damson	Freeze, bottle, pickle or make jam.		

Making Wine and Cider

MAKING YOUR OWN WINE and cider is an excellent way of using some of the produce you have grown or collected, and an extremely cheap way of keeping the cellar stocked. Berries, fruit, flowers, vegetables and herbs can all be used to make wine, although some flowers must be avoided as they are poisonous, and not all vegetables make very palatable wine. Flowers that make very pleasant wine include rose petals, elderflower, mayflower, dandelion, coltsfoot, cowslip, primrose, gorse and meadowsweet. Pumpkin, marrow, potato, lettuce, tomatoes and turnips are the main vegetables that do not make very appetizing wines, although all vegetable wines tend to be something of an acquired taste.

Home wine-making is a hobby and a practice that deserves experimentation, for tastes are very individual and by and large, weights and measures are not too critical. The procedure for turning your produce into wine is much the same whatever the ingredient you use and, although initially you will doubtless follow printed recipes, as you get the hang of it and discover what to add to produce a wine that suits your particular taste, you will find you need to turn to the recipe books less and less.

It is always a good idea to make small quantities of wine each time, little and often being the sensible criteria to follow. About 4.5 litres (1 gallon) or so is the recommended amount; then should some disaster occur during the making, or you find it is not to your taste, it is not such a terrible waste when you have to tip it away.

The two most important aspects of wine-making to keep constantly in mind are absolute cleanliness and considerable patience. All the equipment (see below) should be sterilized before use, otherwise you run the risk of attracting vinegar fly or allowing bacteria to grow in the developing wine. Both will give the wine a strong vinegary taste, rendering it quite useless for drinking purposes. Sterilizing is an easy process and all home

wine-making suppliers sell various sterilizing solutions which carry clear instructions for use. It is a good idea to sterilize equipment when you have finished using it, before putting it away, and then again when you are ready to use it again. After sterilization, rinse the equipment in cold water and leave it to drain, rather than drying it on a cloth.

Patience is extremely important, and many people have never realized their full potential as wine-makers – as well as ruining a good brew – simply because they do not leave their wine for long enough to mature. All wine should be allowed to mature for at least six months before it is bottled, and in many instances it improves still further if left for longer. If you follow the advice of making small quantities of wine frequently, you will soon reach the stage where you always have some fully-matured wine ready to drink, so you do not need to be impatient with the more recently-made vintage.

Basic ingredients

I am presuming here that you are making your wine from your home-produced or collected ingredients, rather than from any of the commercially available concentrates and syrups. Besides the chief fruit, vegetable, flower, berry or herb ingredient, you will need:

water – according to each individual recipe

sugar – it is this which determines the alcohol content of the wine as well as the sweet or dry taste. Sweet or dry wine can be made from any ingredients, the deciding factor being the amount of sugar added. Many recipes – old-fashioned ones in particular – tend to produce wine that is rather sweet, so if your taste is for a drier wine, you may find you need to reduce the amount of sugar quite considerably. As a guide, 250 g of sugar per litre of liquid (2½ lb of sugar per gallon of liquid) produces a dry wine; 300 g of sugar per litre of liquid (3 lb of sugar per gallon of liquid) produces a medium wine and 350 g of sugar per litre of liquid (3½ lb of sugar per gallon of

Making wine: many different flowers, fruits and vegetables can be made into delicious wine. These will vary in potency from being slightly alcoholic to being very strong indeed, and will have varying flavours, according to the ingredients used and the length of the maturing process.

Basic equipment: home wine making can be a simple or extremely sophisticated operation, and this is mainly governed by the amount and type of equipment you buy. Keep it simple at the beginning, and you can then buy more advanced equipment if you wish to continue to make wine. The basic equipment you will need is as follows: **1** demijohns; **2** hydrometer; **3** empty wine bottles; **4** plastic funnel; **5** airlock; **6** corking machine; **7** corks; **8** siphon tube; **9** sterilizer; **10** campden tablets; **11** citric acid; **12** yeast nutrient; **13** pectin-destroying enzymes. In addition, you need yeast, water, sugar and tannin.

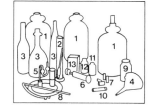

liquid) produces a sweet wine, although this should be slightly adjusted according to the natural sweetness of the chief ingredient. Use ordinary granulated sugar.

yeast – this brings about the fermentation process that turns the liquid into wine. Various types of yeast are available and may be used quite satisfactorily, although some will produce better results than others. Ordinary brewers' yeast can be used, but it is probably better to use one of the special wine yeasts, some of which are sold in sachets already containing the essential nutrient (see below). In addition, there are numbers of yeasts produced in the various wine-growing districts. Experiment with the various kinds to find those you like best.

nutrient – yeast is a living organism and as such needs feeding if it is to grow and do its work. The nutrient it needs to do this job of fermenting the wine is commercially available and the quantity to be added to the wine will be clearly stated on the bottle.

acid – the yeast needs acid conditions to bring about good fermentation. Without them, the final taste of the wine is likely to be impaired. Most home-made wines need acid added to them in the making, usually in the form of citric acid. Follow individual recipes for how much to add – it will depend on the natural acidity of the ingredients. Some need only the juice of one or two lemons to produce conducive conditions.

tannin – this is a substance found in the skins of fruit, particularly those of red fruit. It gives wine its charac-

MAKING WINE

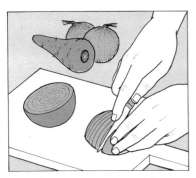

Making wine: 1 Wash and peel the vegetables or fruit you are using for the wine, and then chop into small pieces.

2 Simmer vegetables in water until tender. Steep fruit in a large container of boiling water, cover and leave until fruit is mushy.

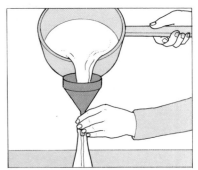

3 Yeast can be added at this stage of the process. It is mixed with fruit juice, sugar and nutrient and added to the wine after a few days.

5 Strain this liquid through a piece of muslin in a plastic funnel into a sterilized fermentation jar or demijohn.

6 Carefully fit an airlock into the top of the demijohn. Half-fill it with distilled water, to which is added a quarter of a campden tablet.

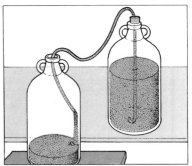

7 When fermentation has ceased, rack the wine by siphoning the liquid into a clean demijohn and seal it firmly with a bung.

teristic bite and, without it, the wine seems to lack some essential quality. Wines made from red fruit and berries – such as elderberries, damsons, plums and sloes – will not need extra tannin; most other wines, even white wines, will benefit from the addition of grape tannin, although if you prefer, you could add some strong, cold tea instead.

pectin-destroying enzymes – these should be added to wines made from fruit that is particularly high in pectin, which can make the wine rather cloudy.

campden tablets – these can be used for sterilizing equipment and they are also added to the wine at a certain stage in the making (see below) to kill off any lingering bacteria.

Basic procedure

As already mentioned, the basic procedure for wine-making is the same whatever sort of wine you are producing. Always choose top-grade, unblemished ingredients that are fresh and ripe. Vegetables should be scrubbed, peeled (if necessary), chopped small and then simmered with the prescribed amount of liquid until tender; berries and fruit should be washed and crushed heavily, put in a container large enough to allow boiling water to be poured over them and then left to steep for up to about four days; flowers or the leaves of herbs should be stripped from the plant, placed in a container

and bruised with a wooden spoon before boiling water is added to them. They, too, are left to steep for a few days. Some recipes will stipulate the addition of the sugar and a campden tablet at this stage (in the case of fruit such as apples, a campden tablet helps to prevent the fruit discoloring or beginning to oxidize). The purpose of this initial exercise is to extract the maximum amount of flavour from the ingredients, and stirring the mixture each day will help to do this. Be guided a bit by your common-sense here: strawberries, for example, turn mushy very quickly and clearly relinquish all their flavour to the liquid; they will only need about a couple of days' steeping. Harder fruits or berries will need a little longer. The container should always be covered during this period.

Prepare a yeast starter bottle; this merely means that you start the yeast working before adding it to the wine (many experienced wine-makers dispense with this operation and add the yeast direct to the liquid). Put the prescribed amount of yeast into a small bottle with some fruit juice, sugar and nutrient, plug the top with a piece of cotton wool and leave it in a warm place. Some types of yeast will begin to activate within a few hours; most take a couple of days.

When the ingredients have steeped for sufficient time, strain off the liquid (through a sieve and muslin) and add all the other ingredients – the yeast, sugar (if not already

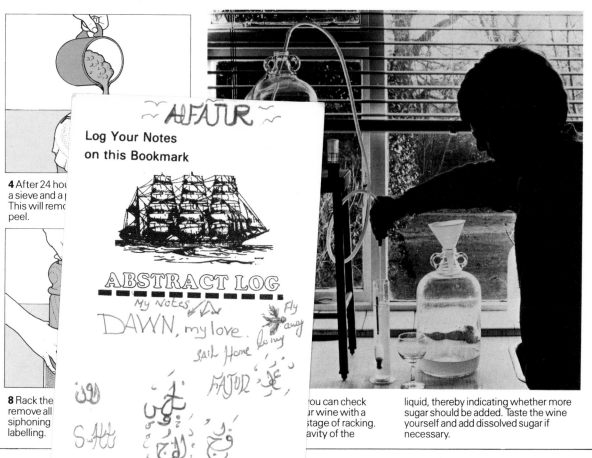

4 After 24 hou...
a sieve and a ...
This will remo...
peel.

8 Rack the...
remove all...
siphoning...
labelling.

...ou can check
...ur wine with a
...stage of racking.
...avity of the

liquid, thereby indicating whether more sugar should be added. Taste the wine yourself and add dissolved sugar if necessary.

adde...
tatio...
eithe...
days...
ferm...

As...
excl...
gase...
airl...
cam...
agai...
cou...
whe...

T...
whi...
the...
crit...
fer...
a r...
del...

mo...
is ...
so...
eq...
complete. Certainly in the early stages of your wine-
making, however, you can take it that once the liquid has

stopped bubbling, fermentation has ceased. Shake the bottle at this stage, and then leave it for another couple of days – no longer, for if the wine is allowed to sit on dead yeast, its flavour will begin to be impaired.

The next stage is to filter the liquid off into a clean, sterilized jar, leaving behind all the sediment at the bottom of the old jar. This process is known as racking, and it is done by placing the clean jar at a lower level and siphoning off the wine from the old jar through a siphon tube. Taste the wine at this stage, for if it is too sharp or dry, you could add some concentrated syrup or sugar dissolved in water. In any event top up the jar with water and add a campden tablet to ensure that no bacteria is allowed to get to work. This jar should then be fitted with an air-tight rubber bung and stored, preferably in a place where the temperature is about 21° C (70° F).

The wine should now be left for at least six months before it is bottled, and if during this time a very heavy sediment forms at the bottom of the jar, it should be racked again in the same way as above. It does not matter how many times you rack the wine – and it is a good idea to do so at least two or three times. The more racking you do, the better the wine is likely to be. It helps to stabilize the wine, thus ensuring that fermentation does not begin again, and it also helps to reduce any risk of the sediment at the bottom of the jar tainting the wine. During the six-month (or more) standing period, most wines will clear naturally, so do not be unduly perturbed if the wine looks very cloudy when you first rack it.

The final process is to pour the wine into sterilized bottles. The corks, too, should be soaked in a sterilizing liquid and, if allowed to soak for about 24 hours in cold, boiled water, they will also soften, which makes them easier to drive into the bottles.

The wine should be filtered and then poured into the bottles so that it comes to a level about 2 cm ($\frac{3}{4}$ in) below the cork. Drive the cork into the bottle, then label the wine with the name and date of bottling. Wine should always be stored on its side, so the cork is kept moist. If it is allowed to dry out, bacteria is able to enter the bottle and the wine will turn vinegary. No wine should be drunk for at least one month after bottling, and it is advisable to leave it much longer if you can.

Making wine from grapes

Most wine aficionados would claim that the best wine of all is that made from grapes, and it is true that grapes are the best type of fruit for wine-making, because they contain most of the essential ingredients themselves. The heavy bloom on their skins is even a type of yeast,

although it is still advisable to add yeast to the must. Most grapes grown in the United Kingdom will also need sugar added to them (those from the wine-growing countries of Europe generally do not), or else the wine will be rather too sharp and acidic.

Red wine is produced by squashing red or black grapes with the skins and steeping them; white wine can be made from white or black grapes, but the grapes are placed in a calico bag before pressing as it is the skins that affect the colour. For a rosé wine, the skins should only be allowed to steep for two days; for a deep red wine they can be left for up to ten. The mixture should be thoroughly stirred every day so that the skins do not gather on the surface and dry out.

Again, the basic procedure for making wine from grapes is the same as it is for making wine from any other ingredient, although you will find individual recipes vary enormously with regard to the amount of water and sugar (if any) used. This is where you must experiment and let your experience guide you.

Cider

If you have a surfeit of apples and have made enough

Making wine from grapes: grapes are the best fruits to be used for making wine because they contain most of the essential ingredients themselves. The bloom on their skins is a type of yeast, and should not be washed off. Some grapes have a very heavy bloom, called noble rot, which contains more yeast.

apple wine, you can turn the remainder into cider. A surfeit of pears can be made into perry. In both cases, it is only the juice of the fruit that is used – no yeast, water or sugar (unless you want to speed the fermentation or produce a very sweet cider). The best cider will be made from a mixture of sweet and more sour-tasting apples, and you will get the greatest amount of juice if you let them soften a little first (this does not mean leaving them to rot; if you have many heavily bruised apples, the cider will not have a good taste).

The apples need crushing, and those who go in for cider-making in a big way will have a cider mill. Alternatives are to hit them hard with a wooden mallet, wrap the pulp in muslin or calico and press it to extract the juice, or to liquidize the apples or put them through a food-processing machine and press them through muslin in the same way. You can even push the wrapped-up pulp through a mangle if you have one.

After that the juice can be poured into a clean, sterilized demijohn or an earthenware jar. A saucer is inverted over the top and the juice is left to ferment. If you want to speed the fermentation process, you can add yeast in the way you would in wine-making, but provided you are patient, it is not necessary. Rack the cider after fermentation has finished, and only bottle it when it has stopped giving off gas. Like wine, it will improve if left in the bottle for some months before drinking.

Making cider: you don't need a lot of expensive equipment to make cider. The apples are first crushed in some way (**left**) before the pulp is left to ferment in a demijohn or earthenware jar (**above**). If you are patient, and allow the cider to mature before drinking, it will taste delicious.

Preserving Goats' Milk

GOATS' MILK can be made into all the dairy products – cream, butter, yoghurt and various cheeses – most usually associated with cows' milk. However, most people are likely to find it fairly impractical to make cream and butter because of the amount of milk needed (plus the quantity of whey left as residue), and the sophisticated, expensive equipment that must be used. Four and a half litres (1 gallon) of milk, for example, makes about 450 to 900 ml ($\frac{3}{4}$ to $1\frac{1}{2}$ pints) of cream; to make good quality butter it is necessary to use cream, and it is hardly worth doing so unless you can use $4\frac{1}{2}$ litres (1 gallon) of cream at a time. To get these sort of quantities of milk, you would need at least four goats in prime milking condition (ie having just kidded), and this would generally be considered too many goats for the average household, even if you had enough land to devote to them. Another point is that cream is really only successfully made using a separator, which is an item of equipment that is not only expensive, but is virtually impossible to find at the current time.

It is possible to get some cream from a goat that has just kidded, without using a separator. Just let the milk stand in the refrigerator for about 24 hours, then skim the cream off the surface and beat it. You will get the maximum amount possible if you put the milk in a shallow container, rather than a deep jug, thereby exposing a greater surface area to the atmosphere. Another way of obtaining cream without using a separator is to heat the milk to 54° C (130° F) immediately after milking; then pour it into shallower saucepans and keep it at a temperature of less than 15° C (60° F) for up to 36 hours. Cream will rise to the surface, which you can then skim off; bear in mind you will get a smaller yield to the litre (gallon) than that quoted above. Clotted cream can be obtained in a similar manner; pour the fresh, strained and cooled milk into a shallow pan, let it stand for about 36 hours to let as much cream as possible rise to the surface and then heat it very slowly to a temperature of 76° to 87° C (170° to 190° F). The top should look oily. Cool the milk quickly and skim off the cream. Again, a separator will make more successful clotted cream.

It is important that milk from different days should not be mixed together. If it is, the milk assumes a very goaty taste very quickly. If you want to have a go at making cream – or even butter, if you have the right equipment – and do not have enough surplus milk from one milking, you can freeze the milk. If frozen within an hour or two of milking, it will not separate out on thawing, and in fact could not be told from fresh milk. Freeze it before the cream has started to rise, in small quantities; this is important as the milk should be frozen solid within three to four hours. When you want it, let it thaw naturally. If you thaw it quickly by standing the carton in hot water or by warming it in a saucepan, small flakes, which will not dissolve, will appear.

Making yoghurt and cheese

The most successful by-products from goats' milk for the small goat-keeper to make are yoghurt and soft cheeses. To make yoghurt, first pasteurize the milk either by heating it to at least 72° C (162° F), holding it at this temperature for a good 15 seconds, before cooling it quickly to a temperature below 12° C (55° F), or by heating it gently to a temperature between 60° to 76° C (140° to 170° F), maintaining this for 30 minutes and then quickly cooling it to 12° C (55° F) or less. After this a yoghurt culture must be added; special goat cultures are available and they will carry instructions for use. The extremely successful alternative is to use shop-

208

bought plain live yoghurt. Just add between a quarter- and a half-carton of plain yoghurt to 575 ml (1 pint) of milk, then leave it covered in a warm place, such as on the side of a solid fuel cooker. An airing cupboard is not really warm enough, so failing this, use either a thermos flask placed in warm water or a special yoghurt-making machine. Leave the yoghurt for up to about eight hours, then put it in the fridge. It will thicken as it cools but goats' milk yoghurt generally has a thinner consistency than shop-bought yoghurt or that made with cows' milk. You can use the yoghurt you make as the culture for more yoghurt for about a week. After that, it will begin to go off.

Both soft and hard cheeses can be made from goats' milk, but again, it is generally more practical to concentrate on the soft cheeses for most home production. Hard cheeses can be made at home, but they take considerably more time (four to six weeks), considerably more milk, and considerably more sophisticated equipment. They are not so likely to be successful and you could end up with a cheese that tastes so goaty that no one will go near it!

Soft cheeses are easy to make, and although some people will advocate the use of sophisticated equipment, perfectly satisfactory results can be obtained without them. There are three easy ways of making soft cheese:
1 Allow the milk to sour naturally by letting it stand in a fairly warm place for 36–48 hours. Then simply wrap it in thick cheesecloth and let it drip into a bowl. After another 36–48 hours, you will be left with the cheese in the cloth and a bowl of whey beneath.
2 Follow exactly the same procedure outlined above, but using yoghurt you have made. This will need to drip for about two days and has a rather sour taste. Try mixing it with garlic, chopped herbs or sesame seeds.

3 In this method, rennet is added to the milk. Rennet is obtainable from health shops and chemists, but make sure it is cheese-making rennet, not that suitable only for making junket. The rennet is likely to carry instructions for use (and will certainly state the correct quantities), but the procedure is to warm the milk to about 32°C (90°F), add the rennet, let the mixture stand for about 30 minutes and then put it through the cheesecloth. It will be ready much quicker than the other two cheeses and has a very mild taste. As it is the quickest cheese to make, the milk has less chance to assume a goaty taste.

The problem with making a lot of cheese (and yet another reason why it is quite a good idea to limit cheese-making and keep it simple), is that you can end up with a great deal of whey, which, by and large, does not have much use. If you are keeping pigs, they will love it and thrive on it. A limited amount can also be fed to your chickens.

There is one other thing you might like to try if you have a lot of whey, and that is to produce a sort of mysost, or Norwegian whey cheese. This is a thick-textured, light-brown cheese, that has a very distinctive, somewhat caramel-like taste, and one which could be said has to be acquired! To produce it, strain the whey into a clean pan and bring it to the boil, stirring constantly. Skim off and retain the thick matter that comes to the surface and coagulates, then continue boiling and stirring the mixture. When it has reduced in volume by about three-quarters, return the coagulated matter to the pan and boil it some more, stirring vigorously. When the cheese has thickened and is a light-brown colour, take it from the heat, but continue beating it until it is cool and too thick to stir any more. Pour it into a greased container and leave it to cool completely and set.

Goats' milk: you can make soft cheese from goats' milk by allowing it to sour before straining it. A basic method of straining is to leave the milk in cheesecloth for a few days **(left)**. An alternative is to drain it in moulds. The whey drains out of the holes **(below)**. The curds form the cheese, which can be flavoured with garlic or herbs **(right)**.

Preserving Rabbits and Hares

RABBITS AND HARES are paunched (de-gutted) and skinned to prepare them for the table. This is done in the same way for either animal, but hares, being game, should be allowed to hang for at least one week before the operation. This does make it an even more unpleasant and foul-smelling job, but those who like the taste of hare generally consider it worthwhile.

Rabbits are not game and therefore do not need to hang. Some people, however, consider that they are better if they are hung for 24 hours or so after killing, but if you choose to do this, you must paunch the animal first or the innards will taint the meat. Skinning can be done later (although it is actually best to skin a rabbit soon after killing it, as the skin comes away easier while the carcass is still warm and soft).

Immediately after killing a rabbit, it should be hung by its hind legs to allow the blood to drain to its head. This keeps the flesh light-coloured; if you want it truly white, stick a very sharp knife through the roof of the rabbit's mouth and place a small bowl or cup beneath the head to catch the blood as it drips. If you have no culinary use for it, put it on the compost heap, where it will be a fine activator.

Hanging and paunching:
unlike hares, rabbits do not need to be hung before paunching, but are generally considered to give a better flavour if they are hung. They must be paunched first, to prevent the guts tainting the meat. Cut through the skin of the belly and then down to the vent, until you are able to remove the innards.

SKINNING AND JOINTING

1 Using a sharp knife, cut off the paws at the knee joints at the beginning of the skinning process.

2 Gently separate the flesh from the skin at the cut in the belly. Continue to cut down the back legs to the knee joints.

3 Peel the skin off the hind legs carefully, and then pull it towards the tail as far as it will go, before cutting this off too.

4 Peel the skin off the body towards the head, cutting around the front legs in the same way as for the back ones.

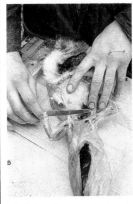

5 Pull the skin up to the head as far as possible and then cut off the head. The skin can be cleaned and treated.

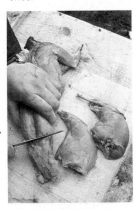

6 Split the pelvic joint and remove any remaining pieces of gut. Either joint the rabbit or cook or freeze it whole.

To paunch the animal, make a cut through the skin of the belly. Do this carefully so as to cut only the skin and not to pierce any of the gut, which will make a horrible mess. Cut down to the vent so as to enlarge the hole sufficiently to allow you to remove the guts (if the animal is still hanging, you will find they fall forward). As you pull them out, take care not to pierce the gall bladder (again, it is attached to the liver) or the flesh could become tainted. If you wish, retain the heart, liver and kidneys, and then dispose of the rest.

There are various ways of skinning a rabbit, all of which are equally easy. It is not a messy job, but it does carry a characteristic smell. If you have paunched the rabbit, separate the flesh from the fur at the incision in the belly by gently prising them apart with your hands. Continue the cut from the vent down the back legs to the knee joint and either cut around the skin here or sever the legs at this point with a sharp knife. Peel the skin off the hind legs, pulling it up towards the tail, then cut this off.

Peel the skin off the body down towards the head (like peeling off a glove). Again, you can either cut round the skin at the knee joint on the front legs, or merely cut them off. Pull the skin down over the rabbit's head, so that it is now completely freed from the body, and cut off the head.

Force the back legs apart, splitting the pelvic joint as you do so. This allows you to remove any final pieces of gut, together with the anal passage. Some people advise against washing the carcass, saying that this spoils the appearance of the flesh, but by and large it is advisable to do so, particularly if the rabbit was a wild one, in case any dirt from the fur has touched the meat. It can then be cooked straightaway (rabbit can be substituted for chicken in most chicken recipes; hares should be cooked according to individual recipes – jugged hare being the most famous, traditional and delicious of all ways to eat it), or frozen, either whole or jointed. To joint it, use a very strong, sharp knife and cut off the front part just behind the shoulder; split this in two. Cut off the rear end just in front of the rear legs and split this into two. Cut the middle portion (ie along the rabbit's back) in two, and split the front part of this section into two by cutting it lengthwise.

Skins can be treated for home use if you want to, or if you have enough of them in good condition you can send them to a pelt-dresser, who will process them for commercial use. The skin needs attention immediately after it has been removed from the carcass; if left in a heap it will soon begin to decompose. Remove the head and tail, and the paws (if they are still attached), then wash the skin to remove any blood or other stains. Cut away all the fat and tissue that you can. Nail the skin to a piece of wood, fur side down, making sure it is taut, but not over-stretched. Nail it out at the four corners first and then nail along the sides, making sure the skin remains taut and smooth. Put the board in a cool, airy, well-ventilated place, well out of the way of foxes and dogs, and leave it to dry. Do not be tempted to dry it in the sun or in front of some source of heat: this will dry the skin too quickly, making it become papery. Any remaining fat must be scraped away after a day or two's drying or it will decompose. The skin is dry when it is quite stiff, and this usually takes about five days or so. If you want it to be supple (to make gloves, for example), it will be necessary to have it dressed professionally.

Cooking: rabbits and hares are used in a number of delicious ways in cookery, from patés to pot roasts. One of the most famous recipes is jugged hare, in which the hare is served in a sauce made of its own blood. Rabbit can be used instead of chicken in most recipes.

Preserving Fish

WHATEVER YOU INTEND to do with the fish and shellfish you catch – cook them and eat them that day, smoke them, salt, pickle or freeze them – you should do it straightaway, as soon as you get the freshly-caught fish home. Fish decomposes very quickly, so it should not be left in the fridge for even a day or two until you get round to dealing with it.

Freezing
Just about all kinds of fish can be frozen, although if this is what you plan to do with them, put them in a cooling container filled with ice as soon as you catch them. The fish can be cleaned and scaled (see below) before freezing, or you can freeze them with their innards left inside. Large fish may be frozen whole or in fillets, steaks or cutlets (see below). In all cases, wipe the fish, then dip it into slightly salted, very cold water and drain it well before wrapping it for the freezer. Rub the flesh of fillets, steaks or cutlets with olive oil before freezing to help preserve the moisture in the fish, and separate them with pieces of waxed paper before wrapping. Fish should be wrapped and sealed very securely, otherwise it is likely to dry out in freezing. Its maximum freezer life is six months, and ideally it should be used before this.

Crabs, lobsters and prawns (shrimps) of various types are really the only shellfish worth contemplating freezing at home, and it is of paramount importance that they are absolutely fresh. They should be killed immediately before cooking, cooled quickly and frozen straightaway. All these shellfish can be cooked by dropping them into a pan of well-salted boiling water; crabs take approximately ten minutes to 450 g (1 lb) of body weight; lobsters about fifteen minutes to 450 g (1 lb) of body

weight; small prawns take about five minutes and large ones (scampi) about ten minutes. Separate the white and brown meat in crabs and freeze them separately; lobster meat can be piled back into the halved shells and frozen in these if you like, or just wrapped in bags and frozen; prawns are shelled and their heads removed before freezing. Shellfish have a freezer life of no more than two months.

Steaks and cutlets
Cutting steaks and cutlets from a large round fish merely entails cutting across the cleaned fish, through the backbone, to give flat, rounded pieces of fish. Cutlets come from the segment of fish between the head and the middle section of the body (down to the incision made for cleaning) and therefore have a hold in the flesh; steaks come from behind this, so the flesh is complete.

Salting
Freshly-caught fish, such as herrings, mackerel and cod can be salted, although unless you are particularly fond of the taste of salted fish, it is probably better to freeze them. Gut the fish, open out smaller fish such as herrings by splitting them down to their tail on the underside, then press them open along the backbone, and fillet large fish. (If you prefer, herrings can be left whole for salting, and may be cleaned later.) Dip the fish into a heavy brine solution, then layer them with coarse salt. Put a heavy weight on the top layer of salt and leave for at least a week (longer for large fish). Remove the fish from the salt and hang to dry – outside if it is sunny and windy; or in a dry, well-ventilated shed if the weather is remotely damp or wet. The dried fish should be stored in wooden crates at

Scaling fish: if the fish has any scales these must be removed before it is cooked or frozen. Cover nearby surfaces with newspaper, because the scales fly everywhere. Using a blunt knife, gently scrape away the scales, working from the tail to the head of the fish **(below)**. Take care not to tear the skin. Rinse the fish under cold water to wash away any scales clinging to the skin **(right)**.

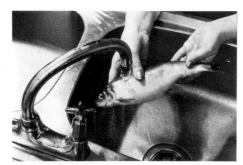

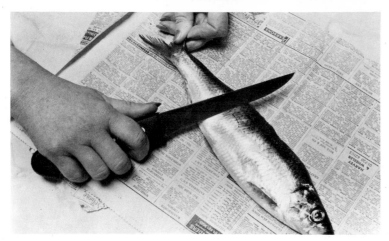

Round fish: 1 Insert a sharp knife into the belly of the fish at the vent and split up to the head.

Flat fish: 1 Cut off the head, thereby opening up the cavity that contains the innards. Scrape these out.

Above: large round fish can be cut into steaks or cutlets once they have been cleaned. Cutlets come from between the head and the middle of the body, and steaks come from the middle to the tail.
Left: whole fish are prepared for freezing by being dipped in slightly salted cold water before being drained, wrapped in foil and labelled. The flesh of fillets, steaks and cutlets is rubbed with olive oil, to prevent it drying out. The individual pieces of fish are then placed between pieces of waxed paper before being wrapped, sealed, labelled and frozen.

2 Scrape out the intestines and other innards, taking care not to damage the flesh.

3 Cut off the head, tail, and fins, and extend cut to the tail. Press flat on a board, skin side upwards.

4 Press hard along the backbone, then turn fish over and ease backbone and side bones away from flesh with a knife.

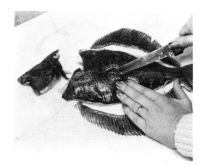

2 Using sharp scissors or a knife, remove the two ridges of fins. Make a cut along the side of the backbone.

3 Holding the knife flat as possible against fish, ease away the flesh from the bones, using short cutting strokes.

4 Turn the fish around and remove the other fillet, then turn it over and remove remaining fillets.

Smoking fish: this can be done either over a log fire **(left)** or in a special smoker **(right).** It is not a method of preservation, however, but merely flavours the fish.
Pickling fish: this will preserve the fish for a short time. One of the most popular forms is rollmop herrings, where raw herring fillets are wrapped around onion rings, bay leaves and peppercorns, secured and then stored in jars with spiced vinegar.

a cool temperature. For quick salting, herrings or whiting can be dipped in salt or sprinkled heavily with it and then hung up to dry somewhere with a good through-draught. They will not keep too long after this, however. Heavily-salted fish should be soaked in cold water for up to 48 hours before cooking.

Pickling

The principle of pickling fish is exactly the same as that of pickling vegetables and fruit – ie using the acetic acid in the vinegar to act as the preserving agent. However, by and large, pickled fish does not last as long as other pickles, although it is a useful and delicious way of preserving fish for a short time. The most common form of pickled fish are rollmop herrings, which are made by cleaning, boning and filleting the herrings before soaking them in brine for about two hours. After this they are rolled up (often with some sliced onions inside), then put in a jar with some bay leaves, chillies, peppercorns and gherkins. Vinegar, boiled up with some pickling spice, is

allowed to cool before being strained over the herrings. The jars should be covered tightly and kept in a cool place, where they will keep for a month or so.

Other fish, cut into pieces, can be pickled in much the same way, although it is sometimes recommended that they should be simmered in the pickling ingredients (ie distilled white vinegar, pickling spice, sliced onions, bay leaves, peppercorns, chillies, etc) for about ten minutes, to make them a little more tender. The vinegar solution is strained over the fish when they have been packed into jars, and a slice of lemon, a bay leaf and some freshly-sliced onions added before the lids are put on.

White fish can be pickled by steeping it in lemon juice for about three days, and salmon can be made into a delicious pickled dish by rubbing it with a mixture of salt, sugar, peppercorns and dillweed and leaving it for not more than five days. In both cases, however, the fish should be eaten when it is removed from the marinade.

Old cookery books, written and published long before the days of freezers, often contain interesting recipes for ways to preserve fish by salting and pickling. If you want to try other methods, search through such sources for inspiration.

Smoking

Home smoking is really best considered as a means of flavouring fish, rather than a form of preservation. By and large, if home-smoked fish is kept for very long, it will decompose and could then cause serious food poisoning. However, smoked fish tastes so good that it is not likely to be kept for long and it is worthwhile trying to smoke your own, treating it as a form of cooking. Smoked fish will freeze well and in this state, it keeps as long as any other frozen dish.

Smoking may be done up the chimney of an ordinary, open, log fire or you can make your own smoker. There are various ways of doing this, using almost any container – old refrigerators or barrels are particularly suitable. The principle is the same whatever type of container you use – there must be a space at the bottom where the sawdust (used to create the smoke) is placed, racks or rods above this where the fish is placed or suspended, and some holes punched in the side and top of the container for the smoke to escape.

If you are smoking in the chimney of the open fire in your living room, the fish can be suspended high up by threading them, through the gills, on to a clipped open wire coat hanger. If there is a recess in the chimney, put the fish in this as it is better if they are not in direct line of fierce heat. They are also out of the line of any rain that might come down the chimney, because it is vital that they are kept dry. The important thing about smoking fish is that the flesh must not melt; in fact, it should barely be warm. The smoke serves to dry the flesh and flavour it, not to cook it by subjecting it to heat. If the fire burns too fiercely, therefore, it is best to remove the fish and return them when the flames have died down and the fire is smoky again. You can make it smoky, incidentally, by sprinkling it with damp sawdust every thirty minutes or so, but if the fire is also designed to keep you warm and make the room cheerful, this may not be practical.

The type of wood you burn will affect the flavour of the fish – oak or fruit being particularly pleasant. Pine is generally not recommended because it will give the fish an unpleasant flavour, and remember not to burn rubbish on the fire – in other words, do not sweep the floor and throw the dust on to the burning logs if you have some fish up the chimney.

Herrings and mackerel are among the most successful fish for home smoking. If you gut and split open the herrings, then salt them in a heavy brine solution for one or two days before smoking them, you will be producing your own kippers and they will keep for at least a week in the refrigerator. The amount of time they need depends on how smoky the fire is and whether you are able to leave them permanently suspended above it during the

process. If you can leave them for 10 to 12 hours, they should be ready; if you have to take them away as the fire gets too hot and then replace them during the night when it has died down, they will probably need a weekend.

Mackerel does not need salting first and it should be given a concentrated burst of smoking – say for about 12 hours – rather than taking it down and putting it back as the fire burns up and dies down. This is because the flesh of mackerel is very thick, and it is likely to decompose rapidly; the smoking process therefore should not be prolonged. Trout is treated in the same way but it may also be salted first.

Salmon can be smoked at home, although do not expect it to have the appearance or flavour of commercially smoked salmon. It should be filleted (see page 212) and the small rib bones removed with tweezers or pincers (a fiddly job!). The fish must then be salted, preferably by rubbing it with salt rather than soaking it in a brine solution. The idea again is to dry out the flesh, so leave it in the salt until it feels fairly hard and stiff. Then put it in a smoker or hang it up the chimney in the usual way, but give it a good concentration of smoke for a good 12 hours or so.

When you remove the fish from the chimney, you will find it is covered in a sooty crust. This can easily be washed off before eating the fish. When smoking was more commonly used as a means of home preservation, this crust helped to deter flies.

PRESERVING PORK

Should you not want to preserve any surplus pork you might have by deep-freezing it (which it will do admirably), you could try your hand at salting it, after which it can be smoked or not, as you like. Whilst some people will tell you that home salting and curing is perfectly safe, I think it is a subject that should be treated with some caution, and it may be better to treat it as a way of flavouring and tenderizing the meat, rather than preserving it for any length of time.

Certainly salting was once widely used as a form of preservation, but one of the reasons that so many highly-flavoured spices were used in the cookery of the Middle Ages was to mask the taste of food that had begun to show signs of deterioration.

There are two methods of salting pork – either by using dry salt or by immersing it in brine, to which various other flavourings can be added. Dry salting will generally preserve the meat for longer, and it involves salt and saltpetre being rubbed well into the meat over a period of days. This should be done five days after the pig has been killed – before this it will not absorb the cure. The meat should be kept in a container with a false bottom during the curing time, through which the moisture can drain as the salt draws it out of the meat. After the curing is completed, the meat is hung to dry for a week or so, before being wrapped in clean cloths and again hung in a well-ventilated place until it is needed.

If a brine solution is being used to cure the meat it will consist of water (or flavouring such as vinegar, beer, etc), coarse salt, saltpetre and generally various flavourings such as treacle, sugar, and spices such as pickling spice, or a mixture of other herbs and spices. It is important that the meat remains totally sub-

Curing hams: salting was once widely used as a form of preserving pork. It is now only used for short-term preserving. Hams intended for Christmas, for example, are cured from pigs killed only the October before. They should be wrapped in muslin and stored in a cool, airy place.

merged in the brine, by weighting it down with a board or plate. The length of time you leave it will depend on the thickness of the meat and whether you are really trying to preserve it for any length of time or merely wanting to flavour it. In any event it is likely to remain in the solution for at least three weeks.

Pork which has been cured by salting can then be smoked, either by suspending it above the chimney in the way described for fish on page 214, or by putting it in a purpose-built smoker. The length of smoking time will depend on whether you want a mild or a stronger taste; a smallish piece of bacon, for example, will taste slightly smoked after a day or so in the smoker; a ham will need several days' smoking.

Preserving Poultry

METHODS OF KILLING POULTRY have already been described. Once dead, the birds must be prepared for the table. This involves plucking (removing the feathers) and drawing (removing the innards).

Plucking is easiest done while the bird is still warm, as the feathers will come out more easily than when the carcass is cold. However, some people feel that the taste and tenderness of domestic poultry is improved if it is hung for 24–48 hours (unless the weather is extremely hot). Hanging is usually done before the bird is plucked or drawn; if the feathers are left on, less flies are attracted to the carcass, and the bird tends to keep better with its innards intact. You can, however, hang poultry after plucking and before drawing, but make sure it is in a cool, airy place where there are no flies.

If you want to hang the poultry for a day or so, you can make plucking easier thereafter by pouring a kettle of boiling water over the bird. Then put it on a clean work surface and pull out the long tail and wing feathers first, jerking them sharply. Pluck systematically from the neck, back, breast, wings and legs, taking a number of feathers between your thumb and fingers each time and tugging them sharply. The tiny pin feathers that remain are easiest to remove using tweezers or by grasping them between your thumb and the edge of a blunt knife. The system of plucking, incidentally, is the same whether you are plucking the bird dry or after you have scaled the feathers.

All poultry is plucked in the same way, but ducks and geese (geese in particular) are harder and take longer as they have a covering of down beneath their feathers. This is removed in the same way, but it flies around everywhere, so put something over your hair and do not wear a woollen jumper or you will end up looking like a snowman! For this reason, it is probably easiest to pluck duck and geese after scalding the feathers; wet down

Plucking: this is easiest to do when the bird is still warm. Pluck the tail and wing feathers first, and then begin plucking at the neck, working your way down to the legs.

does not fly around quite so much. Wash the down and dry it – either in paper bags in a very cool oven or by hanging it in a warm, airy place – and when you have enough, use it for stuffing pillows or cushions. You will find plucking geese very hard on your fingers; a good tip is to wrap sticking plaster round the forefinger of your plucking hand to cushion it.

When the bird is plucked, the head, feet and innards must be removed to prepare it for cooking (or freezing – see below). With the breast side down, insert a knife at the bottom of the neck and slit the skin up to the head. Pull the skin away from the neck, then cut through the neckbone as close to the shoulder as you can, inside the skin. Remove the crop and the windpipe (which go to

Drawing a chicken: 1 Slit skin of neck up to the head. Pull the skin away and cut through the neckbone.

2 Remove crop and windpipe. Discard the head and neckbone. Cut the skin to form a large flap.

3 Turn the bird around and, inserting a sharp knife into the vent, cut up the flesh to the parson's nose.

4 Loosen the innards by placing a couple of fingers each in neck and vent and working them round the carcase.

5 When innards are loose, pull them out through the vent. Keep the gizzard, heart and liver.

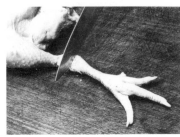

6 Run cold water through the bird. Remove feet at the knee joints. Tuck the skin of the neck under the wings.

make up the giblets), pull out the neckbone and cut round the skin close to the head. This way you leave a large flap of skin which can be folded over the bird's back. (This helps to keep the meat from drying out if you are roasting the bird; if you intend to casserole it in some way, it is not so important to retain this skin.) The neckbone and head are discarded.

Turn the bird round, insert the knife into the vent and cut up to the parson's nose. Loosen the innards by putting a couple of fingers into this opening and then into the opening at the neck end and gently working them round against the inside of the carcass. (This job can be made considerably more pleasant if you starve the birds for 24 hours before killing them.) When you feel the innards are loose, gently pull them out through the opening at the vent. If you keep them all together and work carefully, you should not break the gall bladder; if this does break, it will give the bird a bitter taste.

Run cold water through the bird and dab it dry with kitchen paper. Remove the feet by slitting the skin round the knee joints and twisting the lower legs. Cut through the white sinews. Tuck the flap of skin at the neck under the wing joints.

Separate the heart and liver from the rest of the innards – but take care again, because the gall bladder is attached to the liver. Cut open the gizzard and wash it. This, together with the heart and neck, forms the giblets, and may be used to make stock or soup. The liver is also part of the giblets, but it is best used separately – it can give too strong a taste to stock, for example.

Make sure the innards, head and feet are well wrapped in newspaper before putting them in the dustbin, or they will soon attract flies or predators. If you prefer, you can bury them, but do this deeply or dogs will soon find them.

Poultry freezes successfully, and if this is what you intend to do with at least some of your plucked and drawn birds, you should do so immediately. Make sure all the water has been drained out of the inside of the carcass after washing, then tie the legs together and tuck the wings against the body to make the bird as compact as possible. Make sure there are no sharp bones protruding from the legs which might puncture the wrapping; if there are, cover them with foil. Put the bird in a heavy polythene bag; remove as much air as possible before sealing it; label with the date and weight of the bird and freeze it quickly. Freeze the giblets separately. If you prefer, you can cut the bird into joints and freeze these individually, or make the chickens up into a cooked dish and freeze this. If frozen raw, the poultry must be thoroughly thawed before using.

Game is plucked and drawn in exactly the same way, although it is usually allowed to hang for some while first (see page 181). If the bird is quite high after hanging, you must take care not to tear the flesh whilst plucking – it will be most unpleasant if you do. The plucked and drawn game birds can be frozen in the way described above.

Smoking

Poultry can also be smoked, although this does not actually preserve it for any great length of time. Smoked poultry should be used at once, or it may be frozen for about four months. Soak the poultry overnight in a brine solution in the ratio of 450 g (1 lb) of salt to 1.2 litres (2 pints) of water. Use enough water to cover the bird and place a heavy plate on top to ensure that it remains

Preserving eggs: hard-boiled eggs can be preserved in spiced vinegar, but fresh eggs must be kept in waterglass. They can also be covered with petroleum jelly.

submerged. Dry the bird off the next day and put it in a smoker for at least six hours.

Preserving eggs

If you suddenly find yourself with a surplus of eggs, there are some ways of preserving them. The old-fashioned method is to keep them in a waterglass solution. Waterglass, which is sodium silicate, is available from chemists and it will carry instructions for use with it. It should be poured into a container (preferably stone or galvanized iron) and the fresh eggs placed into it, ideally with their pointed end facing downwards. You can put as many eggs into the container as it will hold, providing they are completely covered by the solution. Remove the eggs and use them as they are needed, but not for boiling.

Another old-fashioned method sometimes used as an alternative to waterglass is to exclude all air from the shell by covering it with a special liquid preparation which consists of fat dissolved in a solvent. A greasy substance, like petroleum jelly, can also be used, but it is vital that the shell is covered and all air excluded.

It is also possible to freeze eggs, although not in their shells. If you want to freeze whole eggs for puddings and cakes, beat them up with a pinch of salt or sugar (according to their intended use), pour into rigid containers and remember to state the number of eggs on the label. Alternatively, you can divide the yolks from the whites and freeze them separately. Just put egg whites into a small container, seal and freeze them. When completely thawed, they will whisk up perfectly satisfactorily. Egg yolks should be beaten with a little salt or sugar (depending on whether you want them for sweet or savoury dishes) before freezing, as this prevents the yolk from coagulating.

The other main method of preserving eggs is to pickle them. For this they must first be hard-boiled, and then peeled and immersed in a spiced vinegar solution. You can use what spices you like to flavour the vinegar – garlic, orange peel, cloves and pickling spice for example. Boil up the vinegar with the spices and flavourings, then let it cool before straining it over the eggs. Allow about 575 ml (1 pint) of liquid for six eggs; make sure the jar is air-tight and leave the eggs for at least six weeks before opening the jar.

Index

ST

V

WYZ